PAUL BEFORE THE AREOPAGUS

Other Books by Ned B. Stonehouse

AUTHOR OF.

J. GRESHAM MACHEN — A BIOGRAPHICAL MEMOIR
THE WITNESS OF LUKE TO CHRIST
THE WITNESS OF MATTHEW AND MARK TO CHRIST
THE APOCALYPSE IN THE ANCIENT CHURCH

EDITOR OF

THE NEW INTERNATIONAL COMMENTARY ON THE NEW TESTAMENT

WHAT IS CHRISTIANITY? AND OTHER ADDRESSES
(*by J Gresham Machen*)

GOD TRANSCENDENT AND OTHER SERMONS
(*by J Gresham Machen*)

THE INFALLIBLE WORD A SYPMOSIUM (*with Paul Woolley*)

PAUL BEFORE THE AREOPAGUS

And Other New Testament Studies

NED B. STONEHOUSE

PROFESSOR OF NEW TESTAMENT IN
WESTMINSTER THEOLOGICAL SEMINARY, PHILADELPHIA

WIPF & STOCK · Eugene, Oregon

Wipf and Stock Publishers
199 W 8th Ave, Suite 3
Eugene, OR 97401

Paul Before the Areopagus
And Other New Testament Studies
By Stonehouse, Ned B.
Softcover ISBN-13: 978-1-6667-4736-2
Hardcover ISBN-13: 978-1-6667-4737-9
eBook ISBN-13: 978-1-6667-4738-6
Publication date 5/5/2022
Previously published by William B. Eerdmans Publishing Company, 1957

This edition is a scanned facsimile of the original edition published in 1957.

PREFACE

QUESTIONS regarding Jesus and the gospel — even in an age largely characterized by secularism and scepticism — are inescapable. There is pathos indeed in the intensive efforts of some men, in spite of radical distrust or repudiation of the testimony to Jesus Christ in the Gospels and the New Testament as a whole, somehow to preserve the essence and relevance of the gospel as the proclamation of the event of Jesus Christ. There is also an element of encouragement, however, in the very fact of concentrated concern with the New Testament. For this offers the hope that the New Testament, because of its self-accrediting testimony, may thus more fully call forth the appropriate response of Christian faith. If the collection and publication of these studies, which have been out of print or generally inaccessible, should make even a slight contribution to the fuller understanding of the New Testament, the author would be amply rewarded.

As the arrangement of the studies is intended to suggest, the chief accent falls on exposition. The study of Paul's Areopagus address, because it is largely exegetical and deals most comprehensively with the New Testament message, is assigned the place of priority and is utilized in the title of the book. Nevertheless, historical and critical questions are also in view to a greater or lesser degree in all the studies. This stems from the conviction that the most fruitful exposition is performed when account is taken of the modern situation and discussion is carried on with the leading representatives of contemporaneous points of view.

The studies of Bultmann and Dibelius, though undertaken several years ago, retain largely such significance as they possessed when they were first written because of the preeminent place of influence which these men have enjoyed in modern New Testament scholarship. This is due to their unique contributions to the method of form criticism but also because of the impact made by their reconstructions of the history and message of the New Testament. Bultmann indeed is even more conspicuous today than when the study devoted to him was first undertaken, occupying as he does the most discussed and controversial place in the current debate about the New Testament. And while this study does not take specific account of the most recent phase of Bultmann's thought, as that is concerned with the evaluation of the apostolic proclamation, the question concerning his conception of Jesus will likely prove to be of more lasting interest. And his later thought is unintelligible apart from an understanding of his conception of Jesus.

A few facts concerning the circumstances of the origin of the several studies may place them in somewhat clearer perspective. The opening study, "The Areopagus Address," was the Tyndale New Testament Lecture for 1949, and was delivered in the Divinity School, Cambridge, England, on July 13, 1949, at a meeting of the Tyndale Fellowship for Biblical Research. It was subsequently published in pamphlet form by the Tyndale Press of London. "Who Crucified Jesus?" and "Repentance, Baptism and the Gift of the Holy Spirit" were published as articles in the *Westminster Theological Journal* in the issues of May, 1943 (Vol. V) and November, 1950 (Vol. XIII) respectively. The study on "The Elders and the Living-Beings in the Apocalypse" is an essay contributed to a volume entitled, *Arcana Revelata*, a *Festschrift* of New Testament studies presented to Professor Dr. F. W. Grosheide of The Free University of Amsterdam on the occasion of the seventieth anniversary of his birth. The volume was published by J. H. Kok, N. V. of Kampen, The Netherlands, in 1951. The articles devoted to Rudolf Bultmann and Martin Dibelius were also published in the *Westminster Theological Journal*, the first in November, 1938 (Vol. I) and the second in May, 1940 (Vol. II). The final study, on "Luther and the New Testament Canon," is a paper delivered before the Evangelical Theological Society at its annual meeting in Chicago on December 30, 1953, and though it was contained in the proceedings of the Society, it was not formally published.

It is a pleasant duty to make grateful mention of several persons who have contributed in one way or another to the publication of this volume. The project developed on the background of interest expressed by students of Westminster Theological Seminary and especially the suggestions of Mr. George W. Knight, III, who also graciously assisted in reading proof. Mrs. Hugh P. Whitted, Jr., my secretary during the academic year 1955–1956, ably assisted in preparing copy for the press. The Reverend Theodore J. Jansma kindly supplied me with a copy of one of the articles which was out of print. I wish also to make grateful acknowledgment of the distinguished services of Paul Woolley and John Murray, who, as editors of the *Westminster Theological Journal* during the first fifteen years of its publication, placed all contributors and readers greatly in their debt. The several publishers concerned are heartily thanked for their readiness to permit republication of the several articles in the present volume. Finally, I wish to express my deep appreciation of the generous cooperation manifested by the publisher of this work at every point of the undertaking.

N. B. S.

CONTENTS

I. THE AREOPAGUS ADDRESS 1
II. WHO CRUCIFIED JESUS? 41
III. REPENTANCE, BAPTISM AND THE GIFT OF THE
    HOLY SPIRIT 70
IV. THE ELDERS AND THE LIVING-BEINGS IN THE
    APOCALYPSE 88
V. RUDOLF BULTMANN'S JESUS 109
VI. MARTIN DIBELIUS AND THE RELATION OF HISTORY
    AND FAITH 151
VII. LUTHER AND THE NEW TESTAMENT CANON 186

CHAPTER I

THE AREOPAGUS ADDRESS

INTRODUCTION

IN venturing upon a discussion of the address of the apostle Paul at Athens, recorded in Acts 17:22-31, I am mindful that I am not entering upon a largely neglected field of investigation. The passage is so replete with exceptional and arresting features that the commentators and the historians of early Christianity have been stimulated to treat it at considerable length. Moreover, a remarkable number of learned monographs have been devoted to its interpretation.

Much as one may learn from what others have written, my impression is that the last word has by no means been spoken, and that the Areopagus address will continue to challenge the Biblical interpreter to press forward to his goal, both because of the variety and intricacy of problems which it presents and because of its far-reaching implications for the understanding of early Christianity. Many modern discussions, moreover, have been absorbed with certain restricted aspects of the narrative such as linguistic or archaeological features. Such studies are indispensable to a proper evaluation of the problems; at certain points account is taken of them here, at others they are presupposed. But they have, perhaps unavoidably, left rather undeveloped the broader questions of the historical and theological significance of the *Areopagitica*, and my purpose is to try, if only in small measure, to improve that situation.

A further impression is that many influential treatises proceed upon the basis of a wrong exegetical method. This appears to be particularly true of representatives of the *religionsgeschichtliche Methode*. While they have the merit of struggling with the basic questions of the place occupied by this address within the context of the history of religion in the Hellenistic Age, it is ironical that in seeking to integrate the narrative with contemporaneous thought and action they end

1

up by displaying sharply divisive tendencies. For tensions and discrepancies are alleged to exist, not only between the Paul of the Athens story and the earliest Christianity, and between this Paul and the Paul of the Epistles, and between this Paul and the Paul of the rest of Acts, but even within the testimony of Acts 17.

Albert Schweitzer gives brief but pungent expression to this general approach in his book, *The Mysticism of Paul the Apostle*.[1] On the background of Norden's learned and challenging work, *Agnostos Theos* (1913), he regards certain features of the address, and especially the quotation, "In Him we live and move and have our being" (17:28), as expressing a God-mysticism which is Stoic rather than Christian, and as having in view an immanentistic and natural view of the world rather than one that conceives of God as transcendent and of history in supernatural terms. This pantheistic God-mysticism is declared to be utterly antithetical to the particularistic, predestinarian Christ-mysticism of the genuine Paul. For this basic reason, as well as for the reason that he judges that there "can never have been such an inscription" as is reported in Acts 17:23, Schweitzer concludes that the speech is unhistorical.

Far more elaborate is the treatment of Martin Dibelius in a monograph published in 1939,[2] which is perhaps the most important study of its kind since Norden's monumental treatise. The body of the address Dibelius regards as distinctly Hellenistic; its general theme the true knowledge of God, a knowledge which is viewed as being accessible to every man inasmuch as his place within the world and the affinity of God must lead thereto. Three principal divisions of the address are distinguished: (a) God, Creator and Lord of the world, requires no temple because He is without needs (verses 24, 25); (b) God made man with the destiny that he should seek Him (verses 26, 27); (c) the affinity of man with God (for we are 'His offspring') should preclude all worship of images (verses 28, 29). All three divisions are thought to betray Hellenistic motifs and the address as a whole is viewed as representing a

---

[1] *Die Mystik des Apostels Paulus* (1930), E. T., 1931.
[2] *Paulus auf dem Areopag* (Sitzungsberichte der Heidelberger Akademie der Wissenschaften, Phil.-hist. Klasse, 1938–39, 2. Abhandlung).

significant development of theology in the soil of Greek culture. The author of Acts is regarded as dealing so freely with the facts that he presents a largely imaginative picture of the manner in which, according to his conception, Paul would have sought to commend Christianity to the heathen. The only Christian feature of the address, according to Dibelius, is the concluding sentence which presents a call to repentance in connection with a declaration of the eschatological judgment, but even this conclusion is thought not to be wholly consistent with the teaching of Paul in the Epistles. The introduction to the address, moreover, is regarded as inconsistent with the mood of the address itself, although not sufficiently to disallow that it could be the work of the author of Acts.

Evaluations such as those of Schweitzer and Dibelius underscore the propriety of seeking to gauge anew what the account actually represents Paul as saying — what the disposition and motif of the address really are. And in treating these matters one is compelled to explore to some extent the larger questions as to the place of this message within the total witness of the New Testament to the teaching of Paul and even within the compass of the still larger question as to the essence of Christianity.

The question of the *Anknüpfungspunkt* is in the foreground of interest. Wherever there is a grappling with the Christian doctrine of revelation and the Christian doctrine of man it will necessarily have to be faced with all earnestness. How can the divine Word, without losing its divine character, be communicated to and apprehended by a finite creature, and especially a creature who, as the consequence of the noetic effects of sin, is viewed as darkened in his understanding to the point where he cannot know the things of the Spirit of God? This urgent theological problem confronts the reader of Acts 17 in a most arresting manner, and though the systematic discussion of the problem would take us far afield, the interpretation of the passage will require some reflection upon it.

The immediate reaction of Paul's hearers indeed does not suggest that *they* recognized that the respective religions had much in common or that the Pauline message found an echo in their own experience. Paul seemed to them to be a setter forth of *strange gods*, to be bringing certain *strange things* into their ears, to be speaking *a new teaching*; and their interest in hearing further concerning it is associated with their characteristic interest as Athenians in something *new* (verses 18-21). It is Paul rather than his pagan hearers who may appear to stress the element of religious commonness especially at the beginning of his address in his observations concerning the altar, and later in his quotations from the heathen poets. Plainly he is at these points doing far more than cleverly applying so-called practical psychology calculated "to win friends and influence people." Paul does show himself to be a masterful public speaker in his ability to arrest attention by linking his message with features of his listeners' own experience, but his apparently favorable judgments concerning their religious beliefs and practices obviously transcend barely formal aspects. The question remains, however, exactly how the element of commonness is conceived. Does the evidence support the conclusion that Paul tones down the antithesis between Christianity and paganism, or at least that the author of Acts represents him as doing so at Athens? Or is perhaps the situation rather that the intolerance of paganism is as unrelieved here as anywhere in the Scriptures, but that the point of contact is found basically to be concerned with judgments regarding the nature of man and his religious responses to the divine revelation?

I. HISTORICAL SETTING AND OCCASION

Although my interest in this study centres upon the Areopagus address itself and it is therefore beyond the scope of this paper to treat all the questions which emerge in connection with the examination of the fascinating context in which Luke presents the address, there are features of the context which are so basically significant for our understanding of the discourse that they must be evaluated, however briefly. The consequences of the address, including especially the intimation that it did not meet with general favor, bear pointedly upon one's final evaluation of it. But no less does the introduction to the discourse in the midst of the Areopagus help towards the understanding of Paul's aim and method as preacher and apologist.

Paul had come to Athens with the purpose of finding a brief respite from the arduous experiences and the perils of his activity in Macedonia rather than to carry forward his apostolic mission. Almost from the beginning of his European ministry he had been harassed by hostile men; in Philippi he and Silas had been severely beaten and imprisoned; at Thessalonica the unbelieving Jews incited a tumult which made further activity impracticable and dangerous; in Berea the advantage of a favorable reception was offset when the Thessalonian Jews arrived once more to stir up the multitudes against Paul and imperilled his mission and person. To relieve this situation Paul was constrained to go to Athens, but evidently it was regarded as a mere stopping place on his way to Corinth. For Silas and Timothy were enjoined to catch up with him as speedily as possible, and, as Acts reports (18:5), the reunion was realized in Corinth, where he remained for a year and a half.[3] Paul accordingly was taking a brief holiday in Athens and did not anticipate the activity which he actually carried on in this brief interlude. An unforeseen circumstance constrained him to speak, and once having made himself heard he came soon to encounter the quite novel situation of giving an account of his Christian faith in the midst of the Areopagus.

Like many men of today on holiday in an historic and illustrious city, Paul had gone to see the sights of Athens. Though it was no longer in its golden age, the spendor of that age was still in evidence. The beautiful setting of the city in the midst of hills on a great bay of the Aegean was

[3] I Thess. 3:1, 6 implies indeed that Timothy must have joined Paul in Athens and returned to Thessalonica before rejoining Paul, presumably at Corinth. Lake and Cadbury, in *The Beginnings of Christianity*, Part I, Vol. IV, in their note on Acts 18:5, among others, find a discrepancy here on the ground that "we ... alone" in I Thess. 3:1 must include Silas whose name is joined with Paul's and Timothy's in the salutation. Although the Pauline language allows for this interpretation, it does not require it. As the usage in I Corinthians, for example, discloses, the inclusion of others besides Paul in the salutation does not govern the decision as to the use of the singular or plural in the Epistles themselves.

quite as stirring as ever, and the magnificent temples and public works added lustre to the munificence of nature. To conclude that Paul had no eye whatsoever for the beauty that surrounded him as he strode about the city would be rash and gratuitous. Nevertheless, his philosophy of life was not such as would permit him to evaluate nature and civilization in detachment from his religious faith. The gigantic gold and ivory statue of Athena in the Parthenon on the Acropolis, for example, could not be viewed by Paul simply as a thing of beauty. The fact that it was an idol stirred Paul far more profoundly than its aesthetic merits.

Paul was struck, moreover, by the fact that Athens was "full of idols" (verse 16). Luke can hardly mean to suggest that now for the first time Paul had come face to face with the prevalence of idolatry in a pagan city, for Luke had reported his residence in Syrian Antioch and he himself probably knew from first-hand knowledge how typically pagan was that city also. Still less can Luke intend to imply that Paul was ordinarily rather complacent towards idolatry. Perhaps the excessive zeal of Athens in this regard, which indeed had become proverbial in the ancient world — especially when considered in the perspective of the intellectual and cultural achievements and pretensions of Athens — contributed to the sharply negative reaction of Paul. But Paul's irritation is referred to not so much that we should dwell upon the novelty or relative novelty of his psychological state as he was confronted with the idolatry of Athens, but in order to explain why Paul could not remain silent in Athens and felt compelled to preach the gospel in spite of his original intention to secure a brief period of relief from the tensions attendant upon his apostolic mission. The special circumstances in Athens merely provided the occasion for Paul's deep indignation; his fervent monotheism was the actual cause of it. And it is not without significance that the word which Luke employs to indicate Paul's feeling is frequently used in the LXX where the Lord is described as being provoked to anger at the idolatry of His people.[4] The zeal of the Lord was eating

---

[4] See the use of παραξύνομαι in Dt. 9:18; Ps 106:29; Is. 65:3; Ho. 8:5; cf. Dt. 29:25 ff., 28.

up His servant Paul, and he was constrained to break his silence in the presence of the presumption of pagan worship. Another significant feature of the Lucan introduction to the Areopagus address is the intimation that Paul's preaching in Athens was by no means confined to the address reported at some length. Even in Athens Paul did not fail to take advantage of the liberty of the synagogue. Evidently, in view of what is to come, Luke treats the ministry there quite summarily, but he can hardly have much less in view than what he has reported, also somewhat summarily, concerning Paul's activity in Thessalonica, when he states that "as his custom was" he went into the synagogue of the Jews, "and for three sabbath days reasoned with them from the scriptures, opening and alleging, that it behoved the Christ to suffer, and to rise again from the dead; and that this Jesus, whom, said he, I proclaim unto you, is the Christ" (17:2-4, R. V.).[5] His reasoning with the Jews in Athens, as in Thessalonica, must have involved a fairly comprehensive presentation of his apostolic message.

Perhaps Luke deals so summarily with the ministry in the synagogue because of his interest in informing his readers of what developed as Paul, taking advantage of the liberty of the market-place, confronted the devotees of pagan religion with the Christian evangel. In contrast with the weekly contact with the Jews, Paul reasoned every day with those who encountered him in the *agora*. But the message during the week was the same as that on the sabbath, for Luke declares that, however novel or trifling the Stoics and Epicureans judged it to be, actually "he preached Jesus and the resurrection" (verse 18). Although perhaps they so far misunderstood that message as to suppose that he was actually proclaiming two divinities,[6] there can be no doubt that Luke

[5] It is of significance that the verb διαλέγομαι is used in both instances (Acts 17:2, 17). See also Acts 18:4, 19, 19:8, 9, 20:7, 9, 24:12, 25. Of further interest is the fact that, while the aorist tense is employed in referring to the activity covering three sabbaths in Thessalonica, the imperfect tense is used in speaking of his ministry in the synagogue in Athens. While the imperfect form may not involve an extensive period, it underscores the impression that Luke by no means restricts his preaching in the synagogue to a single sabbath.

[6] So most expositors suppose. Lake and Cadbury form an exception.

himself regards this phrase as a summary characterization of the apostolic preaching. So indeed all of the sermons previously recorded in Acts might well be designated; so rather precisely Luke has spoken of the apostolic *kerygma* in Acts 4:2 when, in telling of the opposition of the Sadducees to Peter and John, he declares that they were vexed because the apostles "taught the people and proclaimed in Jesus the resurrection from the dead."

It was in the course of this preaching of "Jesus and the resurrection" in the *agora* that the stage was set for the Areopagus address. The question whether Paul was led away from the market-place to the Hill of Ares (the "Mars' Hill" of A. V.) near the Acropolis, or was haled before the supreme council of Athens, known as the Areopagus in view of its former custom of convening upon that hill, is not of decisive significance for the determination of the disposition and meaning of the address itself. For even in the latter case, a broader audience than the constituency of the council would appear to be in view. Nevertheless, the question is of such intrinsic interest and positive bearing upon one's understanding of the historical setting that it may not fairly be passed over in this discussion. My own judgment is that, although perhaps the view that the hill rather than the council is in mind cannot be finally discarded as being beyond the realm of possibility, there are preponderant reasons for concluding that Paul is represented as appearing before the council of the Areopagus. That indeed the philosophers should have desired to take Paul away from the busy market-place to the somewhat isolated hill with a view to a more quiet and leisurely inquiry may well be allowed. But this explanation is not compelling since no adequate reason appears why the inquiry should not have continued there in the *agora* where they were wont to carry on their disputations. If, however, Paul is taken before the Areopagus, probably in the *Stoa Basileios* in the market-place itself, all is intelligible. The absence of intimation of arrest and of distinctly judicial examination disallows the possibility of a formal trial, and if that were the sole prerogative of the supreme council of Athens, the position favored here would have to be rejected. But since the council evidently enjoyed some general prerogatives, including the exercise of some control of lecturing in the market-place, full justice is done to the data of Acts if one understands that Paul was compelled to face the council to demonstrate that his appearance among the public lecturers of Athens was unobjectionable.

The most specific confirmation of this view is found, in my judgment, in the manner in which references to the Areopagus are introduced. Paul is said to have stood "in the midst of the Areopagus" (verse 22), and following the conclusion of his address to have gone out "from their midst" (verse 33). The prepositional phrase "in the midst of" may be used with reference to places as well as persons: Lk. 21:28 refers to those who are in the midst of Judaea; Mk. 6:47 to the boat of the disciples as being in the midst of the sea. But it is exceedingly doubtful that a person or group of persons would be described as being in the midst of a hill. On the other hand, Luke repeatedly speaks of persons as being in the midst of other persons (Acts 1:15, 2:22, 4:7, 27:21; Lk. 2:46, 22.27, 55, 24:36). And the utmost continuity is preserved on this view since Paul is said to have gone forth from *their* midst.[7]

That Paul's address was delivered before the supreme council of Athens emphasizes accordingly the uniqueness of the occasion of its delivery and underscores the necessity of making due allowance for its distinctive contents. Apart from the brief summary of the discourse at Lystra (Acts 14:15 ff.) and such intimations as are provided in Paul's Epistles, the address at Athens provides our only evidence of the apostle's direct approach to a pagan audience. And

---

[7] See especially Ramsay, *St. Paul the Traveller and Roman Citizen* (1903), pp 243 ff., *The Bearing of Recent Discovery on the Trustworthiness of the New Testament* (1915), pp 102 ff., Lake and Cadbury *ad loc*. Dibelius, *op. cit.*, p 9, argues that the hill is favored by the consideration that in Acts 17:19 a change of scene is indicated, and since Paul has been viewed as active in the *agora* he must now be thought of as being taken away from the *agora* to the hill. However, he may quite well be conceived of as being taken from a certain point within the *agora* to the particular place where the Areopagus convened. Moreover, the preposition ἐπί may quite possibly mean "before" rather than "to" at this point, cf the usage in Acts 16:19, 17·6, and the designation of Dionysius as the Areopagite, that is, as a member of the council, is most intelligible on the understanding that the council has been referred to in the preceding context

even this address, though not presented as unrepresentative of his preaching to unconverted Gentiles, is likewise not included as completely typical of such preaching.[8]

II. THE ALTAR TO AN UNKNOWN GOD

At the commencement of Paul's address the attention is unmistakably centered upon the religious devotion of the Athenians. Recalling his tour of the city in which he had been aroused to indignation at the prevalence of idolatry, he singles out for special attention one altar among the many "objects of worship" upon which was inscribed the words ΑΓΝΩΣΤΩ ΘΕΩ ("To an unknown God"). A basic problem facing the interpreter is that of Paul's evaluation of the worship of the unknown God. But a prior question is what such an altar discloses as to the religiosity of the Athenians in the context of their own religious history and outlook, a question which cannot be dissociated from that of the historicity of the book of Acts at this point.

Baur and Zeller as exponents of the Tübingen criticism of Acts, and Schweitzer and Dibelius as representatives of a contemporaneous point of view which retains certain basic evaluations of that school, may be mentioned among the many modern writers who have flatly rejected the testimony of Acts regarding the existence of such an altar. Schweitzer, whose position on this matter is fairly representative, sets forth his view as follows:

> That the speech is unhistorical is at once portrayed by the fact that Paul takes for his starting-point an inscription dedicating an Athenian altar "to an unknown God." There can never have been such an inscription. There is evidence

[8] In passing one may observe how Luke gives evidence of being completely at home in describing the Athenian scene, a fact which is left unaccounted for on certain evaluations of his competence. Lake and Cadbury remark on verse 19: "According to Acts, therefore, just as Paul is brought before the στρατηγοί at Philippi, the πολιτάρχαι at Thessalonica, the ἀνθύπατος at Corinth, so at Athens he faces the Areopagus. The local name for the supreme authority is in each case different and accurate."

in current literature only for altars to "unknown Gods" in the plural, not to *an* unknown God in the singular.[9]

Appealing to the often-quoted allusions in the writings of Pausanias and Philostratus, and recalling Jerome's judgment that Paul had altered the inscription to serve the purposes of his address, he concludes that it was the author of Acts rather than Paul "who transposed the inscription from the plural to the singular, in order to provide Paul with a starting-point for his discourse on monotheism." "Such alterations of traditions and citations," he goes on to say, "were practised without scruple by the religious propaganda of antiquity in its literary forms."[10]

Several critical observations are in order here:

(1) We must challenge the propriety of the assumption that Luke would have felt free to take liberties with historical fact simply because there are evidences that ancient historians sometimes accomodated their facts to their practical purposes. This unscientifically disallows of exceptions to what is said to be characteristic of that age; it begs the question whether the Christian Luke may not have had higher standards; it demands that his specific claim to write accurately and with a view to providing certainty concerning what had actually taken place be set aside as being merely conventional and rhetorical.

(2) This position is most rash, further, in its declaration that "there can never have been such an inscription" on the basis of nothing more than an argument from silence. For even if there were many instead of a very few declarations extant concerning altars to unknown gods, they could never demonstrate that an altar to an unknown god never existed; silence concerning such an altar could prove only that, for one reason or another, allusion to it had not been preserved. Actually, of course, the consideration rests on even less than an argument from silence since the Acts itself, even if doubt were cast upon the Lucan authorship, remains a contemporaneous witness of the first rank. And as it is the testimony of Luke, an intimate associate of Paul, it would be

[9] *Op. cit*, E. T. p. 6.
[10] *Op. cit*, p. 7

rash to set it aside merely because no confirmation of its historicity has been discovered. Schweitzer's dogmatism may be happily contrasted with the statement of Foakes-Jackson in the Moffatt Commentary that "Paul implies that on close inspection he found a single altar thus dedicated, which may have escaped the notice of those who had written about Athens."

(3) It is not as conclusive as many modern critics of the Acts claim that no confirmatory evidence has been forthcoming. While I should certainly not challenge the conclusion that there were in Athens altars dedicated to unknown *gods*, it remains possible to construe the language of Pausanias and Philostratus so as to allow for knowledge of an altar to an unknown god as well, although certainly it was not pertinent to their purpose to distinguish between them. When Pausanias says, for example, that on this visit to Athens (about the middle of the second century of the Christian era) he noticed on the road from the Phaleron Bay harbour to the city "altars of the gods named unknown" (βωμοὶ δὲ θεῶν τε ὀνομαζομένων ἀγνώστων), who can insist that there was not among them one inscribed ᾿Αγνώστῳ Θεῷ? Likewise the statement Philostratus ascribes to Apollonius, that it is the part of wisdom "to speak well of all the gods, especially in Athens where altars are set up in honour even of unknown gods" (τὸ περὶ πάντων θεῶν εὖ λέγειν καὶ ταῦτα ᾿Αθήνησιν, οὗ καὶ ἀγνώστων δαιμόνων βωμοὶ ἵδρυνται), though no doubt applying to altars inscribed with the plural designation, is sufficiently general to comprehend one with the singular form.[11]

(4) Moreover, even if these historical allusions to the religious life of Greece and Athens were exclusive of the Lucan report, there would be powerful confirmation of the credibility of Acts from the well-known story of Diogenes Laertius concerning Epimenides the Cretan, who, when summoned during a plague, advised that white and black sheep should be driven from the Areopagus and that where they came to rest the Athenians should sacrifice "to the appropriate god" (τῷ προσήκοντι θεῷ). As a result the plague was stayed, and Diogenes reports that even in his day (in the third century

---

[11] Pausanias, *Description of Greece*, 1:1, 4; Philostratus, *Life of Apollonius*, 6.3, 5

A. D.) "anonymous altars" (βωμοὺς ἀνωνύμους) were found in the vicinity of Athens.[12] Norden and Dibelius, to be sure, know this story and discuss it in relation to their view that the author of Acts must have altered the plural to the singular in the interest of presenting Paul as an exponent of monotheism, and thus actually invented the altar with the inscription Ἀγνώστῳ Θεῷ. They point out that the story of Diogenes Laertius says nothing concerning an *inscription* upon the altars erected to the appropriate deity.[13] It must indeed be admitted that no precise confirmation of the inscription as reported in Acts is provided by it. This conclusion fails, however, to face the issue in the sharpest terms. It fails to observe that the narrative sheds no light whatever upon the origin of an altar to unknown *gods*. Polytheists might fear that their pantheon was not complete and that there were *gods* who were being deprived of their rightful service because they remained unknown, and thus one may conceive of the erection of altars to unknown *gods*. But the story of Epimenides has in view an essentially different type of situation, in which on a particular historical occasion sacrifice was offered to a specific, though unknown, *god*. Accordingly, though this story does not establish the existence of an altar or altars with the precise inscription found in Acts 17, it furnishes the very background which is required to make it intelligible and bears witness to the prevalence in Athens of the very kind of piety upon which Paul reflects.[14]

The question as to the religious motif which came to expression in the offering of sacrifices "to the appropriate

[12] Diogenes Laertius, *Lives of the Philosophers*, 1:110, cf. Wetstein, *Novum Testamentum*, II (1752), ad loc. Among modern commentators who have utilized this story as a background for the understanding of the narrative mention may be made of Joseph Addison Alexander (1858), Knowling, and Lake and Cadbury

[13] Norden, *Agnostos Theos*, p. 57, n 1, Dibelius, *op. cit*, pp. 16 f.

[14] Lake, *Beginnings*, V, p. 242, says: "There is no evidence for an altar to any one god who was specially called 'the unknown,' but the story in Diogenes Laertius suggests that the singular may have been used in the formula τῷ προσήκοντι θεῷ meaning 'to the unknown god who is concerned in the matter', ἀγνώστῳ θεῷ would be a loose but not very inaccurate paraphrase "

god," and which could have taken the form of worship of an unknown god, needs to be analyzed more specifically. Knowling is representative of the view that "in such an inscription Paul wisely recognized that there was in the heart of Athens a witness to the deep unsatisfied yearning of humanity for a clearer and closer knowledge of the unseen power which men worshipped dimly and imperfectly, a yearning expression in the sacred Vedic hymns of an old world, or in the crude religions of a new."[15] Such a formulation reads much more of positive religious significance into the Athenian piety than is suggested either by the story of Epimenides or by Paul's allusion to the altar to the unknown god. Knowling seems to imply that Paul regarded the polytheistic religion of Athens as a kind of imperfect monotheism, a "knowledge of the unseen power" which needed only to become clearer and more intimate. But how can the readiness to include still another god in their pantheon constitute an approach towards monotheism? The idea of an open pantheon, like that of an open universe in which anything can happen, points to an underlying scepticism and irrationalism rather than to a movement towards the one living and true God.

On the other hand, it may not be overlooked that a measure of awareness of the inadequacy of their own religion is indicated. For the erection of the altar manifested an acknowledgement on a particular occasion that they had to do with a god not previously worshipped, one whom they had neglected and offended, and whose disfavor had to be appeased, and who, for all that, yet remained unknown.[16] The worship of an unknown god, coming to expression within the framework of polytheism, remains the idolatrous worship of one god

---

[15] In the *Expositor's Greek Testament*, II, on v. 23. See also Dibelius, *op. cit.*, p. 19: "Fur den Areopagredner aber ist einzig der singularische Text der Inschrift brauchbar, denn ihm gilt sie als Zeugnis fur das unbewusste Ahnen des wahren Gottes bei den Athenern."

[16] J. H. Bavinck, *Alzoo Wies het Woord* (Baarn, Holland, n. d), p. 175, presents basically this view when he says that the maker of this altar apparently, "hetzij vanwege bijzonderen nood of vanwege bijzonderen zegen, genoopt gevoeld heeft een bepaalden god aan te roepen, maar dat hij niet geweten heeft tot welken god hij zich wenden moest." It is doubtful, however, that he is on equally solid ground in his conclusion that Paul viewed the altar as symptomatic of heathen religion generally.

among many. But the singular expression of idolatry exhibited by the altar which attracted Paul's special attention, intimating as it did its own defectiveness, provided a starting point for Paul's proclamation of the living God who was unknown to them.

III. Paul's Characterization of Their Worship

Paul's own characterizations of the religion of the Athenians serve most immediately to introduce his positive proclamation. They bear pointedly upon one's evaluation of its disposition and thrust, since the question whether he assumes a relatively complacent attitude toward their idolatry, or maintains a mood of indignation, or adopts some other attitude towards it, is in the foreground of interest.

One's attention centers, first of all, upon the fact that he classifies the altar in the focal point of interest among "the objects of your worship" (τὰ σεβάσματα). This word is used on only one other occasion in the New Testament, namely in II Thess. 2:4, where Paul speaks of the man of lawlessness as "he that opposeth and exalteth himself against all that is called God or is an object of worship." While the anti-religious and blasphemous pretensions of the one who sets himself forth as God are thought of as a most direct assault upon the worship of the living God, the use of the compound "God or object of worship" is best explained as having in view the comprehensiveness and absoluteness of his religious claims. Accordingly, Paul appears to be using the term in II Thessalonians at best in a neutral sense and more probably in the unfavourable sense of the idolatrous worship of his day, and there is therefore no hint from the Biblical usage of the term that commendation in the slightest degree is in his mind.[17]

The single instance of the use of the cognate verb "worship" (σεβάζομαι) in the New Testament does not lead to a different result. In fact it does quite the contrary, for in that instance Paul is characterizing the pagan religious outlook with the strongest tones of condemnation: "they exchanged

[17] Considering the usage here and in certain apocryphal writings, Frame, *Thessalonians* (I. C. C.), p. 256, says that it "indicates not a divinity (*numen*) but any sacred object of worship."

the truth of God for a lie, and worshipped (ἐσεβάσθησαν) and served (ἐλάτρευσαν) the creature rather than the Creator, who is blessed for ever" (Rom. 1:25). Although the terms "idol" and "objects of worship" as used by Paul in Acts 17:23 would not necessarily have disclosed to the Athenians Paul's considered judgment concerning such worship, there is, on the other hand, no reason to suppose that his employment of these terms signifies any relaxation of the mood of indignation which Luke attributes to Paul.[18]

Nor is the situation altered by the consideration that Paul uses the verb εὐσεβεῖν to describe their worship of an unknown God when he says, "That which ye worship ... I declare unto you" (verse 23). For this verb with its cognate forms, while frequently employed to express the piety which merits divine approval, was widely used in the Hellenistic world as descriptive of religious loyalty demanded by or offered to the Roman emperors.[19] In the context of Acts the εὐσεβεῖν is the worship of one idol among the many heathen objects of worship.

More significant for our understanding of Paul's evaluation of pagan religion is his general characterization of their cultic piety which resulted from his observations concerning their worship: "I perceive that ye are very religious" (verse 22). The interpretation of the adjective δεισιδαιμονεστέρους reflected in the translation "very religious" is widely accepted today. It is the translation of both the A. S. V. and the new R. S. V. McGiffert suggested the rendering "uncommonly religious." On the other hand, the rendering in the unfavourable sense "superstitious" cannot be ruled out of court in advance. Although the translation of the A. V. "too superstitious" is unacceptable from a linguistic and contextual viewpoint, the same cannot be as dogmatically asserted of the rendering of the E. R. V. "somewhat superstitious," which is also supported in the margin of the A. S. V. And the support which the *Commentary* of Lake and Cadbury gives to the rendering "very superstitious" is indicative of the standing which this evaluation of the word still enjoys.

[18] The verb σέβομαι is used several times in the Acts, usually apparently of the worship of God-fearers, but in 19:27 of the pagan worship of Diana.
[19] Cf. Moulton and Milligan, *Vocabulary of the Greek New Testament*.

No good service would be rendered by embarking here upon a survey of the usage of this word with a view to determining its precise meaning, since this has been done in a thorough way, and it has become clear that the word is sufficiently ambiguous and comprehensive to bear both connotations.[20] That this might turn out to be the case is quite understandable when one keeps in view the difference of subjective evaluation of religions, according as a religion may be one's own cherished faith or another's alleged aberration or defection from a standard of piety. The question whether Paul means that they were uncommonly religious or uncommonly superstitious (allowing for some ambiguity in the term and accordingly for differences of interpretation) will have to be determined, in so far as that is possible, by the evaluation of the context.

Although, in my judgment, there is no evidence within the address or outside of it to suggest that Paul is in the slightest degree complacent towards idolatry, and much that demonstrates his thoroughgoing repudiation of it, it does appear definitely more satisfactory in the present connection to conclude that Paul is underscoring their religiosity rather than their superstition. The observation that their worship of idols included even the veneration of an unknown god provides a ground for calling attention to their extraordinary religiousness, a religiousness which went so far as to include even worship of an unknown god. Such worship, however, would not plausibly be regarded, within the context of polytheism, as an evidence of unusual superstition. On the other hand, to affirm that their religiosity rather than their superstition is prominently in view in Paul's opening observation is not to imply commendation on Paul's part of their religiosity. As has been observed, the very flexibility and ambiguity of the word makes it ill-suited to designate a piety which is favourably regarded; and there is nothing in the present context to warrant the conclusion that Paul's purpose is to compliment them on their worship.

---

[20] See especially Foerster in *Theologisches Worterbuch z. N T* and Lake and Cadbury in *Beginnings*, IV, on v. 22, and their references to the literature.

On this analysis of the Pauline language, his marked interest in the religion and worship of the Athenians may be of profound significance for the understanding of Paul's approach to the heathen. So far as the analysis has proceeded, there is nothing to suggest that Paul acted on the assumption that he needed only to supplement what the heathen already knew or to build upon a common foundation. However, the occupation with the religiosity of the Athenians can plausibly be explained as due to reflection upon the nature of man as created in the image of God and as therefore made to respond religiously to the Creator. However inadequate and even false the religion of the pagan might be judged to be as a consequence of sin, it would still be a fact of profound significance for the proclamation of the gospel that man retained his fundamental character as a religious being, that, as Calvin taught, he possesses as man, inseparable from his very constitution, an indelible *sensus divinitatis*, which the wicked seek to extinguish, but which is still strong and frequently discovers itself.[21]

That the apostle Paul actually held such a view regarding the constitution and nature of men, and therefore of wicked men too, is demonstrated in Rom. 1:19 and its immediate context where he teaches that, in addition to and evidently actually prior to the revelation of God with which all men are confronted in nature round about them, there is a revelation of God "in them." In profound agreement with this thought is his further teaching that the heathen have the law of God "written in their hearts" (Rom. 2:15). The explicit teaching of Paul therefore provides a background which, rather than setting up tensions or contradictions with the address at Athens, sheds welcome light upon his interest in the religion and worship of the natural man.

IV. THE CHARGE OF IGNORANCE

Although, therefore, the reflections upon the worship of the heathen Athenians in Acts 17:22, 23 contain observations concerning the religious state and activity of the natural

[21] *Institutes*, I, 3:1–3

man rather than evidences of positive agreement as to, or of common ground concerning, what true religion is and requires, one nevertheless encounters in this very context one feature which expresses a basic judgment as to the character of their religion. This is found in the indictment that their religion was one of ignorance.

The full impact of the charge is easily obscured in translation. The rendering of the King James' Version: "Whom therefore ye ignorantly worship, him declare I unto you" is particularly unhappy. For besides presupposing an inferior text in the masculine forms "whom" and "him" (for "what" and "this"), it is quite unsatisfactory in translating the participle ἀγνοοῦντες by the adverb "ignorantly," a rendering which lacks precision and, moreover, seems to reflect an emotional reaction not definitely established by the language employed. These defects are overcome in the E. R. V. and A. S. V. which read: "What therefore ye worship in ignorance, this I set forth unto you." Nevertheless, one feature that is still missed is the clear allusion of the participle ἀγνοοῦντες to the adjective ἀγνώστῳ in the inscription which gives real point to the Pauline evaluation. Paul makes the most of their public profession of lack of knowledge concerning the objects of worship by virtually reading it back to them as a characterization of their religion. He says in effect, "That which ye worship *acknowledging openly your ignorance*, I proclaim unto you." The ignorance rather than the worship is thus underscored, and Paul is indicating that he will inform them with regard to that concerning which they acknowledge ignorance. The R. S. V. perhaps reflects the point made here when it translates: "What therefore you worship as unknown, this I proclaim to you." The words, "as unknown," at any rate serve to reflect the inscription "To an unknown god." But even this translation fails to make clear that Paul is characterizing the *worshippers* as without knowledge rather than the object of worship as being, from his own point of view, as such unknown. The original, in any case, demonstrates that Paul, though not censorious, takes advantage of their confession to pronounce censure upon the Athenians and describes their religion bluntly as one of ignorance.

But, how seriously and absolutely is this indictment of

ignorance to be taken? Does Paul maintain a sharp antithesis between the Christian religion and pagan idolatry? Or is he represented here as softening his polemic, accommodating his point of view to the Hellenistic religiosity of his day, and even acknowledging significant common aspects in Christianity and paganism? The latter viewpoint is widely maintained. Dibelius, for example, argues that an attitude towards idol worship quite different from that in Rom. 1 appears in Acts 17. Whereas in Rom. 1:23, 25 Paul is recognized as condemning the pagan entanglement in idolatry with indignation (*"in empórtem Ton"*) he is thought in Acts 17 to be represented as correcting their idolatry in a merely admonishing and reproving tone.[22] On this approach the indictment of ignorance could not be regarded as intended very earnestly.

To advance the clarification of this point it seems advisable to take account immediately of a statement near the close of the address which uses similar language. In verse 30 Paul says that "the times of ignorance God therefore overlooked, but now he commandeth men that they should all everywhere repent." This declaration appears to some, especially in view of the use of the verb "overlook," to express an exceedingly moderate conception of the culpability of the heathen. Thus Percy Gardner states that, while idolatry was for Paul "an utter abomination," to the author of this address "it is only an unworthy way of regarding their Heavenly Father, for men who are the offspring of God who however in past time tolerated such materialism, until a fresh revelation came in the fulness of time."[23] But has the thrust of Paul's language in Acts 17:30 been correctly understood when he is said to have declared merely that God tolerated their materialism?[24]

[22] *Op. cit.*, p. 39.

[23] "The Speeches of St. Paul in Acts" in *Cambridge Biblical Essays* (London, 1909), p. 400

[24] A C. McGiffert expresses a quite different view: "The overlooking of ignorance which is here referred to does not imply that in pre-Christian days God regarded the idolatry of the heathen with indifference or saved them from the consequences of their sins, denounced so vigorously in Romans 1, but simply that the time for the final judgment had not come until now, and that they were, therefore, summoned now to prepare for it as they had not been before" (*The Apostolic Age* [New York, 1903], p 260, n. 1).

Is what Paul states here any different from his utterance concerning "the passing over of the sins done aforetime, in the forbearance of God" (Rom. 3:25)? The overlooking of ignorance, like the passing over of sins, properly signifies an attitude of forbearance, a failure to enter into final judgment with the guilty, but is by no means to be identified with complacency towards, or tolerance of, idolatry.

Those who find a discrepancy between the Paul of the Acts and the Paul of the Epistles at this point should have been forewarned against their divisive conclusions by a consideration of the tone of the Lystra episode where Paul's reproof of paganism is plainly not moderate or restrained! Paul was hardly undisturbed when with Barnabas, following the effort of the people to sacrifice to them, he rent his garments, and sprang forth among the multitude, crying out, "Sirs, why do ye these things?" (Acts 14:14 f.). In this narrative there is a close parallel to Rom. 3:25 as well as to Acts 17:30, for in verse 16 he says that God "in past generations permitted all the nations to walk in their own ways," words which likewise are associated with a call to repentance, that they "should turn from these vain things unto the living God who made the heaven and the earth . . ." (verse 15). Here clearly there is no tolerance of idolatry; the idols are "vain things" which are to be repudiated. Paul does not condemn idolatry more emphatically when he writes that the Galatians had been "in bondage to them that by nature are no gods" (Gal. 4:8; cf. Rom. 1:21, 8:23; I Cor. 12:2).[25]

His permitting the nations to walk in their ways, while perhaps not quite the equivalent of saying, as W. L. Knox has recently stated, that God "handed them over to a reprobate mind,"[26] gives expression to the long-suffering of God who postpones decisive judgment upon sin although men have been deserving of His wrath. In the light of this plain disclosure of how Paul, the Paul of Acts if any one pleases, contemplated the state of the heathen prior to the dawn of the Gentile mission in the new dispensation, it is indefen-

---

[25] K. J. Popma, *De Oudheid en Wij* (Kampen, 1948), pp 96 ff, has effectively pointed out the significance of the Lystra address

[26] *The Acts of the Apostles* (Cambridge, 1948), p 70

sible to force upon his declaration that God overlooked the times of ignorance the interpretation that God was relatively complacent towards idolatry.

The heathen in Athens were accordingly held responsible, according to Paul, for their state of ignorance as they were for their worship of vain things in Lystra. Their ignorance was a sinful ignorance which if persevered in could lead only to imminent judgment; hence the urgency of the call to repentance both at Lystra and at Athens.

The connection established between Paul's characterizations of the state of the heathen in verses 23 and 30 raises the question of the broad disposition and thrust of the address, for that also bears upon the more specific question of the attitude taken towards idolatry. Dibelius' analysis of the address, which has been mentioned, appears to fail in particular to do justice to its coherence. In dissociating Paul's mood of indignation as described in Acts 17:16 from the rest of the address, in isolating likewise the conclusion of Acts 17:30, 31 as a Christian appendage to a basically Hellenistic address (as is supposed), and in formulating the theme of the address proper as concerned with the true knowledge of God accessible to the natural man, the antithesis drawn throughout between the idolatrous religion of the heathen and the true worship of God represented by Christianity is not recognized. The facts are, however, that idolatry was the occasion of Paul's activity in Athens, a particular form of idolatry formed the starting-point for his address before the Areopagus, and the proclamation of God as the sovereign Creator and Ruler of all was directed against idolatry. It established the impropriety of the worship which makes its gods dependent upon men's handiwork, and showed rather that man, owing his life, breath and all things to God, "ought not to think that the Godhead is like unto gold, or silver, or stone, graven by art and device of man." All of this then forms the background for the call to repentance in view of the coming judgment. There are indeed certain features of the address which remain unaccounted for on this analysis, especially the introduction of quotations from the heathen poets in an apparently sympathetic manner. The problems raised by this feature are weighty and they will need to be faced with all earnestness. But it may be observed at once that even these quotations are obviously introduced by Paul to support his principal argument as to the untenability of idolatry, and therefore do not impinge upon the judgment as to the disposition of the address. Paul roundly condemns what he observed as a religion of ignorance.

V. THE APOSTOLIC AUTHORITY

Another fact of fundamental import for the understanding of Paul's approach to the heathen is that he claims that he alone is immediately able to supply their real need, that he alone is able to provide them with a knowledge of the true and living God: "That which ye worship acknowledging your ignorance, I declare unto you" (ἐγὼ καταγγέλλω ὑμῖν). How bold, if not presumptuous and bigoted, his claim must have appeared to his hearers who had already found occasion to ridicule him as a babbler, or at best conceived of him as proclaiming a deity or deities besides those already worshipped among them! But the note of authority to proclaim the true God, however strange and offensive it may have been to his Athenian hearers, is not a novelty. The Christian proclamation throughout the New Testament is never viewed as mere human observations concerning the message of the Old Testament and least of all as human reflections upon the religions of the age, but rather as a divine message, true and authoritative as coming from God Himself. Paul declares that the gospel which he preached "is not after man; for neither did I receive it from man, nor was I taught it, but it came to me through revelation of Jesus Christ" (Gal. 1:11 f.). Faith, Paul taught, is of hearing, and hearing "through the Word of Christ," and this Word of faith in Christ and His resurrection was proclaimed by Paul and others commissioned by God (Rom. 10:8 ff.). And throughout the Acts attention is centered upon the apostolic preaching as carried on by those who were appointed to, and qualified from above for, this task (1:15 ff., 2:42, 6:2, 4 and *passim*). Paul in particular is singled out as having received his apostolic commission by an extraordinary divine intervention: he was a chosen vessel to whom the exalted Christ had appeared to appoint him as a minister and witness both of the things wherein he had seen Christ and of the things wherein Christ would appear to him.[27]

Special interest in this connection attaches to the verb which Paul employs in verse 23 in introducing his proclamation. The verb καταγγέλειν is used frequently in the Acts and the Pauline Epistles of the official apostolic proclamation of the gospel. "The word of God" is proclaimed by Paul and Barnabas (Acts 13:5, 15:36, 17.13); "the testimony of God" was proclaimed to the Corinthians (I Cor. 2:1); "the gospel" is that which is proclaimed by divine appointment (I Cor. 9:14); "Jesus" (Acts 4:2, 17:3) and "Christ" (Phil. 1:17, 18; Col. 1:27 f.) likewise sum up the divine message (cf. also Acts 3:8; I Cor. 11:26). That the publication of the apostolic message was viewed as claiming direct divine authority is furthermore confirmed by the use of the same verb in describing the proclamation beforehand of Christ by the prophets (Acts 3:24; cf. 3:18, 22).

When therefore Paul undertakes to inform the Athenians concerning the sovereign Creator and Judge, and declares that he is proclaiming to them that with regard to which they had in a measure acknowledged ignorance, he sounds the characteristic apostolic note of divine authority. How far he is therefore from stressing supposedly common ground between himself and his pagan hearers! When he says that the state of the heathen was characterized by ignorance of the true God, and he himself boldly asserts his qualifications to provide them with true knowledge, he is accenting, rather than toning down, the antithesis between the pagan religiosity and the Christian religion. When Paul's claim to inform them truly and authoritatively concerning God is taken earnestly, there is no place for the judgment that the thrust of the address is concerned with the knowledge of God and the affinity with God of the natural man, as Dibelius contends, and especially for his asseveration that nothing is said of the claim of the Christian message that the true knowledge of God can be possessed and communicated only by way of revelation.[28] Although the word "revelation" does not appear,

[27] Cf. Acts 9:15, 16, 20:24, 22:14 f., 26:16 ff.
[28] *Op. cit*, pp. 36 ff. and passim. He says: "Von dem Anspruch der christlichen Botschaft die wahre Gotteserkenntnis erst durch Offenbarung

Paul's claim does not fall short of that of the Christian message generally, whether published by the prophets or apostles or by Jesus Christ Himself.

VI. THE SOVEREIGN CREATOR AND LORD

Perhaps the most controversial terrain in the entire narrative lies before us in the study of verses 24–29. The proclamation of God as Creator and Ruler of the world, as has been observed, is often viewed as an affirmation of monotheism, which is thought of as being not distinctively Christian and even as occupying to a large extent common ground with the religious outlook of non-Christians in the Hellenistic age. Although it will not be practicable to consider all the data in detail, certain observations can be made with regard to the main problem. I wish here especially to raise the question as to whether Paul remains on distinctly Christian ground in his positive affirmations and to gauge the implications of his utilization of quotations from heathen poets.

The first observation is that the God whom Paul proclaims the Creator and Lord of heaven and earth, who is self-sufficient, and therefore ought not to be thought of as dependent upon man and worshipped as an idol, is not presented as a matter of fact *in this address* as one whose knowledge may be taken for granted or presupposed or even inferred from a study of the world and history. As has been stressed, Paul proclaims this God as one who is basically unknown to his hearers. Moreover, the appeal is not, at least not in verses 24–26, to natural revelation which would yield these conclusions if properly interpreted. There is nothing, for example, even parallel to the teaching of Paul ìn Rom. 1:20 that "the invisible things of him since the creation of the world are clearly seen, being perceived through the things that are made, even his everlasting power and divinity, that they may be without excuse." Rather the mood is the quite dogmatic one of special revelation associated with Paul's own authoritative claims and reinforced by a direct dependence upon the

---

zu besitzen und mitteilen zu koennen wird nichts gesagt" (p 36) The revelational note appears also with particular force in verses 30, 31

teaching of the Old Testament. Paul may have thought it inappropriate to appeal specifically to the authority of the Old Testament, but the reflection of its language and thought is none the less in evidence throughout. For example, he is on thoroughly Biblical ground in speaking of God as the one "that made the world and all things therein," for this language is a virtual quotation from Ex. 20:11 and has found expression repeatedly in both the Old and New Testaments (cf. Ps. 146:6; Is. 37:16; Acts 4:24, 14:15). Likewise the declaration that God is "Lord" of heaven and earth and "dwelleth not in temples made with hands" is an echo of I Kgs. 8·27 and was previously affirmed in the address of Stephen (Acts 7.48; cf. Is. 46:1 f.).[29] The entire statement concerning God as Creator and Ruler is so obviously a reflection of Biblical perspectives that the argument as to supposedly Hellenistic motifs at most establishes points of contact with the contemporaneous religious vocabulary. Only in the Bible does the doctrine of the sovereign Creator and Ruler, without compromise with immanentistic ideas, come to expression, and this is conspicuously in evidence in verses 24–26.

Paul may perhaps have in the background of his thought his teaching regarding the revelation through nature concerning which he spoke at Lystra in affirming that they had not been left without witness (Acts 14:17), and in Rom. 1·20, where he writes concerning the witness to the everlasting power and divinity in the things that are clearly seen. In so far as the testimony of nature may be in mind, however, Paul would have to be understood as concerned to interpret the natural revelation in terms of special revelation.

Nor is the supposedly common ground of natural religion reached when Paul intimates that God had created the world and ordained its affairs that men "should seek God, if haply they might feel after him and find him" (verse 27). For there is no hint that the heathen are conceived of as having found

---

[29] Other evidences of agreement with Biblical perspectives concerning the divine self-sufficiency, sovereign ordering of events, and the impropriety of idol worship have often been pointed out Cf especially Dt. 32·8, Is. 42:5, Ps 50·12 Even Norden, *op cit.*, pp 8 ff , admits the influence of such passages as these, and declares that the "Grundmotiv" is "judisch-christlich"

God as the result of a groping after Him or as yearning after Him in a manner which had gained the divine approbation. There is no suggestion of a recognition of a kind of "unconscious Christianity." Paul is not describing contemporaneous pagan religion but rather is disclosing the divine purpose regarding man's religious response which was grounded in the creation of man and the divine rule over him. To man was appointed the privilege of religious fellowship with his Creator, and this was to be attained by way of a conscious seeking after God in response to the divine revelation. That goal had always remained, but in "the times of ignorance" it evidently remained distant and had not been reached.

When now Paul adds the concession, "though he is not far from each one of us," he appears to present a new perspective. The concessive character of this statement indeed confirms the conclusion that the goal of finding God had not been attained, but it also reflects positively on an actual relationship of God to all men in the present situation. And what Paul has in mind in characterizing God as being near to all men is apparently regarded as illumined and supported by the more specific affirmations that "in him we live and move and have our being" and that "we are also his offspring." Since the latter quotation is derived from a work of the Stoic Aratus, and the former is almost certainly from Epimenides the Cretan,[30] there emerges most acutely the problem of the propriety of appealing to pagan teaching with the apparent intent of confirming Christian doctrine.

The problem is formidable because the quotations in their proper pagan contexts express points of view which were undoubtedly quite repugnant to Paul. How far removed from the Christian theism of Paul, with its doctrine of the sovereignty of the Creator and Lord and of man as created and fallen, were the heathen deification of man or the humanizing of a god, and the pantheistic mysticism of the Stoics, not to dwell on the irreligious scepticism of the Epicureans! Moreover, Paul would appear to be contradicting his evaluation of the Gentiles, which must have included the poets who are

[30] On these questions see Lake and Cadbury *ad loc* ; Lake, *Beginnings*, V., pp. 246 ff ; and F F Bruce, *The Speeches in Acts* (London, 1942), pp. 16 ff.

quoted, as belonging to the "times of ignorance," and his judgment upon the religion of Athens as one of ignorance. In spite of the antithesis which in fact existed, and which Paul insists upon, can there be a finding of common ground between him and his pagan audience?

A tempting and rather facile solution might be found if Paul could be regarded as virtually Christianizing the quotations in incorporating them into his proclamation. Their language as such indeed would not necessarily compromise the Christian theism enunciated by Paul. In the context of the thought of the preceding verses, the immanence of God expressed in the former quotation could be viewed as deriving its significance from the fact that God is acknowledged by the apostle with full earnestness as the Creator and Lord of all men. That "we live and move and have our being" in God would then be a corollary of the doctrine of the absolute dependence of the creature upon the Creator for life and breath and all things. Similarly, the recognition that man is the offspring of God might enunciate a doctrine which lies at the basis of Paul's reflections in the narrative upon the original constitution of man and his retention of his creaturehood in the midst of his present idolatrous and blameworthy state and acts. Paul then might be regarded as arguing that, if only man had taken due account of his creation in the divine image, he might have recognized the error of his idolatry which conceived of God in terms of dependence upon man's reflection and handiwork.

But is not this approach much too simple? To maintain that Paul has Christianized pagan ideas suggests that propositions which subjectively considered are the antithesis of Christianity might be viewed as being objectively true. K. J. Popma has effectively shown that such a distinction between thought and word, as well as an approach which would allow that the quotations are materially untrue but formally true, sets up dualisms in mind and in history which are intolerable.

When, however, the same writer, on the background of a salutary recognition of the antithesis of Christianity and paganism, argues that the quotations are introduced only with a view to shaking his hearers loose from the apostate religious convictions which the quotations express, it appears that he has not done full justice to all the evidence.[31] This viewpoint overlooks, in particular, the manner in which Paul introduces one quotation, and perhaps both, with the words, "as certain even of your own poets have said" (verse 28). In arguing from the quotations to his Christian conclusions Paul appears unmistakably to be attaching validity to them even while he is taking serious account of their presence within the structure of pagan thought. The formula confirms indeed an observation made previously: it intimates that the quotations are not offered as foundation features of the Pauline proclamation, but only quite subordinately and even incidentally to the main thrust of his address, which stands on strong Biblical ground. The fact remains, however, that, at least momentarily, he appears to occupy common ground with his pagan hearers to the extent of admitting a measure of validity to their observations concerning religion.

This question remains a pressing one, therefore: how can the argument supported by appeal to the quotations of pagan poets be valid even while their pagan origin and character were fully recognized? One will be in an impasse here, I believe, unless account is taken of other teaching of Paul, teaching in the Epistles as well as in the Acts, which provides a broader and richer context of truth. Paul maintained that even pagans remained confronted with the revelation of God in nature, and that this contact with revelation rendered them inexcusable (Acts 14:17; Rom. 1:19 ff.). This confrontation with the divine revelation had not been without effect upon their minds since it brought them into contact with the truth, but their basic antipathy to the truth was such that they suppressed it in unrighteousness (Rom. 1:18).[32] Thus while maintaining the antithesis between the knowledge of God enjoyed by His redeemed children and the state of ignorance which characterized all others, Paul could allow consistently and fully for the thought that pagan men, in spite of themselves and contrary to the controlling disposition of their minds, as creatures of God confronted with the divine revelation were capable of responses which were valid so long as and to the

---

[31] *Evangelie contra Evangelie* (Franeker, Holland, n. d.), pp. 47 ff.

[32] Cf. also γνόντες τὸν Θεὸν in Rom 1:21 with οὐ δύναται γνῶναι in I Cor 2:14.

extent that they stood in isolation from their pagan systems. Thus, thoughts which in their pagan contexts were quite un-Christian and anti-Christian, could be acknowledged as up to a point involving an actual apprehension of revealed truth. As creatures of God, retaining a *sensus divinitatis* in spite of their sin, their ignorance of God and their suppression of the truth, they were not without a certain awareness of God and of their creaturehood. Their ignorance of, and hostility to, the truth was such that their awareness of God and of creaturehood could not come into its own to give direction to their thought and life or to serve as a principle of interpretation of the world of which they were a part. But the apostle Paul, reflecting upon their creaturehood, and upon their religious faith and practice, could discover within their pagan religiosity evidences that the pagan poets in the very act of suppressing and perverting the truth presupposed a measure of awareness of it. Thus while conceiving of his task as basically a proclamation of One of whom they were in ignorance, he could appeal even to the reflections of pagans as pointing to the true relation between the sovereign Creator and His creatures.[33]

One aspect of the criticism of the message attributed to Paul in Acts 17:24–29 remains to be considered. The charge that Paul is represented as introducing an expression of pantheistic mysticism in verse 28 in contrast to a particularistic conception of sonship in his Epistles is presented on the background of the judgment that the body of the address is occupied with a presentation of monotheism which has little or nothing to do with specific Christianity. Assuredly a monotheism which knows nothing of the particularism of divine grace forfeits its right to the name Christian, and hence if living in God and being the offspring of God were intended by Paul in Acts to indicate the sufficiency and validity of a religion of nature, there would be the most violent antithesis to the Christian gospel. However, as has been observed, there

[33] Cornelius Van Til has recently stressed, in connection with a salutary emphasis upon the significance and meaning of history, that the wicked within history, for all of their ignorance of and hostility to God, are kept from being fully satanic. See his "Introduction" to B. B. Warfield, *The Inspiration and Authority of the Bible* (Philadelphia, 1948), especially pp. 24, 32, 38 f. Cf also his *Common Grace* (Philadelphia, 1947).

is no good reason to conclude that Paul means to characterize true religion in these terms. And to come to my main point in this connection, in my judgment a basic fault of modern criticism of Acts 17 is that it supposes that Christianity may exist as a message of grace and judgment apart from monotheism, or from what I should prefer to call a Christian theistic view of the world. This raises a profoundly controversial issue of the modern day which the limits of this paper do not permit me to discuss, an issue so basic as to involve the total question of what Christianity really is. I must be satisfied here with the observation that the message of Paul at Athens, taken in its grand sweep as a message which integrates creation and providence with the teaching concerning Jesus, sin, repentance, the resurrection and the day of judgment, is not confined to this chapter or to the Acts. It certainly may not fairly be ruled out of the thought of Paul of the Epistles.

It is astonishing that Dibelius and Schweitzer apparently fail to take into account the far-reaching implications of I Thes. 1:8, 9, a most precious record of Paul's early preaching in Thessalonica, in which as at Lystra and at Athens he regards as essential to conversion to Christianity a turning unto God from idols to serve the living and true God. However this silence may be explained, one fears that there is at work here, and in much of the modern exegesis, an arbitrary and divisive approach which has disastrous consequences. The modern effort to detach the specific Christian message from the Biblical theism of the Scriptures involves a radical transformation of the Christian doctrines of creation, sin, salvation and consummation, and also the substitution of a modern world view for the one that has been rejected. Hence it represents a thorough-going modernization of Christianity rather than a scientific interpretation of it.

VII. The Consequences of the Address

The conclusion that the apostle Paul remains on solid Christian ground, in complete consistency with his teaching in his Epistles, and yet effectively takes advantage of the religious faith and practice of his pagan hearers in calling upon men to turn from idols to serve the living and true God, is challenged from still another point of view. One might maintain that the narrative is quite trustworthy as a record of Paul's ministry in Athens, but if the apostle himself, as the consequence of the paucity of converts, or because of a revaluation of the propriety or wisdom of his particular approach before the Areopagus, became disillusioned and later determined to follow a different evangelistic method, the address would possess virtually as little relevance for the understanding of the authoritative apostolic proclamation of the New Testament as it would if we held the view that the address is largely imaginative. Such an evaluation of the consequences of the address has enjoyed considerable vogue in recent decades, perhaps as a result of the influence of Sir William M. Ramsay, who summed up his judgment as follows:

> It would appear that Paul was disappointed and perhaps disillusioned by his experience in Athens. He felt that he had gone at least as far as was right in the way of presenting his doctrine in a form suited to the current philosophy; and the result had been little more than naught. When he went on from Athens to Corinth, he no longer spoke in the philosophic style. In replying afterwards to the unfavorable comparison between his preaching and the more philosophical style of Apollos, he told the Corinthians that, when he came among them, he "determined not to know anything save Jesus Christ, and Him crucified" (I Cor. 2:2); and nowhere throughout his writings is he so hard on the wise, the philosophers, and the dialecticians, as when he defends the way in which he had presented Christianity at Corinth. Apparently the greater concentration of purpose and simplicity of method in his preaching at Corinth is referred to by Luke, when he says, 18:5, that when Silas and Timothy rejoined him there, they found him wholly possessed by and engrossed in the word. This strong expression, so unlike anything else in Acts, must, on our hypothesis, be taken to indicate some specifically marked character in the Corinthian preaching.[34]

---

[34] *St Paul the Traveller and Roman Citizen*, p. 252 Recent expressions of this viewpoint are found in Foakes-Jackson *ad loc.* and Finegan, *Light from the Ancient Past* (Princeton, 1946), p. 247. Even G. T. Purves, *Christianity in the Apostolic Age* (New York, 1900), p. 193, though regarding the contents of the address as being of "the highest value, because it presented aspects of truth which were to be of fundamental importance in the coming

The argument no doubt is plausible, and enjoys a measure of popular appeal because of its apparent readiness to be content with the simple gospel rather than with philosophical argument. But my own judgment is that it is quite untenable when the pertinent data are evaluated at their true worth.

In the first place, it is essential to take due account of the Lucan methods and aims in the Acts as the proper background for the estimate of his purpose in introducing this address. In pursuance of his goal to exhibit the manner in which the ascended Lord brought His word to men and established His Church in the face of many obstacles, Luke presents many examples of the apostolic preaching and especially that of Peter and Paul. Without specific evidence to support such a conclusion it is incredible that he should have reported apostolic preaching which was intended to demonstrate how the gospel was *not* to be preached, and it is particularly incomprehensible that the Areopagus address should be regarded in that light when one contemplates the pains which Luke takes to portray the exceptional historical situation in which Paul found himself and the impressiveness with which the address itself is reported. Luke gives every impression of presenting Paul as a masterful orator who knew exactly how to suit his message to a distinctive and challenging situation. That Paul can have been thought of as in reality a failure can be accepted only if the most decisive proofs can be mustered in support of that hypothesis.

When one measures the consequences of the preaching, one must admit that they may not appear impressive. There was the repetition of the ridicule which had been expressed earlier; others continued to show the curiosity that had led to his being taken before the Areopagus (verse 32; cf. verse 18), and thus there is no change in the general situation. There is added, however, the report that certain men joined him and believed, and that among these converts there was a Dionysius who was a member of the supreme council, and a woman named Damaris. Though the number of believers was

---

conflict between Christianity and paganism," speaks of the results as "disappointing" and says that "Paul finally moved on to Corinth resolved to know nothing but Jesus Christ and Him crucified (I Cor. 2.1, 2) "

evidently not great, Luke does not underscore their paucity. It is even possible to suppose that he regarded it as remarkable in the circumstances, with all of the unfavorable religious and philosophical commitments which characterized the Athenians, that there should have been some who were prepared to make a break with views which were in good standing in Athens and to share the ignominy or disdain attached to Paul's faith.

Moreover, even if the results were actually more meagre than Luke shows them to have been, and even if Luke had directed special attention to the paucity of converts, it still would not follow that any blame would be attached to the message of Paul for the failure of a larger company of Athenians to turn to belief in Christ. To the extent that historical factors may have influenced the results, one is on far sounder ground if note is taken of the original purpose of Paul to enjoy a period of rest rather than to preach in Athens, and of the apparent brevity of his activity there.[35] Actually, however, it is most precarious to engage in rationalizing from the number of converts to the correctness of the message. That there were converts at all should be sufficient proof, within the context of the Acts, that the message was regarded as the Christian message. Luke did not share the pragmatism of our day which judges the truth of the message by the criterion of outward success.

Another decisive reason for rejecting the judgment that a causal connection exists between the character of Paul's message at Athens and the meagre results is that the Areopagus address by no means constitutes the only preaching Paul undertook there. As I have previously observed, his activity there included preaching in the Jewish synagogue and in the market-place, and his apostolic message was summed up in the terms "Jesus and the resurrection," a most apt and succinct characterization of the preaching of Paul and Peter

---

[35] Ramsay, *St Paul*, p. 239, himself says that "the lack of results at this stage is . . fully explained by the shortness of time Paul's stay in Athens can hardly have been longer than six weeks, and was probably less than four, and the process described in verse 17 was brought to a premature close by the great event of his visit, which the historian describes very fully"

as reported in Acts.[36] It is quite unjustifiable, accordingly, to insist that there were few converts in Athens because Paul preached somewhat distinctively before the Areopagus. Even if this address were quite at variance with Paul's usual message, one would still have to reckon with the fact that in his general approach to the Athenians he had evidently followed a fairly stereotyped pattern.

Although, accordingly, the narrative affords no hint that Paul was on the wrong track at Athens, it is averred that a contrary impression is given by other data in the Acts and in I Corinthians. Paul himself is thought in I Cor. 2:2 to reflect upon his ministry in Athens and to be expressing a new determination to know only "Christ and him crucified" in contrast to a philosophically oriented message. And in Acts 18:5 Luke is viewed as likewise indicating that at Corinth Paul adopted a different, simpler approach. In the latter passage Luke indeed characterizes the early phase of Paul's preaching in Corinth in a somewhat unusual manner when he says that "when Silas and Timothy came down from Macedonia, Paul was engrossed in the word, testifying to the Jews that Jesus was the Christ."[37] And it is possible that a contrast of some kind is being drawn with the description of his activity in the preceding verse where, following a reference to his labor with Aquila and Priscilla at his trade as a tentmaker, the narrative reports that "he was reasoning in the synagogue every sabbath and persuading Jews and Greeks." If a contrast between two phases of his preaching to the Jews is actually in view, it would be completely gratuitous to explain this development in terms of a simpler, less philosophical approach in the second phase. There is not a trace of a suggestion that this was in mind, and it would furthermore imply that at Corinth, in the beginning, Paul was preaching to the Jews in a form suited to the current philosophy! It would be far more in point to suppose, as Lake and Cadbury do, for example, that the coming of Silas and Timothy somehow

---

[36] See p. 7 above

[37] The E. R V and A S V translate the phrase "was constrained by the word," but most commentators more satisfactorily render it substantially as given above The new R S. V reads "was occupied with preaching." The A V. "was pressed in the spirit" is based upon an inferior text

relieved Paul of the necessity of engaging in earning his living and that he began to be engrossed in the word in the sense that he gave all of his time to preaching. Even the latter view, however, is largely inferential and rather forced, since Luke does not qualify his reference to the preaching activity by stating that he could now engage in it *every day*. Inasmuch as Luke says that Paul was occupied with preaching to the Jews when Silas and Timothy came to Corinth, and thus may be understood as virtually repeating the description of Paul's activity among the Jews in 18:5, it is more satisfactory to conclude that 18:5 is a résumé of 18:4 introduced in order to indicate that, as 18:6 immediately goes on to disclose, soon after the arrival of these men, the Jews turned so sharply against his mission that he turned to the Gentiles (cf. Acts 14:44 ff.). At any rate, there is no foundation whatsoever for the interpretation that Paul's being engrossed in preaching to the Jews reflects a rejection or modification of his message and method in preaching to the pagans in Athens.

Nor does the appeal to I Cor. 2:2 rest upon a firm basis. Paul does not say that, when he came to Corinth, he adopted a new evangelistic approach, and there is no suggestion that he had accommodated his message of "Christ and Him crucified" to his hearers at Athens and now regretted it. There is no hint even that he ever preached any differently than he did at Corinth, but Paul takes pains to remind the Corinthians that he had not come with "excellency of speech or of wisdom"; his gospel was not one that commended itself to the wise in Corinth, but was foolishness unto them. And so indeed his message had largely proved to be to the Athenians.[38]

There remains the consideration, however, that the message says nothing concerning Christ crucified or of salvation by faith in Him. Does not the address, therefore, even if its content is quite unobjectionable, appear to stop short of being a well-rounded Christian proclamation of the gospel? In

---

[38] This interpretation is even more emphatically supported by the original, for Paul does not say, "I determined not to know ..." (A. V, E. R. V.), or "I decided to know nothing ..." (R S. V), but "I did not determine to know ..." See also Lightfoot, *Notes on Epistles of St. Paul* (1895), p 171, who renders it, "I had no intent, no mind to know anything."

considering this question, one may reckon with the distinct possibility that Luke intends to intimate that Paul was interrupted before he had reached his real conclusion. When his hearers heard mention of the resurrection, some mocked while others indicated an interest in hearing Paul at a later time, and Paul thereupon departed out of their midst (17·32 f.). Moreover, when a comparison is made between the address and Paul's summary of his message to the Gentile world in I Thes. 1:9, 10, it may plausibly be argued that there is agreement in the declarations concerning conversion from idols to the true God, the return of Christ, and the resurrection of Christ but that the feature of deliverance by Christ from the wrath to come alone fails of mention at Athens. On this approach one might well maintain that Paul had preached Christ and Him crucified, and deliverance through Him from the wrath to come, in his earlier preaching in Athens, but that in the instance of the Areopagus address the offence taken at the doctrine of the resurrection, disclosing as it did the chasm that separated their thinking from Paul's, was so profound that they precipitately and impatiently closed their ears, as it were, to the proclamation of salvation through Christ.[39]

There are weighty reasons, however, for judging that this evaluation of the conclusion of the address, for all of its plausibility and attractiveness, is not firmly established. In the first place, Luke clearly does not say that Paul's hearers interrupted his address before he had finished. The reactions of his audience may be fully understood as being expressed following the completion of his message, just as similar reactions developed after Paul's earlier proclamation of Jesus and the resurrection (17:18). Secondly, one is not on incontestable ground in assuming that all of Paul's preaching would have conformed to a stereotyped pattern, and especially that the address on the extraordinary occasion of his appearance before

---

[39] On this point and the argument that the Athenian audience definitely broke off his address before it was completed, see Bavinck, *op. cit*, pp. 126 ff., 139 f , 122 ff , 183. Bavinck goes so far as to say, "Als Paulus over de opstanding der dooden begint te handelen, roepen de intellectueele fijnproevers van Athene hem tot orde en breken zijn rede af" (p 183)

the Areopagus would not have expressed a certain formal and material individuality.[40]

Another approach to the problem which escapes these particular difficulties appears to be definitely tenable, one which, rather than inferring that the address was abruptly terminated by his hearers, takes account of the exceedingly compressed character of the reports of the speeches in Acts.[41] If one once recognizes that the addresses must be regarded as condensed accounts of speeches that lasted considerably longer than the time it takes us to read them through, one may be prepared to face the question whether the several reports, while indicating accurately the disposition and contents of the addresses in summary form, do not imply as much as they actually state. As applied to the situation confronting us here, this observation suggests that Luke means to imply that the message of salvation through Christ is being intimated in epitome in Paul's proclamation of the divine command that all men everywhere should repent. "The times of ignorance therefore God overlooked; but now he commandeth men that they should all everywhere repent; inasmuch as he hath appointed a day in which he will judge the world in righteousness by the man whom he hath ordained; whereof he hath given assurance unto all men, in that he hath raised him from the dead" (verses 30, 31).

There can surely be no doubt that Paul is proclaiming here the wrath to come. The day of judgment is announced on the authority of an apostle of Christ as a day when God will judge the world in righteousness. The One through whom the divine judgment will be executed has already been designated. And not only has the commission to execute judgment been bestowed upon One especially chosen, but there

---

[40] It is necessary to guard against exaggerating the stereotyped character of Paul's preaching in general. "To await his son from heaven" (I Thess. 1:10) strikes the eschatological note, but it has a somewhat different orientation from that in Acts 17:31 which centers upon the coming judgment. The preaching of Paul in Pisidian Antioch (13:16 ff.), while stressing the resurrection of Christ and declaring remission of sins through Him, appears to omit the distinctively eschatological feature.

[41] Bruce, *op cit.*, p. 27, takes note of this characteristic of the speeches of Acts in its bearing upon their trustworthiness.

has also already been a sign of the coming of that day and of that Judge. For in raising Christ from the dead God had revealed with sufficient clearness that the age to come had begun to be realized and that the One who had gained preeminence by the divine power which raised Him from the dead was One with whom men were compelled to reckon as a unique servant of God.

But the proclamation of the *dies irae* also brings to Paul's hearers a message of grace. Favor had been expressed in overlooking their ignorance; now there was manifested the goodness of God which confronted the Gentiles with the revelation of the day of judgment and urgently warned them — "all men everywhere" — of the necessity of repentance. But this command to repent expresses more than the thought of the inevitability of divine judgment upon men who fail to repent. It discloses also that the days before the dread day of judgment would come are days of grace and salvation, when men may still repent for their sins and escape the wrath to come.

That the proclamation of the divine command to repent may be understood as a preaching of the glad tidings of salvation is confirmed by the manner in which it is introduced in the apostolic preaching generally. Peter, for example, declares: "Repent ye therefore, and turn again, that your sins may be blotted out . . ." (3:19; cf. 2:38). And Paul informs Agrippa that he was not disobedient to the heavenly vision, but declared to Jews 'and to Gentiles that they should repent and turn to God, doing works worthy of repentance' (26:20; cf. 14:15). Repentance is described not only as a turning unto God, but also as a 'repentance unto life' which God granted to the Gentiles (Acts 11:18), and also as giving assurance of the forgiveness of sins (5:31; cf. 24:47).

And since Paul points to Christ as the One whose resurrection establishes His credentials to judge among men as to their acceptance with God, one may at least read between the lines that those who are to share with Christ the blessedness of the world to come are faced with the necessity of being assured of a favorable relationship to Him who guards the portals of eternal life.

The gospel of Jesus Christ, according to Luke, as disclosed

in both his Gospel and the Acts, is the gospel of the crucified One. But since the divine action of salvation is viewed as reaching its consummation in the exaltation of Christ, there is a profound occupation with the resurrection of Christ as serving to sum up even more pointedly than the cross the decisive saving work of God. This accounts for the prominence given to the resurrection in Luke's record of that which Jesus did before His ascension; it also explains the emphasis which falls upon it in the records of the apostolic preaching. In the Areopagus address the declaration concerning the profound significance of the resurrection of Christ appropriately subsumes the fact of the cross. Thus also in the Epistles Paul, who wished to know only Christ and Him crucified, preaches Christ as the one "that died, yea rather, that was raised from the dead" (Rom. 8:34).

CHAPTER II

WHO CRUCIFIED JESUS?

THE title of this article coincides with that of a recently published book which answers the question in a fashion so arresting and novel and withal so far-reaching in its implications for the understanding of the gospels that the reader is compelled to face the question for himself.[1] While the question superficially considered may appear to concern only a peripheral historical detail, further reflection will disclose that no one can make any affirmation about Jesus Christ, and least of all one that relates to his death, without taking a position, explicitly or implicitly, on the decisive issue of faith or unbelief. Consequently, whether we come to agree or to disagree with the thesis of this book, it serves the highly useful purpose of stimulating us to observe with greater alertness what the records actually say on this momentous subject.

Professor Zeitlin must be credited, we believe, with a rare achievement. For here is a book devoted to a phase of antiquarian research which turns out to be a tract for the times. Our interest is aroused by the fact that a noted Jewish authority on Rabbinics writes on the ever-fascinating theme of the crucifixion and we know in advance that his treatment can hardly be stereotyped. We soon discover, moreover, that in spite of all that has been written on the subject he comes forward with a brand new thesis concerning the condemnation of Jesus which absolves the Jewish people from implication in this event which has come to be weighted down with tragic meaning for hosts of the sons of Jacob. To add to its appeal the author effectively challenges the reader to observe that "history is the teacher of life" (to use the phrase which he borrows from Cicero), which means in this instance that the study of the struggles between

---

[1] Solomon Zeitlin: *Who Crucified Jesus?* New York and London: Harper & Brothers. 1942. xv, 240. $2.50.

absolutist and tyrannical powers and the representatives of decency and piety will provide sound insights for the solution of our problems as we today pass through catastrophic and world-shaking experiences. In a time when Chaucer and Latin are held by some political leaders to be a waste of time, and Josephus and Hebrew would probably receive even less complimentary characterization, it is refreshing to read a defense of the study of history. In particular Dr. Zeitlin appeals to history to fashion an impressive appeal for the elimination of anti-Semitism as unworthy of the democratic spirit and as based upon an unhistorical judgment of the responsibility of the Jews for the death of Jesus.

The thesis of the book, negatively stated, is that the Jews did not crucify Jesus, that in fact this accusation against the Jews "is a tragic libel evilly wrought on an innocent people" (p. 179). Obviously, to lend plausibility to this negative proposition the author must seek to establish a positive explanation of the actual nature of the developments leading to the crucifixion, an explanation which will stand the test of scrutiny, and herein is discovered the chief novelty of the book. Expressed in its barest outline his position is "that neither the modern Jew nor his ancestors were responsible in any way whatsoever for the death of Jesus. For Jesus fell victim to a cruel pagan imperialism whose malign spirit is as much alive today as it was in the days of ancient Rome" (p. xiv). In other words, Jesus was not the victim of the hostility of the Jews, but like the Jews in ages since suffered at the hands of a ruthless political system.

Does Zeitlin then mean to imply that no Jews whatever were involved in the sordid business? Well, not quite. For the high priest of the day and certain associates do not come off very well; in fact, they are likened to the Quislings of our day. It is insisted, however, that the Jewish people as a people cannot be held responsible for the action of one who was ready to sell out his country for the sake of personal advantage. To quote a fuller statement of the author's conclusion:

> "Jesus was crucified as the King of the Jews. The Jewish religious Sanhedrin and the Jewish people had nothing to do with the trial of Jesus. The high priest who

actually delivered Jesus to the Roman authorities either was compelled to do so to save himself so as not to be accused of being an accessory to the rebels; or, most likely, Caiaphas, the high priest, played the rôle of a Quisling who proved ready to sell out Judea to the Romans for personal gain" (pp. 171 f.; *cf*. pp. 210 f.).

We should gladly admit of course that, if the Jewish people actually dissociated themselves from the high priest and repudiated his actions, in so far as he was an accomplice of Pilate, we could not fairly charge the Jews with even a measure of moral responsibility for the crime. But of course such dissociation and repudiation would have to be established.

The reader who has any acquaintance with the Biblical records is likely to interpose at this point a further question: how is it permissible to require the high priest to shoulder all the blame, in so far as any blame attaches to the Jews at all, when actually Jesus was condemned *by the Sanhedrin*, the highest official body of the Jewish people? In answering this question the author displays his greatest originality. The official sanhedrin had nothing whatever to do with the judicial process, he insists; so to understand the records is to fail to make them intelligible. Jesus was condemned, not by the official sanhedrin which could in truth have acted on behalf of the Jewish people, but by a political sanhedrin summoned by the high priest for the special purpose of dealing with Jesus, and this subservient assembly, a kind of outlaw body which was not subject to the control of a defined judicial procedure, and was operating under the protection and with the encouragement of the capricious procurator Pilate, was responsible for the condemnation of Jesus as a political offender against the Roman state. On this view the circle of Jewish Quislings of course is seen to include several persons in addition to the high priest, and the Jews do not get off scot free. Still one can conceive of the possibility that a small company of persons whose action would be at variance with the wishes of the people might engineer a plot against Jesus, and we should in that event be most ungenerous to attribute the blame for Jesus' death to the entire Jewish people.

Actually of course no one can fairly derive from the New

Testament the notion that the Jews bear sole responsibility for the death of Jesus. Jesus was put to death by Pilate and endured a Roman form of death penalty. It is true, nevertheless, that a reading of the New Testament leaves the distinct impression that the leaders of the Jews, including both Pharisees and Sadducees, were deeply implicated and shared the moral responsibility for it. The initiative is distinctly not assigned to the Roman government, and apparently not to a small company of traitors who were influenced solely by political considerations. Are we mistaken in these impressions? What is the evidence that the death of Jesus was an act of Pilate in which Jewish participation was restricted to the actions of a few persons who were members of a special political court completely dominated by a Quisling high priest?

Were There Two Sanhedrins?

The evidence which is held to substantiate the conclusion of Professor Zeitlin is presented in two nearly equal divisions, the former being concerned with a sketch of the background of Jewish history based principally on Jewish sources, and the latter with a discussion of the New Testament record. With the detailed treatment of the political, economic, social and religious background we are not concerned here but for one significant exception. That exception is the chapter devoted to the subject of "The Two Sanhedrins" wherein the author attempts to establish his case for the judgment that alongside of the sanhedrin which had jurisdiction over the religious affairs of the Jewish people there was another sanhedrin "whose main function was to try offenders against the state", which might well be designated "the political Sanhedrin" (p. 76). This sanhedrin, it is contended, was distinguished from the official sanhedrin not only by the types of cases which came before it, but also in other important respects. Its constituency was not made up of scholars but of men amenable to the wishes of the state; no specific statutes guided its time of meetings and procedure; it was called together for special sittings when a case arose but did not hold sittings at regular times (pp. 77 f.).

Without doubt the proved existence of such a distinct sanhedrin would constitute a fact of highly significant bearing upon our understanding of the process in which Jesus was condemned. It remains true, however, even if the existence of such political courts can be established, that it would still be subject to debate whether such an outlaw body rather than the official court of the Jewish people must be charged with the responsibility of condemning Jesus and securing the sanction and services of the Roman governor for his execution.

The terminology employed by Zeitlin to distinguish the two sanhedrins, namely, "the religious Sanhedrin" and "the political Sanhedrin", it should be borne in mind, is altogether his own. He does not refer to any document which makes such a distinction, nor for that matter to any record which distinguishes them under any other designations. Apart from the confirmation which the New Testament is held to provide, all the evidence appealed to in order to prove the existence of the political sanhedrin is found in the writings of Josephus. Seven different contexts are cited as demonstrating that Josephus had knowledge of a distinct political sanhedrin (pp. 79–83). In view of the decisive bearing of this appeal upon the thesis of the book, each passage must be scrutinized in turn.

The first four passages relate to actions of Herod the Great against the deposed king Hyrcanus, his wife Mariamne, his sons, and his sister-in-law. In the first case Josephus relates how Herod was determined to do away with the threat to his security represented by the ex-king. He apparently fabricated a letter which would implicate Hyrcanus in treachery, and then summoned his victim into his presence. And when Hyrcanus denied any guilt, Josephus concludes, Herod "showed the letter *to the sanhedrin* and put the man to death".[2] Here certainly there is no solid grounding of Zeitlin's thesis: there is not a word of the summons of a sanhedrin, nothing of a trial. Herod merely on his own authority dispatched the object of his fear and hate; only he thought enough of his reputation to manufacture evidence, confront his victim with it, and, failing to secure a confession of guilt, to advertise

[2] *Ant.* XV, 6:2 (173); ed. Niese, III, p. 290.

his scrupulous zeal for justice by exhibiting the "evidence" to the sanhedrin. This context therefore is far from disclosing the existence of two sanhedrins or of a specially constituted political sanhedrin.

In the second case there is indeed more of the semblance of a trial by a specially created court. The company which Herod assembled for the trial of Mariamne is described as consisting of his most friendly relations (τοὺς οἰκειοτάτους αὐτῷ). And in reporting their decision Josephus says merely that when "the company" (οἱ παρόντες) had heard Herod's intemperate accusation and was "at length satisfied that he was so resolved, they passed the sentence of death upon her".[3] The jury accordingly was packed and the charges were trumped up. But was the court a Jewish sanhedrin? Was it "the political sanhedrin"? It is not designated as a sanhedrin, and what is more important it was certainly not a company that could have been confused in any way with the official Jewish sanhedrin.

The third instance in some respects comes nearer to supplying the requirements which Dr. Zeitlin sets down for the political sanhedrin. Herod is permitted by the Roman emperor to deal with his sons, but is advised to provide for an examination of the plot against him in a public court (κοινοῦ συνεδρίου), which in the context is also referred to as a δικαστήριον. Following Caesar's advice it was constituted of Herod's own relatives, the governor of Syria and other prominent officials. Of Herod's relatives his sister Salome and his brother Pheroras receive special mention, while Archelaus is specifically excluded as being regarded with distrust. Moreover, we learn that on the emperor's direction the court met at Berytus (Beirut).[4] The court therefore is designated as a συνέδριον, and yet is clearly not the official Jewish sanhedrin. It was a mere tool of Herod since it was packed with those who were known to be ready to carry out his wishes. In spite of these considerations, however, we fail to understand how anyone can seriously propose that this narrative bears in any way whatsoever upon the question whether in Pales-

---

[3] *Ant.* XV, 7:4 (229); Niese, III, p 298.
[4] *Bel. Iud.* I, 27:1, 2 (537 ff.); Niese, VI, pp. 95 f.

tine there existed alongside of the official sanhedrin another sanhedrin of a politicial character. At most the incident proves that capricious and jealous rulers were not unknown to gain their political ambitions by going through the form of bringing their enemies into mock courts whose sentence was determined in advance.

The final case associated with Herod in similar fashion tells of Herod's methods of dealing with another relative who had threatened his security. In this instance he charged his sister-in-law with alienating the affections of her husband, Pheroras, for Herod — a quite unmodern triangular collision. In his indignation, we read, "he assembled a council (ἀθροίσας οὖν συνέδριον) of his friends and relatives" and accused her of many misdeeds.[5] The Greek word συνέδριον is employed here to describe the assembly, but of course it is used in Greek literature to designate a great variety of assemblies, and does not constitute evidence that we have to do here with a Jewish sanhedrin. Moreover, in the present situation there is no intimation of the conduct of even the semblance of a trial. There is no formal decision against the wife of Pheroras. Nothing more evidently than a kind of family council is in view, and consequently nothing is established as to the existence of a political sanhedrin in Judaism. These passages accordingly cast a gloomy light upon Herod and his times, but they add nothing particularly to our knowledge of the circumstances in which Pilate at the instigation of a Jewish sanhedrin consented to the crucifixion of our Lord.

The other three passages from Josephus deal with situations which developed, considerably after the death of Jesus, when the political circumstances had altered in certain important respects. The great-grandson of Herod the Great, Agrippa II, is now king. In the first of these contexts Josephus relates that many of the Levites who were singers of hymns persuaded the king to assemble a sanhedrin (καθίσαντα συνέδριον) in order to gain permission to wear linen garments as well as the priests, appealing to the king's vanity by reminding him that he might be remembered for this novelty. They succeeded in their plan, Josephus adds, for the king

[5] *Bel. Iud.* I, 29.2 (571); Niese, VI, p. 102.

"with the consent of those that came into the sanhedrin" granted this privilege. The paragraph ends with the solemn observation that this action, like certain others, was contrary to the paternal laws (τοῖς πατρίοις νόμοις).[6] With regard to this case Zeitlin concludes: "this Sanhedrin could only have been political. The demands of the Levites to wear linen garments in the Temple were motivated by social reasons not by religious ones" (p. 80). A second reason for maintaining that this sanhedrin, like the others mentioned above, was political is that it was *summoned*, whereas, according to Zeitlin, the provisions for the religious sanhedrin provided no occasion for a special summons "since it held its sessions daily, except on Saturdays and on holydays" (p. 80; *cf.* p. 71). To this latter consideration we must protest that the regulations of the Mishna, even if they belong to the Tannaitic period, cannot, because of their written codification at a much later time, be regarded as establishing positively the procedure of the sanhedrin at the time of Christ. Professor Zeitlin is himself a witness to the sharply varying fortunes and circumstances of the Jewish people and their government in the chaotic and turbulent situations which preceded the fall of Jerusalem. It is clearly impossible to prove from the Talmudic regulations of the sessions of the Sanhedrin that it was so continuously in session that it could never have been summoned by a king or by a high priest. And, turning to the former consideration, namely, that which appeals to the social motivation of the request of the Levites, we regard the evidence as showing unmistakably that the issue was fundamentally religious rather than political. To note that the request of the Levites was motivated by social ambition does not alter, in our opinion, the fundamental fact that they requested the abolition of religious regulations, and that consequently the decision represented a transgression against the "paternal laws" of the Jewish people rather than against the laws of the state. We do not see how Josephus could have expressed more unambiguously his judgment that the king had erred in bending the official sanhedrin to his will so that it was ready to set aside a distinctly religious enactment.

[6] *Ant.* XX, 9·6 (216 ff.); Niese, IV, p. 263.

Nothing in truth is said as to the constituency of this sanhedrin. Perhaps Josephus implies that not all the regular members took part in the decision. But in any case there is nothing to suggest that he chose the members of it in order to secure a political end.

The sixth passage relates how the high priest Ananus in the interval after the death of the procurator Festus, and before the arrival of his successor Albinus, A. D. 62, "assembled a sanhedrin of judges", brought James, the brother of Jesus, and certain others before it, and accusing them of having transgressed the law, delivered them to be stoned. The whole matter was brought to the attention of Agrippa and Albinus with the result that Ananus was quickly deposed from the high priesthood. It is also pertinent to observe that Albinus was informed, according to Josephus, that it had been unlawful for Ananus to summon a sanhedrin without his consent.[7] Now Zeitlin concludes on what seems to us completely inadequate grounds that James must have been tried for a political offense and that consequently the court must have been a political sanhedrin. The evidence appealed to is that Ananus *convened* a sanhedrin and that James was "most likely" accused as a follower of the new sect, the Christians (p. 82). As we have observed above, the mere fact that a sanhedrin was summoned, in this case illegally, is not of sufficient weight to establish this hypothesis. Moreover, in this context, as in the previous passage, Josephus seems clearly to mark the offense of which Ananus thought James guilty as a transgression of the Jewish law rather than as an offense against the state, for he contrasts the severity of the Sadducees with the greater moderation of others who were better informed as to the law (meaning, apparently, the Pharisees). And if Ananus were exhibiting here the zeal of a Quisling rather than of a religionist, it would become difficult to explain why he is represented as having seized the opportunity provided by the absence of the Roman procurator to accomplish the death of James. If he had waited for the arrival of Albinus he might, on the assumption that the alleged offense of James was political, have insured the good will of the Roman governor

[7] *Ant.* XX, 9:1 (197 ff.); Niese, IV, pp. 260 f.

by accusing James before him. His precipitate action points therefore most naturally to the assumption that his quarrel with James concerned a religious issue between the Sadducees and the Christian church. And it is interesting to observe that in this case at least the high priest took the initiative in bringing about the death of a follower of Jesus, and that therefore blameworthy actions of this kind were not in every case the result of pressure which the Roman procurators laid upon them to suppress every movement that might be suspected of political disloyalty.

The final passage cited by Zeitlin envisages a completely distinctive situation when, during the revolt against Rome, the Jews gained their independence momentarily. Josephus, who became a first-rank appeaser himself, writes without sympathy for the Zealots, the revolutionary party, and he accuses them of having instituted various mock courts and trials (δικαστήρια καὶ κρίσεις) when they wearied of massacres, and in particular tells how, when they determined to do away with a certain prominent citizen named Zacharias, they summoned seventy of the leading men to the Temple to act as judges. When Zacharias made a successful defense before them and was acquitted of the charge of treason, the historian states that the Zealots became indignant that the judges had not understood that their authority had not been that of an actual court of justice (δικαστήριον), but was given merely in pretence. Later on two of the Zealots slew Zacharias in the midst of the temple.[8] This incident then provides an example of a mock court constituted to carry out the murder of an innocent man. It fails, however, to illuminate procedure under the Roman procurators, and provides no support whatever of the theory that there were two distinct sanhedrins in the Judaism of the days of Jesus, the sanhedrin which dealt with religious matters and another body which was concerned with crimes against the state.

Following his comments upon these seven passages from Josephus, Dr. Zeitlin summarizes his conclusion as follows:

[8] *Bel. Iud.* IV, 5:4 (334 ff.); Niese, VI, pp. 294 f.

"Thus, we have established the existence at the time of Jesus of two types of Sanhedrin, a religious Sanhedrin about which we learn from the *Tannaitic* literature, and the political Sanhedrin, which Josephus records" (p. 83).

This conclusion, in our judgment, is far from being grounded in the evidence. Indeed, we cannot conceal our amazement that this hypothesis, put forward so confidently, appears to rest on such a fragile basis. None of the passages presupposes a political situation like that which existed when Jewish leaders collaborated with the Roman procurator to condemn Jesus to death. In one case Herod considers it prudent to submit an incriminating document to "the sanhedrin", but for the rest he either deals summarily with the victims of his jealousy and hatred, or goes through the form of prosecuting them before "courts" packed with his supporters. Agrippa and Ananus summon sanhedrins, and take advantage of the supineness of their members to secure actions which suited their personal whims, but the contexts point to the supposition that these assemblies definitely exercised religious prerogatives and were apparently constituted of regular members of the Jewish Sanhedrin. And mock judicatories were set up by the Zealots in a time when Jewish life as a whole bore almost no resemblance to the life under the procurators. The distinct existence of "the political sanhedrin" is therefore by no means established and cannot be assumed in approaching the study of the record of the trial and crucifixion of Jesus.[9] Neverthe-

[9] Attention may be directed to the fact that Zeitlin finds confirmation of his conclusion as to the existence of a separate political sanhedrin not only from the record of the trial of Jesus in the gospels, but also from the records in Acts of the trials of Peter and Paul (pp 180 ff.). His claim is that "Peter and Paul were tried by a political Sanhedrin for a political offense against the Romans in the same manner as Jesus, and they, like Jesus, were executed by the Romans" (p. 180).

In the case of Peter the chief evidence relied upon to establish the political character of the court is that he was a political offender. This conclusion is based, first of all, upon the consideration that Peter was arrested "for teaching that Jesus arose after his death and was made by God the *ruler* of the Jews" (p. 184). Perhaps this statement has in view Acts 5:31 where Peter speaks of Jesus as the exalted "Prince and Saviour", in addition to Acts 4:2 where the reason given for his arrest is that "he

less, we can well afford to listen as Professor Zeitlin employs his hypothesis in the interpretation of the gospels.

proclaimed in Jesus the resurrection from the dead". Zeitlin contends that it could not have been a religious offense to maintain that Jesus had been raised from the dead, and that therefore "Peter could only have been tried for associating himself with Jesus who claimed to be the King of the Jews" (p. 184). But this is to ignore the plain implications of the entire context that the issue was religious Zeitlin makes Christianity essentially a political movement at the beginning, as is indicated by his remarks on page 188 that "In due time the followers of Jesus became a religious group. The political aspect of Jesus, as a Messiah who claimed to be the King of the Jews, became less conspicuous". There is not a particle of evidence that Jesus ever interpreted his messianic claims as having political meaning, or that the community which acknowledged him as the Messiah conceived of itself as the Kingdom of the Jews, at least not in a worldly sense. A second consideration calculated to demonstrate that Peter was a political offender is the fact that Gamaliel appeals to the history of the rebels Theudas and Judas (Acts 5:36 f.; pp. 187 f.) But this is to miss the whole point of the argument, which is that "if this work be of men, it will be overthrown, but if it is of God, ye will not be able to overthrow them, lest perchance ye be found fighting against God" (Acts 5:38 f.)

His discussion of the trial of Paul likewise at many points fails to grasp the fundamental and decisive religious issue which led to the opposition of the Jewish leaders to Paul. One example of his interpretation of the evidence must suffice here. The fact that, according to Acts 23·6, the sanhedrin before which Paul was brought consisted of both Sadducees and Pharisees is said to prove "undoubtedly that the Sanhedrin was not a religious body, but a political Sanhedrin, and that Paul was brought before it for a political offense. It would be unthinkable to assume that a religious court would consist of Sadducees and Pharisees, since their beliefs were so diametrically opposed to each other, for what would appear to the Pharisees a religious offense would not be so considered by the Sadducees ... But if we assume that Paul was brought before a political Sanhedrin ... we can understand why its members consisted of Sadducees and Pharisees. It was quite proper for the head of a nation to convene citizens of different religious beliefs for the purpose of trying a man for a state offense" (p. 199). This argument is certainly extraordinary if one recalls Zeitlin's admission on page 75 that Sadducees sometimes became members of the official sanhedrin but were required to render decisions according to the Pharisaic interpretations. Nor is there any evidence that the sanhedrin was specially constituted by the representative of the Roman government. According to Acts 22:30 the chief captain "commanded the chief priests and all the sanhedrin to come together" in order that he might discover the nature of the accusation of the Jews against Paul, their opposition to Paul being inferred not from any charge of political infidelity, but from the tumult in the temple (*cf.* 23:26–30).

The Testimony of the Gospels

We shall perhaps clarify the discussion of the records of the trial of Jesus if we observe the general approach to the gospels which this book takes. We shall hardly expect Zeitlin to share the presuppositions and approach of Christian orthodoxy. It develops, however, that he is also rather far from assuming the most common critical judgments of unorthodox scholars in our day. He does indeed insist that the records contain discrepancies and that they are characterized by a "theological accent" (pp. 101 ff., 161) rather than by historical fidelity. On the other hand, most modern critics of the New Testament would find him rather naive in affirming as much as he does. For example, he argues quite like an orthodox scholar when he insists that Jesus could not have repudiated the Old Testament, both in view of his statement recorded in Matthew 5:17-20 and in view of his messianic claims which are "based on the validity of the Bible" (pp. 114 f.). The typical criticism of our day, which regards the gospels as consisting essentially of theology rather than of history, commonly appeals to these very features of the gospel record as evidence of the theologizing action of the Christian church.

We doubt, moreover, whether many New Testament scholars of whatever theological tendency would regard his handling of textual questions as satisfactory. On the basis of his judgment that the variant readings in the manuscripts and versions frequently represent theological bias, he proceeds at several points to draw far-reaching conclusions from readings which possess exceedingly slender support (*cf.* pp. 102 f., 138, 172 f., 176). For example, he declares:

"That the Jews had a share in the guilt of the crucifixion of Jesus, the reader of the Passion story may be erroneously convinced on a surface reading of the Synoptic Gospels. However, on examining the readings of the manuscripts such a conclusion is not justifiable. Matthew 23:34, the Revised Version reads, 'Wherefore, behold, I send unto you prophets and wise men and scribes and some of them ye shall kill and crucify and some of them shall ye scourge in your synagogues.' The words, 'and crucify and some of them ye will scourge in your synagogues,' are omitted from some of the manuscripts, which indicates that they were not in the original Matthew" (p. 176).

Even if the evidence for the omission were far greater than it actually is (the edition of Legg notes only two cursive manuscripts as omitting the words in question), we fail to understand what conceivable justification there is for leaping to the dogmatic conclusion without further argument, that the words were not in the original Matthew.[10]

To do Professor Zeitlin justice we must not leave the impression that his case rests solely, or even mainly, upon a theory of interpolations into the text of the gospels of a view which implicates the Jews in moral responsibility for the death of Jesus. His method is in truth often arbitrary and is employed without the advantage of a carefully conceived judgment as to the place occupied by the gospels in the history of Christianity. His main argument nevertheless remains to be considered. In brief, he rests his case on the judgment that the records make sense only if the entire procedure, including betrayal, arrest, accusation, condemnation and execution, is observed to be a purely political matter (pp. 144 ff.). Jesus was executed as "King of the Jews" by Pilate who must therefore have found him guilty of an offense against the Roman state. The high priest and his associates, acting as Quisling supporters of the authority of Rome, must have made the charge that Jesus was a rebel when they brought Jesus before Pilate. Previously, meeting at night as a political sanhedrin under the domination of the high priest they had conducted a preliminary examination wherein the basis of this charge must have been determined. Still earlier, because of their bond with the Roman procurator they had been able to enlist the aid of a Roman cohort of soldiers in order to arrest Jesus (Jn. 18:3). And, finally, it is maintained that the

---

[10] His judgment that the synoptic gospels were written exclusively for Jewish Christians, and John for Gentile Christians, is clearly not established (pp. 107 ff.). In connection with his view of early Christianity as consisting of two distinct groups, Jewish and Gentile Christian (pp. 194 f.), these conclusions as to the gospels are made the basis of far-reaching judgments concerning their testimony (e. g , pp. 140 ff.).

action of Judas in informing the high priest concerning Jesus must have been in the form of a report that the disciples of Jesus were about to declare him to be King of the Jews, an estimation which Judas himself found irreconcilable with his own acknowledgement of Jesus as the Son of God (pp. 162 f.)! The rôle ascribed to Judas is wholly conjectural,[11] but for the rest we may admit that this reconstruction has the advantage of providing a very simple and apparently plausible explanation of the trial of Jesus. The question is, however, whether it is actually borne out by the evidence, whether this simple theory does not constitute an extreme oversimplification of a complex historical development.

The Political Situation

Passing over many details of the argument we shall concentrate on two broad criticisms. Our first fundamental objection to this reconstruction is that, although the issue is judged to be purely political, it fails even to take adequate account of the complexity of the political situation. Of course Pilate's only interest in the case was occasioned by its political complexion. Not that he was a scrupulous and honorable judge, but his decision to consent to the death of Jesus was dictated by the demands made upon him to maintain tranquillity in Judea. From what we know of his ruthless and capricious actions it is clear that the maintenance of *Pax Romana* was not subordinated to the establishment of *Iustitia Romana*, not to speak of a higher justice. It is altogether

---

[11] Judas is made to side with Paul against the other disciples! "We may add that the Gospel of John states that the disciples of Jesus wanted to make him king while Jesus was still in Galilee. Paul did not eliminate Judas from the twelve apostles. In his letter to the Corinthians, he still speaks of the *twelve* It is indeed strange that Paul should still include Judas, the so-called betrayer, among the twelve. But we must not overlook the fact that Paul never regarded Jesus as the 'King of the Jews'. To Paul Jesus was the Son of God" (pp. 162 f.). Passing over the allegations as to Paul's attitude towards Judas as too absurd to require refutation, we may point out that John 6:15 does not state or imply that the eleven wanted to make Jesus king, but that the people did, and this became the occasion of Jesus' withdrawal from the crowds and of intimate contacts with the inner circle.

plausible that he should have been prepared not only to suppress any revolutionary movement that appeared on the scene but also to cater to Jewish leaders whose support in handling the delicate situations occasioned by Jewish piety must have been recognized as a most valuable asset.

The high priest and his immediate associates may well have been as bad as Zeitlin makes them out to be, that is, appeasers and Quislings. As such they obviously had an important stake in maintaining the *status quo*, and any new movement that threatened their position of privilege would have been regarded as a menace to be dealt with in drastic fashion. We need not suppose then that they felt any necessity of taking their cue in each concrete situation from the Roman procurator; as Quislings they were in the advantageous position of taking the initiative as they saw fit when public order, as they conceived of it, was disturbed.

But is it true that the Pharisees could not have participated in the action against Jesus? Could not a sanhedrin, consisting of Pharisees and Sadducees, and perhaps even dominated so far as its purely religious decisions were concerned by the Pharisaic point of view, have instituted proceedings against him? Professor Zeitlin seems to consider the Pharisees as above any such political action, and accordingly is confident that the sanhedrin before which Jesus was hailed and where he was condemned could not have been the official sanhedrin of which they formed a large majority. The fact is, however, that the Pharisees, in spite of their radical differences from the Sadducees on religious questions, were characterized in this period by a readiness to appease the Roman government. In a situation where they were the acknowledged religious leaders of the people, they also had a great stake in the maintenance of the *status quo*. Zeitlin himself calls attention to the fact that the Pharisees had lost their revolutionary ardor and had come to adopt a policy of quietism (pp. 43 f., 87 f.). It may be recalled, moreover, that the Pharisees were unsympathetic with the policy of the Zealots, and that Josephus identified his point of view with that of the Pharisees. The sanhedrin which tried Peter, regarded by Zeitlin as a political sanhedrin (pp. 181 ff.), included Pharisees, and in fact they apparently dominated the council inasmuch as the advice of Gamaliel was followed. Although this advice showed greater moderation than that of certain other members, there is no doubt that he, no more than the high priest, was willing to encourage revolutionary movements like that which centered about Judas of Galilee (Acts 5:37). Likewise the sanhedrin which tried Paul, which Zeitlin also considers a political body and not the official Jewish Sanhedrin, included many Pharisees (Acts 22:30; 23:6; *cf.* pp. 195 ff.). Hence when the gospels refer the initiative in the process of Jesus to the sanhedrin, we may not exclude the Pharisees from participation in its actions.[12] Perhaps then the greater initiative in maintaining the supremacy of Roman authority would have come from the high priest and his party, but all that we know of the Pharisees agrees with the supposition that they would have been willing to cooperate with the Sadducees in indicting Jesus as a disturber of the peace and as threatening revolution

If then the Pharisees, as well as the Sadducees, who together made up the membership of the official Sanhedrin, cooperated with the Roman state in maintaining order, there is nothing incongruous in the statement of John 18:3 that a Roman cohort participated in the arrest of Jesus. Zeitlin points to this datum as evidence that we have to do with a purely political case (pp. 151, 155). But he himself admits that the Roman cohort was at the disposal of the high priests "in seizing all suspicious elements against the Roman state" (p. 156). Clearly then there is no implication that the arrest of Jesus was due to the initiative of the Roman state, but only that the high priest because of his position of favor could take advantage of the presence of the Roman soldiery at this season in dealing with a situation which he regarded as a threat to the peace. That John's mention of the Roman cohort does not presuppose that the apprehension of Jesus was conceived of as the action of a Quisling high priest is confirmed incidentally by the fact that John in this very passage specifically mentions "the Pharisees" as associated with "the high priests" in the arrest.

---

[12] The Pharisees are specifically associated with the action against Jesus in Mt. 27:62 and Jn. 11:47, 57; 18:3, and must be chiefly in mind when repeated reference is made to the actions in which "the elders" participated.

The recognition of the great stake which the Pharisees as well as the high priests had in preserving their prestige and authority will account, moreover, for the unseemly haste and other "irregularities" of the trial. Zeitlin contends that the Sanhedrin which tried Jesus could not have been the official Jewish Sanhedrin because the procedure of that body was determined by statutes which excluded such irregularities. This claim involves two presuppositions, neither of which can be granted: (1) that the regulations set down in the Mishna many decades after the time of Christ necessarily represent the procedure of the Sanhedrin *circa* A. D. 30, and (2) that, assuming their currency at that time, they would necessarily have been consistently applied. The latter point is particularly doubtful. A Sanhedrin which was compelled to take cognizance constantly of the autocratic authority of Rome and which apparently cooperated actively in maintaining order against all threats of revolution would not be likely to be under a strong compulsion to adhere to the letter of the rabbinic regulations. And even the Mishna, as Billerbeck and Dalman have pointed out, allowed for exceptions, especially if it was thought that the non-observance of the law at one point might appear to be the means of its confirmation as a whole.[13]

The Religious Issue

Our second main criticism of Zeitlin's approach to the question of the crucifixion of Jesus is that, in seeking to resolve the issue into a purely political conflict, he neglects all the evidence that the division between Jesus and the Jewish leaders, including Pharisees as well as Sadducees, was at bottom grounded in their religious differences. To construe the conflict as merely political requires one to pass over the consistent testimony of the evangelists on this matter. It moreover confronts the historian with the necessity of accounting for a sudden and abrupt outbreak of action against Jesus on political grounds in spite of all the evidence that Jesus

---

[13] Strack-Billerbeck, *Kommentar zum N. T*, II, pp. 815–827; Dalman, *Jesus-Jeshua*, E. T., pp. 98–106.

himself never interpreted his messianic claims in a worldly or political sense. The hostility of the high priest to Jesus was indeed, as admitted above, grounded partially in the threat which he discovered in Jesus to his position of authority in the order of the day, and it was accordingly motivated by political considerations, but alongside of the issue of political power, and even transcending it in significance, there was the conflict of religious authority. It is after all the religious authority associated with the office of the high priest which alone accounts for the readiness of the Roman government to capitalize upon his subservience, as indeed for the willingness of devout Jews to tolerate him. There can be no doubt that the high priest and his aristocratic associates regarded the claims of Jesus to exercise authority in religious matters as a force that would tend to jeopardize their already precariously situated leadership. Zeitlin virtually admits this point when he says that Jesus' action in driving the moneychangers from the temple "was a challenge against the authority of the high priest who ruled over the Temple precincts like a dictator" (p. 160), but this can hardly be construed as the first instance in which the high priest took cognizance of the religious claims of Jesus. Consequently, the New Testament records present an altogether congruous account when they represent the fundamental issue between Jesus and the Jewish leaders as religious, and yet show how, when they appeared before Pilate, they could construe it as political.

While then Zeitlin's construction, in our judgment, oversimplifies the issue between Jesus and the aristocratic opportunists who belonged to the circle of the high priest, in that the profound dispute over authority in religious matters is neglected, he errs even more conspicuously in practically discounting the conflict between Jesus and the Pharisees as a factor in the development of the final climax. Since the official Jewish Sanhedrin was composed to a large extent of Pharisees, the effect of Zeitlin's claim, that not this body but a political group dominated by the high priest must be charged with complicity in the death of Jesus, is to exonerate the Pharisees altogether. As a matter of fact, along with a readiness to castigate the high priestly circle as appeasers and Quislings, this author presents a stout defense of the Pharisees whom he considers to be the "saviors of Judaism" (pp. 142 f.). The record of Jesus' conflict with the Pharisees, it is maintained, is colored considerably by a later attitude. In particular it is not allowed that Jesus himself could have called the Pharisees "hypocrites".

With this important question of the relation of Jesus to the Pharisees, which has been in the foreground of discussion in recent decades, we cannot concern ourselves to any great extent in the present discussion. Even to expound and evaluate Zeitlin's treatment of the subject in connection with his exceedingly interesting chapters on "The Sermon on the Mount" and "Jesus' Controversies with the Pharisees" (pp. 114-143) would demand more space than is available here. On many individual points he is decidedly worth hearing. On the other hand, he fails to impress when he argues that various references to the Pharisees as "hypocrites", especially in Matthew 23, must be regarded as interpolations into the original document (pp. 138 ff.). The evidence of a sharp divergence between Jesus and the Pharisees is so pervasive that the decision cannot be made to depend upon the authenticity of certain phrases. The fundamental fault on this point is, we believe, that he has failed to grasp the real import of the teaching of Jesus.

So far as the Pharisees are concerned Zeitlin virtually admits their legalism, externalism and casuistry. These characteristics are placed, however, in a perspective which discloses that they are assets rather than liabilities. The fundamental motive of the Pharisees appears to be that the authority of the divine law should be maintained, and yet that the law should be adjusted to the practical situation in which weak and sinful men live, even if in effect such adjustments set aside the law. The Pharisaic approach to religious and ethical questions is illustrated in a variety of ways. For example, seeking to set aside the *lex talionis*, the Pharisees achieved their end by a "legal fiction", that is, by limiting the right of a man who suffered the loss of an eye to take out an eye exactly like his own in size and color. This of course abolished the law (p. 120). The utilitarianism of the Pharisees receives pointed expression in the appraisal of their attitude toward the Sabbath: "The Pharisees were always ready to amend the laws of the Sabbath and to make it possible for the people to observe the Sabbath" (p. 130).

Jesus, on the other hand, is represented as an impractical moralist, who was unconcerned with human society and made no concessions to human nature, and who "relied entirely on ethics and ethical exhortation to change human nature" (p. 122). The differences between Jesus and the Pharisees, as expounded by Zeitlin, come to especially significant expression in connection with the discussion of oaths:

"And the Pharisees maintained that if a man took a *corban*, a vow, not to honor his father or his mother, he must keep that vow. By this Jesus claimed the Pharisees themselves were nullifying the Pentateuchal law of God.

"In these charges and countercharges is reflected the philosophy of the Pharisees and Jesus concerning the nature of society. The Pharisees were the leaders of the religious Sanhedrin. As such, they had to take cognizance of the weaknesses of human nature, knowing that a person may transgress a precept; and therefore, it was their duty to find a way to give the person the opportunity for repentance and readjustment. Jesus, on the other hand, believed a person should be taught that he should never transgress the laws, not taking into consideration the weakness of humanity.

"*The corban, the vow.* According to the Pharisees a vow must be kept since it is written in the Pentateuch that a man should not break his word. But if a man took a vow against the Biblical precept he must keep his vow, and not observe the precept for which, according to them, he would be punished for not observing the precept. However, to avoid a clash between two commandments in the Pentateuch, namely, 'Honour thy father and thy mother' and 'He shall not break his word,' the Pharisees introduced a legal fiction. If a man took a vow not to honor his father and his mother, he could absolve himself of his vow. This is called, in the *Tannaitic* literature, the 'invalidation of vows.' According to Jesus, however, no vow could be taken against a Pentateuchal precept, thus disregarding human weakness that a man might transgress, and take a vow against a Pentateuchal precept" (pp. 134 f.).

Professor Zeitlin's estimate of Jesus is correct, in our judgment, when he indicates that Jesus went beyond the externals of conformity to the law to appeal to the motive behind the act, but like many Liberals, he fails to plumb the depths of Jesus' teaching chiefly because its God-centered character escapes him. The message of our Lord will never be comprehended if it is conceived as a mere moralism which appeals to men's consciences and aims to bring about moral reform through human effort. Against the externalism and casuistry which in a purely formal manner upheld the authority of the law of God only to set it aside by legal fictions, and which failed therefore to enunciate the radical implications of the commandment of love to God and to one's neighbor, Jesus brought men into the very presence of God by confronting them, not with an ethic constantly ready to adjust itself to human weakness and sin, but with the absolute demands of a holy and righteous God. Of course, the ethical message of Jesus does not comprise the whole of his teaching, for, alongside the message of the claims of the holy God for an absolute and whole-hearted obedience, there was also the proclamation of the coming of the rule of God with its gracious bestowal of the gifts of forgiveness and fellowship. But Jesus and the Pharisees are seen to be poles apart even in their teaching concerning the law of God. Occasionally indeed Zeitlin seems to admit that the differences between Jesus and the Pharisees was deep-seated, since they did not recognize his claim to speak with messianic authority and could not countenance his rejection of the traditions of the elders on the ground of their conflict with the law of God (*e. g.*, p. 132). But these admissions fail to carry with them their full implications. For nothing less than an entirely different attitude toward religion and life is expressed by these differences.

Now Zeitlin objects strenuously to the testimony of the gospels that Jesus at times characterized the Pharisees as hypocrites (p. 143). It may be admitted that the word "hypocrite" as used today carries a somewhat harsher connotation than the Greek word ὑποκριτής. A "hypocrite" as used in the New Testament signifies one who pretends at something, that is, who is a play-actor, and hence one whose actions are not in conformity with his actual claims about himself. Paul even accused Peter and certain others of dissimulation (ὑπόκρισις) when they failed to act in consistency with their own principles (Gal. 2:13). This is not to say that the application of the term to the Pharisees in the gospels represents a mild rebuke. Quite the contrary. While it does not imply that the Pharisees without exception were completely lacking in sincerity, it does involve the judgment that their professions and practices were inconsistent. In our judgment, as much as this is established even on the basis of the admissions of Zeitlin. What was so repugnant to Jesus was that they set themselves up as teachers and guides for the religion of others, and yet did not fulfill the fundamental requirement of a teacher of religion that he should confront men with God himself, with the divine law and with the divine grace. Their "legal fictions" disclose the sad fact that they were not teachers of genuine religion at all, but only of a kind of practical ethic which countenanced all kinds of compromises with sin. In making the pretence of upholding the law of God, and yet using their energies to set it aside, they established the charge which Jesus made. The righteousness which Jesus demanded, on the contrary, bore no resemblance to the righteousness which the Pharisees enunciated, simply because it was the righteousness of God himself.[14]

It is because of his failure to gauge the profound religious issue which separated Jesus and the leaders of Judaism that Zeitlin's reconstruction of the judicial process in terms of purely political considerations appears unrealistic. The crucial question of the actual nature of that process, as attested by the evidence, must nevertheless be considered. The Jews, we admit, did not actually perform the act of crucifying Jesus. That was Pilate's responsibility. The question to be faced, however, is whether the Jews share the moral responsibility for the act inasmuch as they condemned him and prevailed

---

[14] Cf. Mk. 7:6 ff. and Mt. 15:7 where, quoting Isa. 29:13, our Lord condemns as hypocritical and vain the worship of God which is accompanied by a setting aside of his commandments. The instances in Mt. 23:13 ff. and Lk. 13:15 are similar in import. In Mt. 22.18 and Mk. 12:15 Jesus accuses them of hypocrisy because they came with hostile purpose, in order to ensnare him, and yet addressed him as a Teacher who was true and taught the way of God Cf. Lk. 12:1.

upon Pilate to put him to death. What was the basis of the sanhedrin's condemnation of Jesus? Did its condemnation rest on religious or on political grounds?

THE ACCUSATION OF BLASPHEMY

As remarkable as any feature of the entire book is the manner in which the author, despite his acceptance of the historicity of the charge of blasphemy against Jesus, construes the process before the sanhedrin as political and not religious. That this is the author's meaning appears most clearly from his comment on John 19:7, which he treats as an integral aspect of the actual development of events. The words of the accusers to Pilate, "We have a law and by that law ($κατὰ\ τὸν\ νόμον$) he ought to die because he made himself the Son of God" refer undoubtedly, he claims, to Roman law rather than to Jewish law, and therefore must be understood as meaning that "Jesus' reference to himself as Messiah and the 'Son of God' was tantamount to challenging the authority of Caesar over the Jews" (pp. 168 f.). But what is the basis for the conclusion that Roman law must be in view? There are two principal considerations advanced to support this proposition. The first is that "there is no Jewish law, either in the Bible or in the *Talmud* to the effect that a person who claims to be 'Son of God' is liable to capital punishment" (p. 168). And the second is derived from the fact that the text reads "the law" rather than "our law" (A. V.). On the latter point, it seems absurd to claim that, when the Jews say, "We have a law", and then proceed to speak of the particular law which they have in mind, they are to be understood as referring to a Roman law rather than to a Jewish law. And as for the former consideration, it seems clear that the law against blasphemy as formulated in Leviticus 24:16 must be in mind rather than an infringement of a Roman law against insurrection.

We receive the impression, moreover, from the Matthaean and Marcan records of Jesus' appearance before the Sanhedrin that he was accused of blasphemy and on that account judged to be liable to death (Mt. 26:63–66; Mk. 14:61–64). Since this charge of blasphemy is evoked by Jesus' acknowledgment of his divine sonship, and by his immediate interpretation of that sonship as involving rule at God's right hand and an appearance with theophanic glory, it would seem impossible to construe the record so as to support the theory that the charge against Jesus was fundamentally political rather than religious. As a matter of fact we cannot regard Zeitlin's discussion as having actually faced this issue in any adequate fashion. His argument is to the effect that the facts do not agree with the presupposition that the body before which Jesus appeared was the official Jewish Sanhedrin. These alleged facts are two in number: (1) the language of Jesus was, he contends, not strictly a cursing of God but merely abusive language, which under Tannaitic regulations was not subject to the death penalty, and (2) the official Sanhedrin could have carried out the death sentence. Hence, it is argued, the offense could not have been a religious offense properly speaking, and the court must have been the political sanhedrin which did not possess the prerogative of carrying out the death sentence (pp. 152 ff.). Our answer is simply that if the regulations of the Mishna, understood in this fashion, are taken as decisive for the procedure at the time of Christ, we had better reject the New Testament account as unhistorical rather than invent the explanation that, in spite of all appearances to the contrary, the charge of blasphemy was understood in a political sense.

Although then Zeitlin seems to interpret the charge of blasphemy as not constituting a religious offense, there is one point in his discussion where the confession of Jesus before the sanhedrin is judged to bear a religious aspect (p. 164). Here it is maintained that the entire assembly is viewed as judging that one who spoke such abusive language against God was obviously a person *of no special worth or importance*, and, considering the danger that Pilate might punish the Jewish people as a whole because of the claims of Jesus to be the king of the Jews, they accordingly felt no compunctions of conscience in delivering such a person to Pilate as a rebel who was worthy of death. The implication seems to be that if Jesus had not spoken as he did, there might have been some hesitation on their part in making him a scapegoat in order to free themselves of suspicion. Considered in that fashion the issue remains, according to Zeitlin, essentially political, from the point of view of the sanhedrin as from Pilate's, and the religious aspect is completely subordinate. As a political sanhedrin they had no jurisdiction over religious matters, and hence could not have sought to condemn him on religious grounds. We cannot regard this reconstruction as borne out by the evidence. The subordination of the religious charge to the political is not derived from the accounts of the appearance of Jesus before the Jewish authorities, for there the main point is precisely that at last the Jewish judges discovered a religious ground for his condemnation to death.

The extremities to which Zeitlin must go in seeking to carry out consistently this thesis that the charge against Jesus was essentially non-religious are further displayed in connection with his discussion of the condemnation of Stephen as a blasphemer (pp. 188 ff.). Strange to relate, the trial of Stephen is held to have been for a purely religious offense, the charge being that "he spoke words of blasphemy (abusive language) against God and Moses" (p. 189). On the basis of this conclusion, and because of the statement of Acts 6:12 that "they brought him into the sanhedrin" (that is, one that did not have to be assembled), he affirms that the trial judicatory must have been the official, or "religious", Sanhedrin (p. 190). Wherein then does the charge against Stephen appear to be religious whereas that against Jesus is considered political? The charge against Stephen was that in his testimony to Jesus he had spoken blasphemous words against Moses and against God (Acts 6:11 ff.) and apparently it was his testimony that he saw the glory of God and Jesus standing at the right hand of God (Acts 7:55 f.), which confirmed their judgment that he was a deceiver and a blasphemer. Obviously his offense was religious. But was not the conflict between Jesus and the Jewish leaders, including Pharisees as well as Sadducees, precisely that he spoke "as having authority and not as the scribes", that is, as possessing the right to declare authoritatively the will of God, and that he set aside the traditions of the elders? And did he not at the trial, in acknowledging his Messiahship, speak of his person in a way that evoked the charge of blasphemy? On this question Zeitlin is not completely silent. He says:

"There is a vast difference between the words of Jesus and the statement of Stephen. Jesus made a prediction while Stephen made a statement that he saw the Son of Man standing on the right hand of God; that is, he considered Jesus the founder of a new religion" (p. 191).

Can one seriously propose that the formal difference between a prediction and a statement is of sufficient weight to establish a qualitative difference between the Jewish conceptions of the offense of Jesus and of that of Stephen? So far as the reference to the session at God's right hand and the coming with theophanic glory is concerned, Zeitlin admits that both as spoken by Jesus and as affirmed by Stephen they were held to establish the proof of the commission of blasphemy. In our opinion, on the assumption that Jesus had no right to make such transcendent claims of superhuman dignity, the blasphemy involved in ascribing such glory to one who no longer lived among men was far less evident than in the instance of one who claimed *for himself* such authority and dignity that his Jewish judges would be compelled to recognize his transcendent power and glory. As we have observed above, the religious differences between Jesus and the Jewish leaders were so profound that, even though the break with Judaism had not been consummated, there must have been an awareness that the acknowledgement of the claims of Jesus involved a fundamentally different view of religion from that represented by current Judaism.

In concluding our discussion of the religious aspects of the conflict between Jesus and the leaders of Judaism, we may profitably observe that the evangelists at no point disclose any awareness of the participation of any other assembly than the official Jewish Sanhedrin in the trial of Jesus. Matthew and Mark describe the trial court as consisting of "the high priests and the whole sanhedrin" (Mt. 26:59; Mk. 14:55; 15:1). Zeitlin indeed makes ingenious use of the Lucan phrase "their sanhedrin" (Lk. 22:66) as an argument for his thesis that the trial sanhedrin was constituted of persons who were merely "rubber stamps" of the high priest. He declares: "This was his Sanhedrin, as the Gospel of Luke states clearly, 'And the scribes assembled and led him into *their* Sanhedrin' " (pp. 163 f.). If the Lucan passage actually stated that the sanhedrin was "his", that is, the high priest's, it would seem to suggest that in some special sense the high priest could claim it as his own. Since however the text reads "their" rather than "his", the claim made on the basis of Luke's declaration is astonishing.

As a matter of fact the more closely Luke 22:66 is scrutinized, the less support it actually offers for the theory that the trial court was a special political tribunal. What Luke actually says is this: καὶ ὡς ἐγένετο ἡμέρα, συνήχθη τὸ πρεσβυτέριον τοῦ λαοῦ, ἀρχιερεῖς τε καὶ γραμματεῖς, καὶ ἀπήγαγον αὐτὸν εἰς τὸ συνέδριον αὐτῶν.... In order to construe the meaning of "their sanhedrin" correctly, it is necessary to examine the implications of the antecedent language. A comparison of the phrase τὸ πρεσβυτέριον τοῦ λαοῦ with πᾶν τὸ πρεσβυτέριον in Acts 22:5, as well as with πᾶν τὸ συνέδριον in Acts 22:30, will show that this phrase is Luke's designation of the Sanhedrin, which he says gathered together as soon as it was day. That he mentions the chief priests and scribes as constituting its membership, but does not mention "the elders" (οἱ πρεσβύτεροι), is apparently due simply to the fact that he has already characterized the assembly as "the *presbyterion*". That the "elders" are not meant to be excluded receives confirmation from the manner in which Luke at other points includes them among those who rejected Jesus (Lk. 9:22; 22:52). In view of these considerations, the final clause must be understood as meaning that, the *presbyterion* having come together, Jesus was led "into their assembly", the word συνέδριον being employed here in a non-technical sense. The expression "their assembly" implies then that it was the assembly of the entire company of the members of the Sanhedrin. It may be observed therefore that Lk. 22:66 not only offers no particular support of the theory that the sanhedrin in some special sense was dominated by the high priest, but it also presents positive evidence that the sanhedrin which tried

Jesus was not a special political court of the kind that Zeitlin contends for. Such a political body of Quislings could never have been described as "the *presbyterion* of the people".[15]

When the thesis of the work we have been examining is tested by the pertinent evidence, we are convinced that it falls far short of being established. We wish to add, however, that the recognition that the official Jewish Sanhedrin condemned Jesus and secured his crucifixion at the hands of Pontius Pilate by no means provides a tenable basis for anti-Semitism. The popular and official repudiation of Jesus' claims by the Jewish people as a whole, and the resultant visitation of a divine judgment upon them, never carried with it the implication, according to the New Testament, that the Jewish people might with impunity be made the objects of hatred and persecution. On the contrary, there is everywhere the insistence that the divine plan required the missionaries to preach "to the Jews first". The deep yearning of the apostle Paul for the salvation of his Jewish compatriots is eloquent on this subject. The repudiation of anti-Semitism does not depend upon a radical revision of the New Testament. There is a far deeper guarantee in Christianity of the rights of the Jew than any revision of one's estimate of the actual course of the events connected with the death of Jesus could provide.

---

[15] It may be recalled also that Zeitlin maintains as a criterion for distinguishing a political sanhedrin that it had to be specially summoned while the official sanhedrin is represented as being in regular session five days a week. In this case the theory would break down, for here certainly there is no implication that the sanhedrin was constituted and convened for this occasion. They convened when it became day.

CHAPTER III

REPENTANCE, BAPTISM AND THE GIFT OF THE HOLY SPIRIT

THE title of this article is suggested by the language of Acts 2.38, a passage rendered in the RV as follows: "Repent ye and be baptized every one of you in the name of Jesus Christ unto the remission of your sins; and ye shall receive the gift of the Holy Spirit". And the purpose of this study is to reflect upon some of the basic problems with which these words of the apostle Peter confront the reader of Acts. In particular I have in view certain questions that relate to the teaching concerning the Holy Spirit as that comes to expression in this verse and in the larger context of this Lucan writing. Repentance and baptism will be under discussion very largely only as that may be required to illumine the basic question of the nature of the operations of the Holy Spirit.

An advantage of this approach is that, whereas such matters as repentance and baptism are not reflected upon with sufficient frequency and fulness to allow dogmatic formulations of these doctrines on the basis of the data of Acts alone, there is a pervasive occupation with the doctrine of the Holy Spirit. The distinctive approach of Luke to the history of the Christian church which he records may be summed up in terms of an interpretation of its origins and development as being basically and conspicuously the work of the Holy Spirit. Pentecost is viewed as the foundation of all that follows. The age depicted in Acts is the age of the Spirit, an age that stands apart as "the last days" of prophecy (Acts 2:17) which have been decisively introduced by the divine action in "pouring out" the Spirit.

Acts indeed is not narrowly pneumatological. The promise of the Spirit is "the promise of the Father" (1:4; Luke 24:49). And it is the exalted Christ who pours out the Spirit (2:33), and thus is understood as carrying forward his ministry following his ascension through the Spirit (*cf.* 1:1 f., 4 f., 8). The work of the Spirit is thus integrated with that of the Father and of the Son. Nevertheless, it is the baptism and enduement of the Spirit that is pervasively and most conspicuously in the foreground.

So much would perhaps be generally admitted today as to the general approach of Acts to Christian history. But thereafter divergent viewpoints emerge, and many such differences appear in connection with the exegesis of Acts 2:38. With a view to a clarification of the issues at stake it is well to try to observe that some are much more basic than others. And one of such more basic issues concerns the question whether "the gift of the Holy Spirit" has in view saving operations of the Spirit upon the heart of man or certain extraordinary manifestations of the Spirit of a more external character.

On the supposition that Peter is speaking particularly concerning salvation in this passage and its immediate context, and that "the gift of the Holy Spirit" also must have in view the Spirit's saving action, the passage might appear to suggest a number of interesting possibilities. According to Smeaton,[1] the reference "is plainly to the sanctifying gifts of the Spirit and to His gracious inhabitation", a view that would be quite compatible with the classic Reformed conception of salvation by grace alone. If, however, the gift of the Spirit were understood as signifying regeneration in the narrow sense, the passage would appear to have a Pelagian flavor. Or, if the reference to the reception of the Spirit were construed precisely and pointedly with the requirement of baptism, baptism could be understood as effecting regeneration or salvation in general, and the passage would seem to support certain high-churchly views of the sacrament.

More commonly today Acts is thought to have in view in this passage and in similar references the special and extraordinary manifestations of the Spirit such as the gift of tongues and that of prophecy. On such an estimate of the gift of the Spirit, Acts 2:38 points up quite distinctive per-

[1] G. Smeaton: *The Doctrine of the Holy Spirit* (Edinburgh, 1882), p. 30.

spectives. The soteriological difficulty mentioned above disappears. If the passage deals with the endowment of Christians with special powers it cannot be understood as impinging upon the doctrine of salvation by grace alone. On this approach, however, other problems emerge. Though baptism would not then be understood as effecting regeneration, it still might be regarded as, *ex opere operato*, conferring miraculous gifts.[2] And thus disturbing questions as to the New Testament teaching regarding baptism would be thrust upon us. But even more basic problems come into focus, problems relating to the distinctive viewpoint of Acts concerning the real nature of the Christian faith and practice. It has been widely held in modern times, for example, that for Acts the significance of the Spirit is wholly or largely exhausted in the bestowal of miraculous gifts, and that thus its doctrine of the Spirit is radically at variance with the Epistles which dwell upon the Spirit's saving influences upon the hearts of men in regeneration and sanctification.[3] And the prominence of miraculous and charismatic features in the portrayal of early Christianity raises acutely the old problem as to whether such elements of "enthusiasm" belong to the original and essential nature of Christianity.

Of special interest is the extensive discussion of Jackson and Lake in connection with their treatment of primitive Christianity in the first volume of their monumental *Christian Beginnings*.[4] Concerning Acts 2:38 they assert:

> The obvious meaning is — just as in Acts xix.1-7 — that the gift of the Spirit is conditional on baptism; but this sudden introduction of baptism seems quite inconsistent with what was stated: the disciples had received the Spirit without having been baptized for that purpose, and the words of Jesus in Acts i.4 imply a baptism in Spirit as a substitute for baptism in water, not as a consequence of it.

[2] *Cf* F J. Foakes-Jackson: *The Acts of the Apostles* (London, 1931), pp. 18 f.; C. Gore: *The Holy Spirit and the Church* (New York, 1924), pp. 53, 126 f.

[3] See especially H. Gunkel: *Die Wirkungen des heiligen Geistes, nach der popularen Anschauung der apostolischen Zeit und nach der Lehre des Apostels Paulus* (Gottingen, 1888).

[4] F. J. Foakes-Jackson and Kirsopp Lake: *The Beginnings of Christianity, Part I, The Acts of the Apostles*, Vol. I (London, 1920), pp. 337 ff.

The redactor, however, like all his contemporaries in the Gentile Church, regarded baptism in the name of Jesus as necessary for admission to the Christian society and its benefits, of which the gift of the Spirit was one of the chief; it is therefore not strange if he introduced the references to baptism in ii.38 and 41.[5]

This interpretation of Acts 2·38 presupposes the judgment that baptism is presented in Acts from several contradictory points of view. Three are specifically distinguished: (1) "Baptism in water conferred the gift of the Spirit, but only f administered in the name of the Lord Jesus"(p. 337). This is said to be the viewpoint of Acts 19:1–7 and 9:17 f. as well as 2:38. (2) Sharply opposed to this is allegedly the view of Acts 1:4–2:4 that the Christian baptism foretold by John the Baptist is by the Spirit and not in water, and this is thought to have been fulfilled on the day of Pentecost. This view is thought to be farthest removed from the outlook of the "redactor" of Acts who is said clearly to have regarded baptism as a Christian practice from the beginning. The sources of Acts 2 and 10–11 contained nothing concerning baptism in water, it is held, but "it was found in the sources used for the second part of Acts, and the redactor, regarding it as a primitive custom connected with the gift of the Spirit, adapted the earlier narratives to agree with the later ones".[6] (3) Agreeing with neither extreme is the view that in Acts 8:8–19 "Baptism in water, even in the name of the Lord Jesus, did not confer the Spirit, which was given only by the laying on of hands by the apostles".[7] On the background of this analysis Jackson and Lake conclude with the conjecture that Christian baptism in water does not go back to the time of Jesus and his immediate disciples, but owes its origin to the Seven and likely arose in the environment of the Hellenistic Diaspora, possibly through the influence of magical ideas and practices.[8]

We encounter in this discussion, accordingly, the judgment

[5] *Ibid.*, pp 339 f.
[6] *Ibid.*, p 341.
[7] *Ibid.*, p 338 *Cf* C. K Barrett: *The Holy Spirit and the Gospel Tradition* (London, 1947), p 142.
[8] Jackson and Lake: *op. cit.*, pp. 341 f.

that Acts 2.38, particularly in its teaching concerning baptism and the gift of the Holy Spirit, is sharply at variance with the point of view of the Pentecost narrative, and that it is not completely reconcilable with other representations of Acts on the subject. At Pentecost there was a baptism with the Spirit with nothing said about water baptism; in Acts 2:38 and at other points, according to this approach, the gift of the Spirit is viewed as following upon, and even as being conferred by, water baptism. This analysis is regarded, moreover, as supporting a skeptical estimate of the origin of Christian baptism together with a conception of it as conferring benefits, including the Spirit, *ex opere*. This disparaging evaluation of the sacrament, as well as the divisive exegesis offered in support of it, will be recognized as rather characteristic of the modern approach to the subject of Christian origins.

Acts 2:38 assuredly confronts the interpreter with weighty problems. In order to evaluate the passage correctly it will be imperative to take account of all or most of the passages which have been mentioned, for thus only can one hope to do justice to the terms employed and to deal concretely with the questions raised concerning the alleged discrepancies of viewpoint in Acts. I shall pass in review four events or episodes which bear upon the understanding of Acts 2:38: (1) the Pentecost narrative in Acts 2; (2) the salvation of Gentiles in Acts 10 and 11; (3) Samaria's reception of the Word of God in Chapter 8; and (4) the episode concerning the disciples in Ephesus recorded in Acts 19. There is no want of diversity in these accounts; there is perhaps even more than is commonly recognized. But the question remains whether, if the distinctiveness of the several situations is discerned, one may not account for the diversity and still avoid the skeptical and divisive conclusions of such constructions as those proposed by Jackson and Lake.

(1) *The Pentecost Narrative*

Pentecost, intimating that the prophecy of Joel concerning the outpouring of the Spirit has received fulfillment, is the foundation of all that follows. Peter interprets the days of the Spirit as constituting "the last days" (Acts 2:17), and this eschatological evaluation of Pentecost gives perspective to the ensuing history.

Pentecost itself is not repeated. It stands apart from what follows as an event that occurred once for all when the ascended Christ decisively sent forth the Spirit to inaugurate the new order. Indicative of this fact is the consideration that the phenomena of the day of Pentecost were not repeated. In what follows there is nothing comparable to the "tongues as of fire" or the "sound as of a mighty wind being borne along". And evidently the speaking with tongues described in Acts 2 is not repeated. At any rate it is not the ecstatic speech which required the gift of the interpretation of tongues to be intelligible, which Paul refers to in I Corinthians, but a speaking in various languages which were understood immediately by representatives of various nationalities who were present on the occasion. Men heard in their own languages the proclamation of the wonderful works of God. This phenomenon accordingly has more in common with the gift of prophecy than with that of tongues.

It is entirely in keeping with the unique nature of Pentecost, therefore, that nothing is said immediately of persons coming to be baptized in water. The baptism with the Spirit on that day constituted a unilateral, eschatological action on the part of Christ, as immediate and miraculous as the resurrection of Jesus. If human cooperation or a human response had been indicated as being of the essence of what took place, the foundational significance of Pentecost would have been obliterated or obscured. Nevertheless, on the background of the unique happenings of that day, it would be entirely understandable that there should be subsequent mediations of the Spirit's gifts and actions on various occasions, and that these should be brought into intimate association with the baptism of Christian converts.

(2) *Salvation of the Gentiles*

The consideration of Pentecost prepares for the evaluation of Acts 2·38 and the response of 2:41, but a richer context is given by the narrative of Peter and Cornelius in Acts 10 and

11. Though this narrative contains various biographical features which illumine the career of the apostle Peter, it is evident that Acts dwells upon this story because its purpose is to delineate the main stages in the early expansion of Christianity and it regards the development in Caesarea as constituting an epochal phase of that history. It became clear once for all that the Gentiles in becoming Christians did not virtually have to become Jews first and conform to the Jewish manner of life, as Peter at first supposed. Peter's problem was not that of the salvation of the Gentiles as such, for on this both the teaching of the prophets and of the Lord was plain, but that of the possibility of their coming directly to Christ without the necessity that the wall of partition between Jew and Gentile should be broken down first.

Following Peter's vision, and while he was still proclaiming the message concerning Christ to the Gentiles

> the Holy Spirit fell upon all those who heard the word. And they of the circumcision who believed, as many as came with Peter, were amazed because that on the Gentiles also was poured out the gift of the Holy Spirit. For they heard them speak with tongues and magnify God (Acts 10:44 ff.).

The epochal significance of the reception of the Holy Spirit on the part of the Gentiles is underscored by the observation that Peter justified his actions before the Church at Jerusalem virtually by characterizing this development as a repetition of what had happened at Pentecost. He declares:

> As I began to speak the Holy Spirit fell upon them, even as on us at the beginning. And I remembered the word of the Lord how he said, John indeed baptized with water, but ye shall be baptized in the Holy Spirit. If then God gave them the like gift as he did also unto us when we believed on the Lord Jesus Christ, who was I that I could withstand God? (Acts 11:15 ff.).

It is remarkable that Peter not only closely identifies the gift which the Gentiles received with that which the Christians had received at the beginning, but he even characterizes it as the baptism of the Holy Spirit, in fulfillment of the word of the Lord (*cf.* Acts 1:5). In linking up the developments in Caesarea with those of Pentecost, the epochal significance of the salvation of the Gentiles is powerfully emphasized. As at Pentecost when suddenly there was a sound from heaven manifesting the supernatural action of the coming of the Spirit, here the action of the Spirit does not wait upon the deliberations or actions of apostles, but immediately and directly initiates a new order of dealing with men. Indeed, in this instance the Spirit encountered the resistance of an apostle, and thus there was an additional reason for the action to take the form of a divine interposition. Yet, in spite of certain parallels with Pentecost, the development in Caesarea is undoubtedly viewed as somewhat subordinate to it, and as actually intimating the significance of Pentecost for the salvation of the Gentiles. Since the company at Jerusalem had been confined to Jews (*cf.* 2:5, 14, 22, 36), its concrete significance for the Gentiles had to await disclosure until the gospel moved out beyond the Jerusalem scene.

That "the gift of the Holy Spirit" has in view extraordinary, miraculous actions of the Spirit is rather evident from the context. When the Jews "heard them speak with tongues and magnify God", they were assured that the Gentiles had received this gift. These gifts were probably glossolalia and prophecy (*cf.* Acts 19:6). That they were of an external nature appears from the observation that the Jewish believers who accompanied Peter were able to discern what was taking place. These gifts did not produce faith in a miraculous fashion, for the Gentiles were those who had heard and believed the word which had been spoken (*cf.* Acts 10:44; 11:17). But these events did serve to prove that the Gentiles were true believers, that "God had also granted unto the Gentiles repentance unto life" (11:18). They were thus the divine seal upon these believers and the evidence to Peter that a new era in God's dealings with men had dawned.

There is also special interest in the fact that we are confronted with the administration of Christian baptism in a context where another baptism, the baptism of the Spirit, has been in view and has been closely identified with the gift of the Holy Spirit. Baptism with water is introduced in this narrative as a practice that is virtually taken for granted where there was evidence of Christian faith. Thus

Peter, having received evidence of the presence of the Spirit, asks, "Can any man forbid water that these should not be baptized, who have received the Holy Spirit as well as we?" (Acts 10:47 f.). Jackson and Lake suggest that the story is illogical in introducing the baptism with water after Cornelius had received the Spirit since, it is alleged, no apparent reason remains for baptism after the Spirit had been decisively conferred.[9] But this is so only if baptism is understood as bestowing the Spirit more or less magically. Though indeed baptism and the gift of the Spirit are intimately associated in Acts, there is no evidence, as will be observed more fully below, to support the conception of baptism as an *ex opere operato* sacrament. And the narrative under consideration itself offers evidence that the relationship between baptism and the gift of the Holy Spirit is not viewed in the rigid and stereotyped fashion that is often supposed. The administration of Christian baptism, as Acts appears to assume throughout, followed upon evidence of faith in Christ, and Peter had had to be assured of the presence of such faith by evidence of the extraordinary presence of the Spirit.

(3) *Samaria's Reception of the Word*

The proclamation of the gospel in Samaria also represented a significant stage in the expansion of the Christian church, as Acts 1:8 has suggested and as the account of the preaching of Philip in Acts 8 brings into sharp focus. As a result of Peter's preaching and healing work a company of men and women believed and were baptized (Acts 8:5 ff., 12 f.). Evidently, so far at least as Philip was concerned, no special evidence was required that the Samaritans might hear the Word and be received into the Christian church on the basis of faith. Though the beliefs and practices of the Samaritans were somewhat distinctive, they were not classified as Gentiles. The proclamation of the Word to them and their acceptance of it was a distinct step forward in the unfolding of the divine plan. But it was not such a radical

[9] *Ibid.*, p. 340.

development as was to take place in the approach to Cornelius the Gentile, and thus one may understand that the extraordinary evidence of divine approval given in Caesarea was not demanded in Samaria. Their faith in the Word was itself taken as evidence that they were *bona fide* members of the Christian community. And when the apostles take account of developments, their verdict is the same. The faith of the Samaritans was all that was needed to support the judgment that "Samaria had received the word of God", momentous though this evaluation was for the apostles who had come down from Jerusalem for the purpose of judging for themselves of the progress of the gospel.

In Samaria likewise baptism is regarded as the normal Christian practice following upon faith, just as in the story of Cornelius. There is little or no reflection upon the doctrine of baptism in either narrative. Nevertheless, one fact stands out sharply in both, a fact that is the more remarkable in the light of the exceedingly diverse situations which unfold. That fact is that in Samaria as in Caesarea baptism is not regarded as *ipso facto* conferring the gift of the Holy Spirit. In the case of Cornelius the gift was given first and baptism came at the end; in Samaria baptism preceded the bestowal of the gift of the Spirit, but that bestowal waited for the coming of the apostles and their direct action through imposition of hands upon the baptized converts. The diversity in the administration of the special gifts of the Spirit is accounted for, therefore, by the diversity in the historical situations. In both cases one may regard the sanction as divine, but there is the difference that in Samaria the sanction was mediated by apostolic action when the apostles were persuaded by what they saw, while in Caesarea the sanction was directly given by the Spirit when Peter required proof that what was taking place under his eyes was indeed in accordance with the divine plan.

The Samaritans are described as not having received "the Holy Spirit" though they had believed and had been baptized. Only after the apostles prayed and laid their hands upon them did they receive the Holy Spirit (8:16, 17). This terminology pointedly calls attention to the special manner in which the doctrine of the Holy Spirit is being and may be set forth in Acts. What gift or gifts of the Spirit were being bestowed upon the Samaritans is not specified, but that they were external, miraculous gifts is plain from the reactions of Simon the sorcerer. "Now when Simon saw that through the laying on of the apostles' hands, the Holy Spirit was given, he offered them money, saying, Give me also this power that on whomsoever I lay my hands, he may receive the Holy Spirit" (8:18 f.). Such gifts as prophecy and tongues evidently had been conferred, and Simon had been able to observe their manifestations. At this point at least, therefore, there is no reflection upon the relation of the Spirit to the origin of faith and the growth of the Christian life. To us that may seem baffling because the theological questions are of paramount and perennial interest. But one may not insist that the writer of Acts had to reflect upon these questions in our terms, and one must recognize the peculiar appropriateness in a volume largely concerned with the external course of early Christian history of centering attention upon the extraordinary miraculous power of the Spirit in the accomplishment of the divine plan for the people of God.

(4) *The Disciples in Ephesus.*

The extraordinary incident recorded in Acts 19:1–7 may also illumine the basic problems before us, for there, likewise, the elements of faith and baptism and the coming of the Holy Spirit are in the foreground. The decisions are somewhat complicated by difficulties of translation and interpretation connected with the understanding of the incident as a whole, and some attention must be paid to them.

One problem concerns the identity of the disciples who stood in astonishing isolation from the main stream of the Christian church. They not only had not been baptized with Christian baptism but they also seem strangely ignorant of the Holy Spirit. Can they nevertheless be regarded as Christians? The suggestion has been made that they were in fact disciples of the Baptist rather than of Jesus, but this view must be rejected. The term "disciples" in Acts 19:1 stamps them as Christians in view of the manner in which

Luke thus designates Christians again and again (*cf.* Acts 6:1; 9:10; 11·26) Moreover, they are spoken of simply as "believing" (19:2), and this terminology is consistently applied by Luke to Christians (*cf.* Acts 2:44; 4:4, 32; 18:8, 27). It is incredible that Luke should have used these terms without qualification if he were referring to non-Christians.

If, however, the disciples are Christian believers, their isolation from Christian history is the more difficult to explain. Nevertheless, all is intelligible if they were a small company of disciples who had not been in touch, especially at the time of their coming to faith in Christ, with developments following the resurrection and including particularly the happenings on the day of Pentecost. To the question of Paul, "Did ye receive the Holy Spirit when ye believed?", they answer, "Nay, we did not so much as hear whether the Holy Spirit was given". This rendering of the RV is indeed not literal, for the original literally reads, "We did not so much as hear whether there was a Holy Spirit". But the RV must be recognized as giving the true sense of the Greek. The force of the passage is like that of John 7:39 which is rendered in the RV by "the Spirit was not yet given, because Jesus was not yet glorified".[10] These passages have in common the eschatological perspective given by the discernment that, through the exaltation of Christ, the messianic age, the age of the Spirit, was realized. On the background of Joel's promise of the outpouring of the Spirit, his coming could be spoken of as an absolutely new coming, though all the while it would be taken for granted that every one knew that the Spirit had been active during the old dispensation.[11] In

---

[10] John's οὔπω γὰρ ἦν πνεῦμα as a didactic statement is even stronger than the judgment of the Ephesian disciples: Ἀλλ' οὐδ' εἰ Πνεῦμα Ἅγιον ἔστιν ἠκούσαμεν.

It is remarkable that the RSV, which is not distinguished for the literalness of its translation, renders Acts 19:2b, "No, we have never even heard that there is a Holy Spirit", but in John 7:39 adopts the translation "for as yet the Spirit had not been given".

[11] Similarly John 1:17 states that "grace and truth came through Jesus Christ", as if grace and truth had never previously been present in the world in any degree, and Galatians 3:23 speaks absolutely of the old dispensation as an order of affairs "before faith came", though Abra-

declaring that they had not so much as heard whether the Holy Spirit was manifested, the disciples accordingly disclosed that they had not heard of the fulfillment of the promise of the coming of the Spirit at Pentecost.[12]

In the main the developments at Ephesus correspond closely with those in Samaria which have just been reviewed. Following upon Paul's inquiries and his instruction as to the inadequacy of their baptism, they "were baptized into the name of the Lord Jesus" (19:5). Paul at Ephesus like Peter in Caesarea and Philip in Samaria evidently assumes the necessity of the administration of Christian baptism following upon faith in Christ. Moreover, in this context likewise baptism is not represented as conferring the gift of the Spirit for it was only after Paul had laid hands upon them that "the Holy Spirit came upon them, and they spoke with tongues and prophesied" (19:6). The parallelism of the developments here with those in Samaria is marked, the only difference being that in this instance apostolic action followed baptism without delay while in Samaria it awaited the arrival of Peter and John from Jerusalem.

The gift of the Spirit is described in Acts 19:6 in much the same terms as in 10:46, and confirms the earlier conclusion that in all of these situations the gift is understood as having in view extraordinary, miraculous effects.

When now one turns back to a more particular consideration of Acts 2:38, most or all of the problems with which it

ham's justification *by faith* has been a leading feature of the argument in this very chapter.

[12] It may be objected to the argument that the Ephesian group was Christian that they had been baptized with the baptism of John (19:3), and therefore would more naturally be understood as being disciples of the Baptist than of Christ. Some matters concerning the relation of the baptism of John to Christian baptism are obscure, but evidently specifically Christian baptism began only with the establishment of the Christian church following the exaltation of Christ. On this view the baptism by the disciples of Jesus mentioned in John 4:1 ff. may best be understood as a continuation of John's baptism Accordingly, the Ephesian disciples could be early believers in Christ who were baptized by John or, more probably, with his baptism by another See G. Vos: *Biblical Theology, Old and New Testaments*, (Grand Rapids, 1948), pp. 341 f.

confronts the interpreter will appear to have been under review. And the disadvantages bound up with the brevity and summary character of this passage in Peter's discourse are largely overcome by taking stock of the information gained from a study of the other contexts in which the same features appear.

In Acts 2 two forms of baptism appear, that of Pentecost itself and the sacrament which Peter invites those who repent to undergo and which subsequently those who heard the Word underwent (Acts 2:38, 41). But the proximity of these two kinds of baptism does not point to a discrepancy of viewpoint or set up tensions within the narrative. In the perspective of Acts Pentecost forms the foundation for all subsequent actions and provides a distinctive perspective for all of the history that is recorded, and hence is in an entirely different category from the sacrament of baptism which was to be received by individual believers following upon their faith.

One may conclude with confidence that Acts 2:38 is not to be understood as teaching that the gift of the Spirit was conditional upon baptism, even though the command to receive baptism is followed with the promise, "and ye shall receive the gift of the Holy Spirit". In the several contexts where it has been possible to evaluate the question of the possible relation between baptism and the bestowal of the Spirit, it has been unmistakably clear that baptism is not conceived of as conferring the Spirit. The two are intimately associated, and the gift of the Spirit may well be regarded as the normal concomitant of baptism, but it never appears as the inevitable or immediate consequence of baptism. It would therefore be rash to insist that the words, "and ye shall receive the gift of the Holy Spirit" in 2:38 indicate that baptism as such confers this gift.[13]

---

[13] Jackson and Lake: *op. cit*, p 338, also contend that Acts 9:17 f. supports the view that baptism in the name of the Lord Jesus confers the Holy Spirit. Ananias tells Paul that the Lord had sent him "that thou mayest receive thy sight and be filled with the Holy Spirit". And immediately, when Ananias laid hands on Paul," he received his sight and he arose and was baptized". Like Acts 2:38 this passage is so brief that it is difficult to come to final conclusions regarding the relation of baptism and

Moreover, Acts 2:38 itself provides a reason for resisting the conclusion that the gift is conditional upon baptism. For it must be underscored that Peter's basic and primary demand is for *repentance*, and his thought may be that the promise of the Spirit is assured upon the basis of conversion rather than merely as the consequence of baptism. This interpretation is given support by noting Peter's appeal in Acts 3:19: "Repent ye, therefore, and turn again, that your sins may be blotted out that so there may come seasons of refreshing from the presence of the Lord". Repentance will bring refreshing from on high, evidently through the work of the Spirit. But nothing is said of baptism. Similarly in Acts 2:38 baptism may be subordinated to repentance. That the accent falls more on repentance than upon baptism also gains support from the observation that in Luke 24:27 the gospel to be preached in Christ's name to all the nations is summed up in terms of "repentance and remission of sins".

That "the gift of the Holy Spirit" in Acts 2:38 must have in view miraculous powers will hardly appear doubtful when one recalls the other references to the gift of the Spirit which have been considered. And it may be significant that the very same word for gift ($\delta\omega\rho\epsilon\dot{\alpha}$) is employed in Acts 8:20 where Peter condemns Simon for supposing that he could obtain "the gift of God" for money; in Acts 10:45 in connection with the amazement of the Jews that "the gift of the Holy Spirit had been poured out upon the Gentiles"; and in Acts 11:17 where Peter speaks of it as "the like gift" which God gave to them.

The question remains, however, whether possibly on certain occasions, and particularly in Acts 2:38, the designation "the gift of the Spirit" may not be employed somewhat

---

the bestowal of the gift of the Spirit solely on the basis of its contents. Jackson and Lake state that there is a clear implication that the baptism of Paul was the fulfillment of the promise that he would be filled with the Holy Spirit Even if that were the implication, it would not follow that baptism is regarded as *conferring* the Spirit. Actually the account is silent regarding the bestowal of the Spirit upon Paul, and it is entirely possible that the baptism of Paul is introduced as an additional development, while the Spirit is regarded as having been previously given in connection with the recovery of his sight.

more comprehensively than is suggested by the above. May it not include gifts of a more distinctly religious and ethical character in addition to the miraculous *charismata*? Though Acts gives great prominence to the miraculous activity of the Spirit, and on occasion seems to refer to the Spirit as if there were no other kind of activity for which he was responsible, it is equally clear that the fruits of Pentecost are not restricted to miraculous activities. All of Christ's work is viewed as accomplished through the Spirit, and this would quite well allow that all of the gifts bestowed upon the church and upon individual Christians would be regarded as the gift of the Holy Spirit.

It would be particularly appropriate to regard the qualifications of wisdom and faith mentioned in connection with the appointment of the Seven as fruits of the Spirit (*cf.* Acts 6:3, 5). But it may be that salvation itself, considered comprehensively as the total saving work of God, is understood as the work of the Spirit. The quotation from Joel concludes with the intimation that the age of the Spirit is to be a time of salvation (*cf.* 2:21). The "seasons of refreshing" in Acts 3:19 also appropriately describe the joyous benefits of salvation experienced by those who turn to the Lord.

The external gifts, moreover, serve the purpose of affording evidence that God's saving purposes had been effectually realized. Thus Peter regards the extraordinary working of the Spirit among the Gentiles as proof that "to the Gentiles also hath God granted repentance unto life" (11:18). Similarly, even the pouring out of the gift of the Holy Spirit upon the Gentiles, referred to in Acts 10:45, may look beyond the gifts of tongues and prophecy themselves (v. 47) to the total application of Pentecost to the Gentiles. And thus one can hardly exclude the possibility that in Acts 2:38 "the gift of the Holy Spirit" promised to believers may comprehend the saving benefits of Christ's work as applied to the believer by the Spirit.

If, however, gifts of salvation and spiritual gifts in general may be comprehended in "the gift of the Holy Spirit", no support of a synergistic conception of salvation is forthcoming from the teaching of Acts. Acts 11:18 specifically recognizes that "repentance unto life" is the gift of God. It is the Lord who adds daily unto his church those who are saved (2:47). And those who believed are recognized as being such as were ordained unto eternal life (13:48).

The situation in Acts, in view of all these considerations, is not as varied from that of the Epistles of Paul as has been often supposed. Paul as distinctly as Acts, as Gunkel also recognized, testifies to the presence of the miraculous work of the Spirit in the early church. Paul does dwell more fully and explicitly upon the ethical and religious work of the Spirit and through his teaching greatly enlarges our understanding of the doctrine of the Spirit. Because his epistles were concerned with the faith and life of his converts they could be the vehicle for such teaching in a way that Acts, largely absorbed as it was with the external course of Christian history, could not be. But even Acts is not without reflections upon the decisive divine ordination and accomplishment of salvation, and envisages the work of salvation as the fruit of Pentecost. Acts, therefore, has its own peculiar forms of expression and differences of emphasis in dealing with the Holy Spirit, but a broad unity of perspective with the rest of the New Testament also is evident.

Integrated with these historical and exegetical questions concerning the Spirit and the church is the divisive issue of supernaturalism. Such phenomena as the gift of tongues and prophecy, not to reflect particularly upon the many other miracles recorded in Acts, conspicuously center attention upon it. In the light of all the facts it appears that these miracles are not presented as isolated happenings, nor are they to be explained either as evidence of the penetration of magical notions and of a popular enthusiasm into the Christian church or in terms of a philosophy of irrationalism. For they are instances of decisive divine interposition in history which are aspects of a comprehensive divine plan that has in view the certain realization of God's saving purposes, pointing to goals and demanding responses which are profoundly religious and ethical. Pentecost undergirds the new dispensation, and thus gives perspective to all the individual instances of the supernatural and intimates their meaning in and for Christian history. Since these elements of the supernatural pervade the entire New Testament expression of Christianity, they cannot be evaluated except as one judges Christianity as a whole. If one recognizes Christianity to be the supernatural religion of individual and cosmic redemption, and its goal the transformation of men and the world by God almighty through his grace in Christ Jesus, the miracles will not appear as a burden or liability to Christian faith. They are, rather, significant aspects of that redemptive and revelational action of God in transforming the world, are indicative that that transformation has been begun and even has been realized in a significant manner, and point to the consummation of "new heavens and a new earth, wherein dwelleth righteousness".

CHAPTER IV

THE ELDERS AND THE LIVING-BEINGS IN THE APOCALYPSE

THE Apocalypse has been a book particularly for times of *Sturm und Drang*. One may recall, for example, that the persecution of Septimius Severus was the occasion of the occupation of Hippolytus, at the beginning of the third century, with the contents of Daniel and Revelation. Similarly, a century later, the commentary of Victorinus, the martyr, appeared during the reign of Diocletian. On the other hand, during the latter half of the 19th century, marked as it was by an unbounded optimism regarding the supposed progress of man and society, when even much of the Church fell under the spell of a wholly *diesseits* evaluation of its mission, the Apocalypse was not widely regarded as containing a message of vital relevancy. In such an atmosphere academic treatises might indeed be produced because of an interest in the nature and origins of early Christianity, but many scholars would leave the book largely alone if they did not attack it as "Jewish" or "chiliastic" or "fantastic." The earth-shaking impacts of two world wars, and the fears of perhaps even more catastrophic events to come, however, have substantially changed human perspectives. The Apocalypse now appears to stand much closer to us because we live day by day in the consciousness of being involved in a stupendous crisis in which the destinies of peoples and nations are being finally determined.

Another reason why the Apocalypse may be expected to attract the sustained interest of serious students of the Bible is that the march of thought concerning Christian history has resulted in an absorption with the study of eschatology. This interest in eschatology may indeed be explained partially in terms of the outward course of events in the present century to which reference has been made. But there have at any rate been some independent factors of a more academic character. The new attention to eschatology and apocalyptic which, with varying degrees of influence and differences in interpretation, took its rise with Baldensperger and Johannes

Weiss and Schweitzer, was to introduce perspectives into the modern study of the New Testament which have affected exegetical and historical judgments in significant fashion. Though Schweitzer did not, like Baur and Ritschl, become the head of a school, the force of his impact upon the study of the New Testament remains unspent after fifty years. It now seems incredible that men will ever return to a completely non-eschatological interpretation of Christianity and the Christian message. So long as Jesus could be understood essentially as Harnack viewed Him, as one for whom the eschatological hope was at best of peripheral concern, the Apocalypse would necessarily appear to be utterly at odds with Jesus' message and would be looked upon as a fantastic intruder into the New Testament. There are indeed substantial remnants of the older Liberal view still in evidence. C. H. Dodd, for example, in keeping with his one-sided "realized eschatology," critizes Revelation as characterized by an "excessive emphasis upon the future" which has "the effect of relegating to a secondary place just those elements in the original Gospel which are most distinctive of Christianity — the faith that in the finished work of Christ God has already acted for the salvation of man, and the blessed sense of living in the divine presence here and now."[1] Nevertheless, the total situation has improved immeasurably for it is widely acknowledged that, in studying the Apocalypse, one must be occupied with the very subject of eschatology which constitutes a central aspect of the teaching of our Lord and of the New Testament as a whole.

To the beginner no part of the New Testament seems so bewildering as the Apocalypse. This is due no doubt both to the strangeness of much of its language and imagery and to the exceedingly voluminous literature which, by the very diversity of its viewpoints, seems to make the initial confusion worse confounded. And even a somewhat older scholar, who spends any considerable amount of time with the literature, may conclude that he must remain rather non-committal on many basic questions of interpretation. No doubt there has been progress toward a truer understanding. And Reformed

[1] *The Apostolic Preaching*, 1936, p. 88.

interpreters have made their own particular contributions. But many questions remain; and differences, even among Reformed exegetes, continue unresolved. It is to be hoped that in these days there may be a new stimulus to fresh study of this portion of Scripture.

Some larger objectives are in view in this brief study of the significance of the twenty-four elders and the four living-beings. The study is justified for its own sake as one considers the diversity of judgment that has prevailed concerning their identity and meaning. But it may also serve to emphasize certain basic matters, relating to the text and its interpretation, which are essential to progress in understanding Revelation as a whole. In view of limitations of space no attempt will be made to reflect upon every fact or argument that may bear upon the final decision. However, the considerations which seem most decisive will be reviewed and some note taken of published opinions.

The position taken here is that both the elders and the living-beings are to be understood as celestial beings of a rank superior to the angels in general, like the cherubim and seraphim of the Old Testament if they are not to be identified specifically with them. Such an interpretation is indeed not a novel one for it has had its representatives for centuries. In the present century it has been generally held by interpreters who have adopted the approach of the *religionsgeschichtliche* School, and thus objectionable features are commonly associated with it. For example, Gunkel had influenced many commentators to conclude that back of the representations of the Revelation there stand astral deities of Babylonian mythology and similar pagan religious conceptions.[2] Such evaluations of the origin of the imagery and conceptions are,

[2] H. Gunkel, *Schopfung und Chaos*, 1892, pp. 302 ff ; *Zum religionsgesch. Verstandnis des N. Ts* , 1903, pp. 42 f Cf. the expositions *ad loc.* in Bousset (1906), Holtzmann–Bauer (1908), Moffatt (1910), J. Weiss (3te Aufl. 1920), Peake (1919), Case (1919), Charles (1920), Beckwith (1922), Kiddle (1940). Lohmeyer (1926) appears to reject the interpretation of the elders as astral deities, but finds the origin of the conception of the living-beings in Babylonian astrology. Anderson Scott (1902) regards both elders and the living-beings as angels, but stresses Biblical and Jewish rather than Babylonian backgrounds.

however, not essential to the view that celestial beings are in mind. Zahn among the Lutheran commentators and Ringnalda among the Reformed afford rather recent proof of this fact.[3]

Nevertheless, traditionally, evangelicals have rejected the conclusion that these beings are angels or celestial spirits. For the most part the elders have been interpreted by them as symbolizing or representing *the church*, and the living-beings *creation*, as they unite in worshipping God about His heavenly throne. Since this viewpoint has received the support of such able and influential expositors as Hengstenberg, Düsterdieck, Alford, B. Weiss and Swete, it is not surprising that it apparently continues to enjoy considerable popular favor.[4]

Chief Factors Affecting the Decision

As one weighs the arguments which have been advanced by those who are assured that Revelation cannot have angelic beings in view, several considerations appear to have been of decisive influence.

(1) One gains the impression that the *textus receptus* of Rev. 5:9, 10, (with the older vernacular translations based upon it) has been responsible to a remarkable degree for the repudiation of this interpretation and for the resultant search for explanations that would appear to satisfy the data. As will be recalled, the older translations represent the elders and living-beings as singing a new song to the Lamb in which they say:

---

[3] Zahn, *Kommentar*, 1924, A. Ringnalda, *Het Koningschap van Christus*, 1939. W. H Simcox in *Cambridge Bible*, 1893, and W Hendriksen, *More Than Conquerors*, 1939, regard the living creatures as cherubim, though they do not reject the traditional interpretation of the elders as signifying "the glorified embodiment of the people of God" (Simcox) or "the host of the redeemed" (Hendriksen). Cf. also C. A. Briggs, *The Messiah of the Apostles*, 1895, p 397.

[4] Hengstenberg (Eng. Trans. 1851); Düsterdieck (1859 ff); Alford (1861 ff.); B Weiss (1902), Swete (1906 ff). Similarly in Lange (1871), Milligan (1889), de Moor (1926), Pieters (1937), Schlatter (5te Aufl. 1938). For somewhat different views, which agree, however, in understanding the elders as redeemed men, see also C. Vitringa (1728), M. Stuart (1845), J. A. Seiss (1865 ff), and R. C H Lenski (1935).

> Thou art worthy to take the book, and to open the seals thereof: for thou wast slain, and hast redeemed us to God by thy blood out of every kindred, and tongue, and people, and nation; and hast made us unto our God kings and priests: and we shall reign on the earth.[5]

In these terms it is plainly a song of *the redeemed* who personally praise the Lamb for their redemption. Quite understandably Vitringa, Hengstenberg and Seiss appeal to this form of the text as decisively excluding a reference to angels.

Modern expositors such as Alford, B. Weiss, Swete and Greijdanus, to be sure, reject the received text, and accept substantially the following rendering:

> Worthy art thou to take the book, and to open the seals thereof: for thou wast slain, and didst purchase unto God with thy blood *men* of every tribe, and tongue, and people, and nation, and madest them to be unto our God a kingdom and priests; and they reign upon the earth.[6]

But my impression is that the traditional interpretation associated with the *textus receptus* had become generally so attractive to Christian expositors, especially because of its immediate, personal religious relevancy, that it survived in spite of the fact that this text had been rejected. At any rate, as I shall seek to show below, the late expositors do not appear to do justice to the implications of the current critical text which records a song celebrating the redemption of a diverse multitude *but which evidently ascribes the song to beings who are distinguished from the redeemed.*

(2) A second consideration that has been appealed to as decisively eliminating the interpretation of these beings as angelic is based upon Rev. 5:11, which distinguishes "many angels" from the living-beings and the elders, and upon Rev.

---

[5] Quoted from the Authorized Version of 1611. Thus also the Staten Vertaling.

[6] Quoted from the Revised Version of 1881. The printing of "men" in italics indicates that the word is not found in the Greek text underlying the translation. The Nieuwe Vertaling is similar. Three variations are principally in view: (1) ἡμᾶς or its omission in v. 9, (2) ἡμᾶς or αὐτούς in v. 10, (3) βασιλεύσομεν or βασιλεύουσιν (or βασιλεύσουσιν) in v. 10. No attempt will be made in this study to decide between the present and the future forms of the verb "reign."

7:11, which pictures "all the angels" standing round about the throne and about the elders and the living-ones. Vitringa, Düsterdieck, Greijdanus and Lenski may be mentioned as commentators from earlier and later modern times who have leaned heavily upon this argument. Since, as nearly every expositor has recognized, the description of the living-ones, including their designation as living-beings ($\zeta\tilde{\omega}a$) is derived largely from the representations of the *cherubim* in Ezekiel 1:5 ff.; 10:20 ff. (Rev. 4:6 ff.), and since it borrows as well certain details from the vision of the *seraphim* in Isaiah 6.2 f. (Rev. 4:8), the *prima facie* impression is that Revelation has in view celestial spirits. Nevertheless, this natural and obvious interpretation is commonly rejected simply, or chiefly, on the ground that if John had cherubim or other celestial spirits in mind, he could not have distinguished them from the "angels" referred to in Rev. 5.11 and 7:11.

(3) One may also notice at this point the influence of a basic approach to the interpretation of the language of Revelation that deserves discriminating evaluation. Having observed that the description of the living-beings is in such close agreement with Ezekiel's language that one can hardly resist the conclusion that *in some primary sense* they must be regarded as cherubim, many expositors seem to suppose that they are compelled to discover behind and beyond the obvious primary identity of the living-beings a more remote symbolism. Thus Alford admits that the four living-beings "are in the main identical with the cherubim of the Old Testament," but he follows this conclusion with a broad inquiry as to "their symbolic import." The question arises whether one does not in this fashion unnecessarily complicate and burden the interpretation of this book, inviting arbitrary and subjective judgments which result in increased obscurity rather than promoting a sober drawing out of the true sense of a passage or detail.

(4) The view that the living-beings refer to creation or nature, moreover, appears to be so little required by the precise data relating to them that one gathers that this interpretation is based, to a significant extent, upon an inference drawn from the supposed meaning of the twenty-four elders. If one once judges that the elders must signify the church or the company of the redeemed, and one then takes account of

the manner in which the living-beings, though distinguished from the elders, yet join with them in worship and praise about the throne, it is understandable that within the context of Christian theology no other entity would seem to qualify so well as creation or nature to join in the adoration and praise of Him who is upon the throne and of the Lamb. Referring to Rev. 4:8–11, Swete declares:

> The two actions are coòrdinated as simultaneous. Nature and the Church must ever unite in the praise of God... This concurrence of the *kosmos* and the *ekklesıa* in the worship of God was keenly realised by the Ancient Church... There is certainly not less cause for its recognition in an age which like our own is replete with new revelations of the wonders of the physical universe.

But would the thought that *nature* is represented by the living-beings have come to mind were it not that the *church* was previously thought to be clearly intimated by the description of the twenty-four elders?

(5) Though the judgment has been expressed above that the identification of the elders with the redeemed apparently has been strongly influenced by the *textus receptus* of Rev. 5:9, 10, one may not fairly maintain that nothing further may be said in commendation of this view. B. Weiss perhaps sums up the other evidence most succinctly when he comments as follows on Rev. 4:4:

> Surrounding the throne of God there are seated upon thrones the twenty-four elders, the heavenly representatives of those who have prevailed, to whom this seat had been promised in iii.21, since they carry the white garments of immaculate righteousness and the golden crowns of victory... It is the congregation of God which has existed through all times, and is represented by twelve elders from the people of the twelve tribes and twelve from the congregation of the twelve apostles, since the former began what was completed by the latter.

However suitable such terms may appear to be as descriptive of the redeemed people of God, one must nevertheless ask whether they apply exclusively to the redeemed, and whether perhaps they are not at least as fitting when regarded as intimations of the purity and dignity of a superior rank of heavenly spirits.

THE TEXT OF REVELATION 5:9, 10

Since the text presupposed by the rendering of the Revised Version quoted above is adopted by the leading modern editors, including Tischendorf, Westcott and Hort, B. Weiss, the Nestles and Baljon, as well as by modern translations and commentaries, the discussion of the question here might appear to be a work of supererogation. Its significance for the subject under discussion, as suggested above, seems, however, to justify an evaluation of it. Moreover, in spite of the almost perfect unanimity of opinion as to the correct text, H. C. Hoskier, who appears to have given more time to the study of the text of Revelation than any other scholar, evidently insists that "us" ($\dot{\eta}\mu\tilde{a}s$) should be retained in Rev. 5:9.[7]

Hoskier emphasizes the fact that "us" in Rev. 5:9 is omitted only in Codex Alexandrinus and the Ethiopic Version. He declares, moreover, that this Greek MS. "drops the word between the two columns;" and he dismisses the support of the Ethiopic on the ground that it "is unreliable in such a matter, frequently baulking at any difficulty."[8] Hoskier clearly has a right to be heard in view of his monumental work in the description and collation of MSS. and the incomparable *apparatus criticus* he has supplied for the Apocalypse. His classification of MSS. into families is also of interest though not decisive, and his warning that individual late cursives may prove to be of fully as much value as the early uncials is well taken. Whether, however, he may be credited with good judgment in the evaluation of readings, manuscripts and families is another matter.

In certain respects the determination of the text of the Apocalypse is of exceptional difficulty, in others it is much simpler than that of other portions of the New Testament.

[7] *Concerning the Text of the Apocalypse*, 1929, Vol. I (751 pages, chiefly collations); Vol. II (649 pages, chiefly apparatus). Hoskier's opinion concerning the variations in v. 10 is apparently not indicated.

[8] Vol. I, p. 26. See also p. 28, note, where he says that B. Weiss "puts himself right out of court by omitting $\dot{\eta}\mu\tilde{a}s$ in Apoc. v. 9, a purely clerical omission of A, alone of all MSS. and authorities." Nevertheless, on the very next page he praises Weiss and Bousset for their method and scientific spirit.

That it is somewhat simpler is reflected in the very substantial agreement among modern editors today. This is no doubt due to the fact that the principal types of text are less distinctive in Revelation than in the other parts of the New Testament.

Whereas the "Western" text witnessed by Codex Bezae and its allies and the "Alexandrian" text of Sinaiticus-Vaticanus and their allies diverge substantially in Acts and also significantly in the Gospels, and a comparable situation to that in the Gospels obtains with reference to the Epistles of Paul, it is extraordinary that one cannot definitely distinguish a "Western" text of the Apocalypse. Not less striking is the observation that the *textus receptus* is considerably closer to the text of the early uncials in the Apocalypse than in any other part of the New Testament. In spite of the substantial unity of the textual tradition, however, the Apocalypse is not marked by a paucity of variants. The variants are in fact exceedingly numerous but to a large extent they concern orthography, transpositions and other formal details. The considerable diversity in the context of a very substantial unity inevitably complicates the task of classifying manuscripts and therefore also of evaluating families or groups. Consequently, also, the necessity of weighing each textual problem with due regard to intrinsic and transcriptional considerations is perhaps even more evident in the case of Revelation than in that of the other parts of the New Testament. Since Rev. 5:9, 10 involves a rather exceptional instance of substantial variation, it provides one of the most interesting opportunities of taking account of various factors affecting one's final judgment concerning the text as a whole.

Since the witness of Codex Alexandrinus so largely provides the foundation for the omission of "us" in Rev. 5:9, one's judgment concerning it will be of great importance. Sixty years ago the eminent significance of this MS. was established by B. Weiss in an important monograph on the text of the Apocalypse.[9] Subsequently, in 1920, Charles carried this

---

[9] *Die Johannes-Apokalypse. Textkritische Untersuchungen und Textherstellung*, 1891, especially pp. 131 ff. Though Bousset disagreed with Weiss on various matters (*Zur Textkritik der Apokalypse*, 1894, *Kommentar*,

study to the point where he was prepared to speak of "the absolute preëminence of A."[10] Though his observations did not take much account of the cursives, and his treatment as a whole is marred by a tendency to resort frequently to conjectural emendations, his judgment is of considerable importance because, like Weiss, he built his case largely on the basis of a detailed evaluation of individual passages rather than of a merely statistical cataloguing of agreements and disagreements between manuscripts.

Though Charles' estimate of Codex A appears to be somewhat exaggerated, his judgment as to the general superiority of this MS. received significant confirmation from the work of M. J. Lagrange, who took account of a broader base of testimony including the then recently discovered papyrus MS. of Revelation ($\mathfrak{P}^{47}$) in the Chester Beatty collection. Among the significant points made by Lagrange is his observation that this papyrus MS. stands closer to Codex Sinaiticus than to Codex Alexandrinus if one judges merely in terms of statistics of agreements and disagreements, but that such agreements of $\mathfrak{P}^{47}$ with Codex Sinaiticus do not heighten the value of the latter as against A. To a large extent, he observes, the agreements relate to readings which may be explained as due to a scribal concern to smooth over apparent roughnesses, which, however, are retained for the most part in A.[11] Accordingly, though Lagrange expressed his evaluations more moderately than Charles had done, he contributed impressively to the judgment, which could have been supported by an even more detailed statement of the facts, that Codex A often preserves — sometimes alone or almost so — readings which are strongly commended by the application of basic principles to the evaluation of the text.

1906), he agrees substantially with his estimate of Codex A. Cf *Kommentar*, pp. 155 f. Von Soden also praises A, though he regards ἡμᾶς as an omission, in *Die Schriften des N. Ts.*, I, 3, pp. 2070 f

[10] *The Revelation of St. John*, 1920, I, p. 166; cf. pp. 160–183. See also I. T. Beckwith, *The Apocalypse of John*, 1922, p. 414, F. G. Kenyon, *Recent Developments in the Textual Criticism of the Greek Bible*, 1933, pp. 61 f.; and *The Chester Beatty Biblical Papyri*, Fasciculus III, 1934, pp. 12 ff.

[11] M. J. Lagrange, *Critique Textuelle, II La Critique Rationnelle*, 1935, p 591; cf. pp. 579–625.

Returning now to the consideration of the text of Rev. 5:9, 10, one may quite summarily dismiss the distinctive readings of the *textus receptus* of the latter verse. In verse 10 the first person is read consistently at both points of variation only by certain Latin and Armenian authorities.[12] It appears, therefore, that the first person plural forms were introduced into v. 10 fairly late in the transmission of the text to make the verse conform to the then current reading "us" in v. 9. And it seems to be generally acknowledged today — in the light of the early prevalence of the interpretation of the elders and living-beings as *men*, such as apostles, prophets, and evangelists — that it is far more difficult to account for the origin of the reading adopted in the critical texts on the assumption that the "received text" is original than the reverse.

But what of the text of verse 9? Agreement with the contents of v. 10 would appear to demand the rejection of "us" in v. 9 as secondary. Nevertheless, one may well pause to weigh Hoskier's arguments. (1) One must acknowledge, as an examination of Codex A will disclose, that, if the scribe had planned to include "us," this word would have appeared as the first one in the first line of the second column of the page concerned.[13] Nevertheless, this fact by no means establishes the conclusion that Codex A "drops the word between columns," as Hoskier dogmatizes. The presumption is that the MS. is true to its exemplar, a presumption which cannot be set aside by the conjecture that the scribe must have passed over the word "us" when he lifted his pen from the bottom of the leaf to commence the second column of writing. (2) Nor may the support of the Ethiopic Version be dismissed as lightly as Hoskier does. Though this version may not possess great independent value, the fact that it reports the rather

---

[12] According to Hoskier's Apparatus, one cursive (no. 113) reads ἡμᾶς in v. 10 but has βασιλεύουσιν. And two cursives (no. 57 and no. 141) contain the form βασιλεύσομεν. These two cursives are assigned by Gregory to the 16th century, though Hoskier is inclined to ascribe the latter to a somewhat earlier date. But he acknowledges that "all practically agree to contradict the 'received text,'" where by "all" he apparently has in mind textual witnesses rather than editors (cf. I, p. 26).

[13] One column ends with ΗΓΟΡΑΣΑΣ ΤΩ ΘΩ and the next begins with ΕΝ ΤΩ ΑΙΜΑΤΙ ΣΟΥ.

abrupt,[14] shorter reading shows that Codex A does not stand alone.[15] (3) Moreover, there is the fact that Codex 44 and a few other cursives do not have the reading "us" but "our" (ἡμῶν). One possible explanation is indeed that the "our" is a mistake for "us," perhaps substituted through the influence of the same phrase (τῷ θεῷ ἡμῶν) in v. 10. There remains the alternative, however, that Codex 44 and other cursives presuppose the reading of Codex A as original, and that "our" is not a substitute for "us" but an interpolation, plausibly due to the presence of the pronoun in v. 10.

One could therefore visualize the textual history in various stages: (1) the reading of A, Aeth. as original; (2) the reading of 44 as possibly introducing an interpolation; (3) the introduction of "us" into v. 9 at a rather early time in agreement with current interpretations; (4) the adjustment of v. 10 to v. 9 mainly in Latin witnesses. One clearly cannot conceive of the development in reverse order. Nor can one begin at the third stage, and explain very plausibly the other readings as secondary.

A supplementary argument based on the style of the Apocalypse provides further confirmation of the original character of the shorter reading of verse 9. Mention has been made of the judgment that the shorter reading would have appeared rather abrupt to many scribes. This stylistic abruptness of v. 9, it may now be observed, can be shown, when judged in the light of other passages, to be intrinsically unobjectionable and even remarkably characteristic of Revelation. Of special interest are the instances in Rev. 2·10; 3:9; 5·7 and 11:9 of *partitive expressions introduced*, like the reference to "every tribe and tongue and people and nation" in 5:9, *with the preposition "out of"* (ἐκ). The instance in Rev. 5.7, immediately preceding the passage under discussion, forms a striking parallel to Rev. 5:9. For a few cursives and Latin and Syriac witnesses interpolate into the abrupt, shorter text, between the verb and the preposition, "the book" (τὸ βιβλίον) as a

---

[14] Modern translations reflect the abruptness of the original for they supply a direct object: the Revised and Revised Standard Versions read "men;" the Nieuwe Vertaling reads "(hen)."

[15] Unfortunately Codex C, which often agrees with Codex A, and Papyrus no. 47 are defective at this point.

specific object. This was evidently due to the feeling that the Greek in the sentence, "He came and took out of the right hand of Him that sitteth upon the throne," was obscure or unnecessarily abrupt.[16] The English and Dutch renderings are of interest either because they presuppose the interpolation in the Greek text or introduce a noun or pronoun to overcome the abruptness of a literal translation.[17]

Similarly in Rev. 2:10 and 3:9 the Greek texts contain no specific object in the accusative case, but only partitive prepositional phrases introduced by "out of." And in each passage there are instances, almost exclusively confined to versions, of interpolations of appropriate substantives. Of most interest, perhaps, as indicative of the style of Revelation is Rev. 11:9 where substantially the same prepositional phrase which appears in 5:9 as *object* is expressed as the *subject* of the sentence.[18] No wonder that in this case various versions ignore the preposition "out of" and construe the genitives as possessive, and that the modern versions add the word "men" or the equivalent.[19] These passages, accordingly, demonstrate how characteristic such partitive expressions are of the style of Revelation. And at the same time the textual history shows that ancient scribes as well as modern translators naturally altered or paraphrased the text to overcome the abruptness of the original.

The further exegetical discussion in this paper will bring additional confirmation of the intrinsic strength of the text accepted in modern editions of the Greek New Testament. But in my judgment sufficient evidence has been presented to show that the case for this text by no means depends on *a priori* judgments as to the superiority or preëminence of Codex Alexandrinus. The situation is rather that Rev. 5:9

[16] Hoskier's apparatus records that more than a score of cursives insert τὸ βιβλίον at the end of the verse.
[17] Cf. "the book" in A. V.; "it" in italics in R. V.; "the scroll" in R. S. V.; "het boek" in Staten Vertaling; "de rol" in Nieuwe Vertaling.
[18] καὶ βλέπουσιν ἐκ τῶν λαῶν καὶ φυλῶν γλωσσῶν καὶ ἐθνῶν τὸ πτῶμα αὐτῶν.
[19] The Arabic Version e. g. has "videbunt cadavera eorum, populi . . ."; R. V.: "And from among the people . . . do *men* look upon their dead bodies"; Nieuwe Vertaling: "En uit de volken . . . zijn er, die hun lijk zien."

constitutes a remarkably impressive instance of a reading which is so indubitably required on the basis of other than external evidence that the MS. is demonstrated by this very passage to enjoy a certain preëminence among earlier and later witnessess.

As suggested above it is my impression that various modern expositors have remained unduly influenced by traditional interpretations connected to a significant extent with the *textus receptus*, and that justice is hardly done to the implications of the accepted text of Rev. 5:9, 10. It now remains to undertake a somewhat fresh evaluation of the elders and the living-beings in the light of the pertinent evidence.

Some Basic Exegetical Considerations

(1) One may well begin by reflecting upon the manner in which the elders and the living-beings are described as engaging in worship. That this is a conspicuous feature of their activity is shown by Rev. 4:8-11; 5:9, 10, 14; 11:16 and 19:4.

(a) In this connection my first observation is that the elders and the living-beings not only both engage in worship, but that both *do so in the same terms*. They are so intimately joined in worship that it seems impossible to avoid the further conclusion that they are viewed as standing in the same basic relationship to God. The utterances of Rev. 4:8 and 4·11 are of essentially similar import so far as their implications for the understanding of the relationships of the elders and living-beings to God are concerned. There is nothing incongruous in the thought that the church and the creation should both worship, nor in understanding them as agreeing in some respects in their worship of the Creator. But it is extraordinary that the praise ascribed to them at no time reflects the difference in their relationships to God. There are songs which ascribe *salvation* to God and the Lamb, but they are not presented as distinctive of the elders.[20] And in the acts of worship ascribed solely to the elders, there is no suggestion that they are numbered among the redeemed.[21]

[20] Cf. also Rev. 7:10, 12:10 f.; 19:1.
[21] Cf. Rev. 5:14; 11:16 ff.

It is revealing that Alford and B. Weiss ascribe the song of Rev. 5:9, 10 *to the elders alone*, but not without arbitrarily construing "having each a harp" in 5:8 as referring only to the elders. Alford admits that this view is mainly based upon his conclusion that the "right view" of the living-beings is that they represent creation, and thus would not appropriately present the prayers of the saints or offer the praises of the whole church! In view of the fact that Alford himself understands the living-beings as "in the main identical with the cherubim of the O.T.," the insecurity of the interpretation of the elders as the redeemed is underscored.

Milligan evidently has this basic difficulty in view when he concludes that we must understand *creation*, as well as the church, *as redeemed*, and thus as appropriately joining in the persons of their representatives in extolling the redemption wrought by the Lamb. Though there is perhaps a sense in which one may contemplate the "redemption" of the world of nature, that thought is clearly excluded in Rev. 5:9 where everything centers upon the salvation of *men* from every tribe and tongue and people and nation.

(b) Still more decisive is the consideration that the elders and living-beings unite in the new song of Rev. 5:9, 10 in such a manner that *they are distinguished from the redeemed*. They extol the Lamb because of the accomplishment of the redemption of a great company from every tribe and tongue and people and nation, but, on the correct text, they pointedly refrain from identifying themselves with the redeemed. Similarly in Rev. 11:17, 18 the elders refer to "the saints" and "the corrupters of the earth" with equal detachment. How can one possibly account for this *objectivity* of reference to the redeemed, this detached attitude toward them, if we are meant to understand that the redeemed people of God, represented by the elders, are glorifying God for their own salvation?[22]

---

[22] Greijdanus does not, in my judgment, do justice to this factor when, in commenting on 5:9, he says merely: "Er staat geen object bij, om de gedachte zelve van loskooping voor den prijs van's Heeren kruisdood, alle aandacht te doen hebben."

Nor is it satisfactory, as many expositors appear to seek to do, to overcome this difficulty by understanding the elders merely as the *representatives* of the church This approach seems to be fusing two distinct interpreta-

(2) The same distinction between the elders and living-beings, on the one hand, and the saints, on the other hand, appears in Rev. 5:8 where the former are viewed as acting in conjunction with the saints in regard to prayer. For they have "golden bowls full of incense, which are the prayers of the saints." Though the saints are clearly distinguished from the elders and living-beings in this reference, the exact nature of the activity in relation to the saints is not defined. However, the matter is illumined by Rev. 8:3 where an angel similarly appears at the altar before God with a golden censer containing much incense. The purpose is said to be that the angel should "add the incense unto (or, give the incense with) the prayers of all the saints upon the golden altar which was before the throne." The rendering of the verb and the dative ($\delta\omega\sigma\epsilon\iota\ \tau\alpha\hat{\iota}\varsigma\ \pi\rho\omicron\sigma\epsilon\upsilon\chi\alpha\hat{\iota}\varsigma$) is somewhat difficult, but probably the incense is indicated as rising unto God with the prayers. The two are closely joined in thought, as in Rev. 5:8, and thus the angel is regarded as performing a priestly function on behalf of the people. Rev. 8:3 is significant for the interpretation of Rev. 5:8, therefore, not only because the function in view is seen not to be that of the saints themselves, but also because, positively, it is performed *by an angel*. Thus the appropriateness of understanding the activity of the elders and living-beings as that of celestial spirits rather than that of men and nature is confirmed.

(3) In addition to the activities mentioned above, there are other functions performed separately by one or more of the elders and living-beings, and these also are less naturally understood as performed by redeemed men or creation than by celestial spirits. In Rev. 5:5, as John observes the scene unfold about the throne in heaven and is overwhelmed with grief, it appears that no one will be able to open the book with seven seals, one of the elders addresses him, evidently from the vantage point of his nearness to the throne: "Weep not! Lo the Lion of the tribe of Judah, the Root of David, has

tions, one which would distinguish the representative elders from the church on whose behalf they might act, the other which regards the elders as representing the church in the sense that they symbolize the church and are really identical with it.

overcome to open the book." Subsequently, one of the elders who is addressed by John as "my lord," interprets for John the significance of the vision of the company which no man could number (Rev. 7:13 ff.). Nowhere, apparently, is *a man* introduced as John's *interpreter or informer*. An angel acts, however, to tell a mystery which caused John to wonder greatly (Rev. 17:6 ff.). And *an angel* calls to John, carries him away in the spirit, and shows him the vision of the heavenly Jerusalem (Rev. 21:9, 10; 22:1). John is so overwhelmed that he falls down to worship the angel, but he is rebuked and reminded that the angel is a fellow-servant (Rev. 22:9, 10).[23]

The living-beings likewise on occasion act individually. They summon the four horses and their riders to appear on the scene (Rev. 6:1, 3, 5, 7). One also is described as giving unto the seven angels "seven golden bowls full of the wrath of God who liveth for ever and ever" (Rev. 15:7). They appear, accordingly, as agents of God who are instrumental in directing the execution of His decrees, an activity hardly appropriate for the creation, but entirely in keeping with the place assigned to celestial beings.

(4) The conclusion that in referring to the elders the Apocalypse does not have in view the redeemed is strengthened by the observation of the manner in which *the saints* are described. Again and again they are forthrightly named "saints," as they frequently are in the rest of the New Testament, which fact alone should caution the interpreter to avoid the supposition that they will likely be introduced through the medium of obscure symbols.[24] This does not mean that only the designation "saints" is employed. But when saints are described in other terms, one is not left in doubt as to their identity. Thus in Rev. 14:1 ff., the 144,000 who sing a new song "before the throne and before the four living-beings and the elders" are identified as "the redeemed from the earth." Even more illuminating is the fact that, in the great scene which unfolds about the throne, the people of God do not themselves appear

---

[23] "Voices" (φωναί) evidently perform similar functions. Cf. Rev. 4:1 f. with 21:9 f.; 10:8 and 10:9; 19:9 f. with 22:9 f.

[24] "Saints" (ἅγιοι) are referred to in Rev. 5:8; 8:3, 4; 11:18; 13:7, 10; 14:14; 16:6; 17:6, 18:20, 24, 19:8, 20:9; 22:21. Cf. e. g. Acts 9:13, 32, 41; Rom 1:7; 8:27; 12:13; 15:25, 26, 31, 16:2, 15.

until Rev. 7:9, 10. Rev. 5:9, 10 celebrates indeed the redemption of the saints, but in Rev. 7 for the first time do the saints themselves ascribe their salvation to God. This postponement of reference to the participation of the saints in the worship of God is in keeping with the manner in which, beginning with the throne itself and the One seated upon it, notice is taken successively of the presence of elders and living-beings, of the book with seven seals and the Lion of Judah, the Root of David, appearing as a slain lamb, of myriads of angels and of every creature. Moreover, in Rev. 19:1 f. a multitude in heaven shouts: "Hallelujah; salvation and glory and power belong unto our God," whereupon the elders and the living-beings respond by falling down and worshipping God, and saying, "Amen. Hallelujah."

(5) Comparable to the manner in which the redeemed are plainly designated time and again as "the saints" is the matter-of-fact way in which *creation* is referred to in Revelation. That the writer does not think it necessary to designate the created world by the use of symbolic language is evident from the quite didactic manner in which he refers to the divine creative activity and its results. His usage is essentially the same, for example, as that of the Epistles of Paul. The elders, in the very context in which the living-beings have been introduced, ascribe glory and honor and power to God: "for thou didst create all things, and because of thy will they were, and were created" (Rev. 4:11). And in Rev. 5:13 "every created thing which is in the heaven, and on the earth, and under the earth, and on the sea, and all things in them" are indicated as being present and receive mention just before a reference to the living-beings.[25] Recalling once more the observation that the living-beings must be understood, in the light of Ezekiel's description, of the cherubim, and observing the characteristically Biblical way in which the creation is mentioned, one has added reason for judging that it is not only unnecessary, but actually involves labored exegesis, to find a reference to creation behind the description of the living-beings.

[25] Cf. Rev. 3:14; 8:9; 10:6 for other references to creation and created things. See e. g. Rom. 1:20, 25; Col. 1:15, 16; 1 Tim. 4:4. A comparison of Rev. 4:11 with Col. 1:16 is of particular interest.

(6) Finally, brief account must be taken of the objection stated above in connection with the mention of the second of certain factors affecting the decision. If due weight is given to the considerations outlined in the foregoing, the argument will, in my judgment, appear to be specious rather than persuasive. Technically the elders and living-beings are distinguished from the angels in Rev. 5:11 and 7.11, but this may well be due to a rather strict limitation of the term "angel" to mean *messenger*. Then the "angels" may be thought of, principally at least, as "ministering spirits, sent forth to do service for the sake of them that shall inherit salvation" (Hebrews 1:14). The elders and living-beings, on the other hand, are not sent forth to minister but are "throne-attendants of God" who remain near the throne "where they have to give expression to the royal majesty of Jehovah, both by their presence and their unceasing praise."[26] One must also keep in view the possibility that the usage in Revelation is not stereotyped, and that therefore at times the writer could distinguish between the cherubim and the angels while at others, as possibly in Rev. 3:5 and 14:10, he may use "angels" as embracing all celestial spirits.[27]

Concluding Observations

In conclusion, a few general observations and evaluations may not be superfluous.

This study has centered attention upon the significance of

[26] G. Vos, *Biblical Theology*, 1948, p. 167, in characterization of cherubim.

[27] Due to the limits of space I cannot undertake a discussion of the significance of the number 24 as that has been thought to bear upon the main question. The view that this number is formed by the addition of twelve (the number of the tribes) and twelve (the number of the apostles) is to say the least not conclusive. Revelation does not add the numbers, and it is very doubtful whether it reflects upon the people of God under the two dispensations as two separate groups. Rev. 21:12, 14 is often appealed to as proving the contrary because of the reference to the "twelve tribes" and the "twelve apostles" in connection with the description of the holy city. Since, however, the former names are on the *gates* and the latter on the *foundations*, the intention cannot be to suggest that they are *coordinate* and, when added together, make up an entity. Rather these reminiscences serve appropriately to teach that those who will dwell in the holy city will be at once the Israel of God and Christ's chosen servants.

the determination of the correct text with a view to arriving at solid exegetical conclusions. At the same time the indispensability of exegesis to a fruitful practice of textual criticism has also been underscored. Though, with regard to the Apocalypse, there is broad *substantial* unity among the textual witnesses, and remarkable agreement among modern editors, there is no short-cut to correct decisions by way of simple evaluation of manuscripts and other external testimony.

In connection with the interpretation of the Apocalypse two extremes are to be avoided. Strange imagery and symbolic representations abound, and thus may influence the reader to discover symbolism where none is intended. There is more direct didactic teaching and plain language than many interpreters seem to allow. But this is not to suppose that some simple hermeneutical principle will satisfy every exegetical situation. It would be most arbitrary, for example, to judge that one must necessarily construe every detail as literally as possible. Oftentimes the decision between a literal and a figurative interpretation will prove difficult. But one can hope for progress as one seeks to understand the language particularly in the context of the Scriptures. The utilization of Old Testament forms and ideas is evident to all. And the integration with the rest of the New Testament is considerably greater than may appear to the superficial reader. Nevertheless, as there is not a slavish appropriation of Old Testament formulations, there is likewise much in the form of the prophetic message which finds no parallel in the eschatological teaching of the rest of the New Testament. To some extent these distinctive features may be explained in the light of contemporaneous concepts and language, but for the most part the Apocalypse itself, and taken as a whole, will have to be depended upon to illumine the darker passages.

The particular interpretation of the elders and living-beings set forth in this paper may seem to some readers to spell theological and religious loss. For if the exegesis is correct, some fascinating estimates of the conjunction of the church and creation before the throne will have to be abandoned. Nor will the songs of praise ascribed to the elders, including the song of redemption in Rev. 5:9, 10, retain the immediate religious significance that they had on the understanding that the Christian reader might envision himself with all the saints as represented by the elders.

Nevertheless, there is no actual loss. At other points, in quite unambiguous language, the saints appear both in tribulation and glory. And even the song of redemption of Rev. 5:9, 10 does not diminish in meaning because at this point the pure cherubic attendants upon the throne of God, rather than the saints themselves, celebrate with rejoicing the decisive accomplishment of redemption — the redemption by the blood of the Lamb of a multitude from among every tribe and tongue and people and nation that they might constitute a kingdom and be priests unto God. And is there not gain in the turning of our thoughts from the privileges of men and creation to the God of the throne, whose sovereignty, majesty and glory are dwelt upon in the vision as calling forth, not only the grateful praises of the redeemed, but also the adoration of holy angels? Though holy and undefiled themselves, and granted places of extraordinary intimacy and dignity about the throne, these celestial spirits, as the creatures of God, acknowledge that the Almighty and the Lamb alone are the divine objects of worship, and alone are worthy to receive unceasing praise and honor.

CHAPTER V

RUDOLPH BULTMANN'S JESUS

MR. PRESIDENT and Gentlemen of the Board of Trustees:

I wish to take this opportunity to express my gratitude for the honor which you have conferred upon me in elevating me to the Professorship of New Testament. Let me assure you that I am vividly aware of the unique privileges which this position affords, and that I am entering upon its labors with no small measure of enthusiasm. Nevertheless, as I reflect upon the demands which it places upon me, I confess a deep sense of inadequacy.

One factor in the situation that gives me considerable pause is the memory of the one whom I am called to succeed in this great work. Although fifteen months have passed since Dr. Machen found rest from his labors as minister and teacher of the New Testament, the sense of loss, like the sorrow at his departure, has not diminished. I am deeply conscious of the distinction which his presence here gave to the department of New Testament, as to the Seminary as a whole, both through his scholarly attainments and his illustrious success as a teacher. I can follow him only from afar. Nevertheless, my mind does not linger long with these thoughts before I am reminded that our sovereign God, who bestows diversity of gifts, both of kind and of measure, does not hold us responsible according to the standard of another's endowments.

* This article constitutes the inaugural address of the author delivered at Westminster Theological Seminary on April 14, 1938, upon the occasion of his inauguration as Professor of New Testament in that institution

The final reason why my enthusiasm is tempered with trembling is found in the character of the responsibility that has fallen upon me. For the responsibility is to God Himself, and demands first of all faithfulness in the handling of His Word! Today, through the reading of the pledge required of professors in this institution, I dare say that you too have been impressed with the solemn character of this undertaking. Accordingly, that which occupies my mind today is less the exacting demands of true scholarship, however insistent they are, than the call for faithfulness to the Word of God. Not long ago a Calvinistic theologian in the Netherlands spoke aptly of the isolation in which the Reformed man finds himself today as he takes his stand upon the Bible as the Word of God, surrounded as he is by the mediating theology of experience on the one hand, and by the Barthian theology on the other.[1] In this country too we have become conscious of our isolation, but, in humble submission to the authority of God speaking in His Word, and in reliance upon the power of His Spirit, we can go forward in quiet confidence to seek to fulfill our God-appointed task.

I propose to speak to you on the theme: RUDOLF BULTMANN'S JESUS IN THE PERSPECTIVE OF A CENTURY OF CRITICISM. I shall be concerned to examine his approach to and estimate of the testimony of the gospels concerning Christ. To use the familiar modern formulation, my address will endeavor to set forth Bultmann's place in the history of the quest of the historical Jesus.

Lest it should appear that I have chosen a rather narrow theme for an inaugural address, in so far as I am restricting myself to the point of view of a single individual, let me say that the Professor of New Testament at the University of Marburg is not an isolated figure. Rudolf Bultmann's view of Jesus has peculiar significance because in him converge what appear to be the two most noteworthy developments in the study of the New Testament in the past two decades.

---

[1] Berkouwer, G. C. in an address before the 26th General Conference of De Vereeniging van Predikanten van de Gereformeerde Kerken in Nederland, reported in *Gereformeerd Theologisch Tijdschrift*, XXXVIII, 1937, pp. 535 ff.

One development is concerned with a distinctive approach to and treatment of the gospels regarded as sources for the knowledge of Christ, and the other comes to expression in a new estimate of the theological message of the New Testament, and of the figure of Jesus Christ in particular. Through a survey of the former, I shall seek to show how, especially as an advocate of *Formgeschichte*, or form-criticism, Bultmann has come to a position of thorough-going skepticism on the testimony of the gospels to the history of Christ. But alongside of this extreme historical skepticism there appears, particularly in his exposition of the message of Jesus, a positive theology, indeed, nothing less than the theology of crisis, the theology which is being hailed as the answer to modernism and even as a return to the Calvinistic theology of the Reformation.[2] The relation of the historical skepticism and the theological construction is in need of clarification. Whether or not my discussion aids in its clarification — if it be true that historic Christianity has looked upon the history of Christ as its very foundation — the consideration of this

---

[2] President John A Mackay, for example, says· "It is Reformed theologians like Barth and Brunner who have smashed the presuppositions of theological modernism and rekindled faith in the Scriptures and historic Christianity", in *The Princeton Seminary Bulletin*, XXXI, November, 1937, p. 2

In characterizing Bultmann's theological point of view as Barthian, I am far from wishing to imply that there are not noteworthy differences between him and Barth, much less that the details of this discussion of Bultmann's views are meant to apply without qualification to the crisis theologians in general. Barth, *Kirchliche Dogmatik*, I, 1, p. 421, indeed, criticizes Bultmann's *Jesus* for its neglect of the deeds of Jesus, as distinguished from His teaching, and evidently does not follow Bultmann in his extreme historical skepticism. The decisive issue, however, is not that of the extent of historical skepticism but of the evaluation of the history of Christ. Indifference to the history of Christ appears most pointedly on the background of radical skepticism but it may go hand in hand with a relatively high view of the trustworthiness of the gospel records. It will not do summarily to set Bultmann aside as "extreme" in the interest of classifying Barth as "conservative", for they are essentially in agreement on the all-determinative matter of the doctrine of God, including the philosophy of nature and of history. The very radicalness of Bultmann's approach may serve to clarify the relation of the crisis theology to historic Christianity.

theme clearly involves reflection upon the momentous issue of the very nature of Christianity.

Before proceeding to the discussion of Bultmann's application of form-criticism to the gospels and his interpretation of the teaching of Jesus, it will be necessary to note his place in the history of the criticism of the gospels themselves. In order to set this matter in perspective I shall first endeavor to sketch in a few broad strokes the history of modern criticism. Meanwhile the background for an understanding of Bultmann's work as form-critic and as theologian will have been provided, if only in meager outline.

I

HISTORICAL BACKGROUND. ESTIMATE OF THE
TESTIMONY OF THE GOSPELS.

For the purpose of this survey it is not necessary to turn back the pages of history beyond the thirties of the last century. The influence of the rationalism of the Enlightenment had begun to wane, but in its place came the idealistic philosophy of Hegel. Soon after Hegel's death in 1831, his philosophy inspired two notable reconstructions of the origin and early history of Christianity. These were the productions of Ferdinand Christian Baur and of David Friedrich Strauss.

Although Baur's chief writings and the period of the dominant influence of the famous Tübingen School fell in the following decades, it is exactly one hundred years ago that Baur, in an article on the origin of the episcopate, outlined his reinterpretation of early Christian history in terms of the Hegelian dialectic.[3] On this basis the gospels and other canonical writings were regarded as party documents, and were thought to reflect either an early period of hostility or a later period of compromise, with the result that the traditional views of their dates and origin were radically revised. While many of the conclusions of Baur and his followers are regarded today merely as historical curiosities, one may not

[3] "Ueber den Ursprung des Episcopats", in *Tubinger Zeitschrift fur Theologie*, 1838, Heft 3, pp. 142 ff.

overlook the continued influence of their attack upon the unity of the New Testament by way of setting one part against another in incisive fashion. In this connection it is well to recall also that later criticism, while modifying decisively the Tübingen view of the synoptic gospels, generally accepted its judgment that John is quite untrustworthy as a source for the history of Christ.

My interest in this study centers more directly upon Strauss, pupil of Baur and eighteen years his junior, whose *Leben Jesu* appeared in 1835, when he was only twenty-seven. The reason for attaching greater significance to Strauss in this connection is that his monumental work is absorbed with the testimony of the gospels themselves, an approach which is most characteristic of our own times and, while open to serious criticism because of its neglect of the testimony of early tradition, serves to center attention most quickly upon the issues that are at stake. Because of the drastic character of his attack upon the testimony of the gospels, the work of Strauss was an immediate sensation, so much of a sensation, indeed, that, since he forthwith lost his position as *Repetent* at the famous *Stift* in Tübingen, it put an end to an academic career that had hardly begun.

The main thrust of the criticism of Strauss was directed against the miraculous elements in the gospels. On the basis of the consistent naturalism of the Hegelian philosophy, maintaining that "the absolute cause never disturbs the chain of secondary causes by single arbitrary acts of interposition",[4] he rejected in decisive fashion a great portion of the testimony of the gospels. Disdaining the highly subjective and arbitrary interpretations of the rationalists like Paulus along with the mediating approach of Schleiermacher, he developed his mythological theory to account for the origin of most of the contents of the gospels. The myths which made Jesus a supernatural figure were produced, according to Strauss, by the early church, not indeed as pious frauds nor as conscious fiction, but as the unconscious products of faith. In this process Strauss attributed decisive significance

---

[4] *Das Leben Jesu*, 4te Aufl., 1840, I, p. 100 (E. T., *The Life of Jesus*, 1846, I, p. 88).

to a subjective experience of the disciples in Galilee which led them to believe in the resurrection of Jesus, and to their application to Jesus of passages from the Old Testament which were interpreted messianically. Radical as Strauss was in his skepticism, it must not be forgotten that he affirmed the historicity of the messianic consciousness of Jesus, regarding that consciousness and its disclosure to the disciples as the necessary presuppositions of their belief in the resurrection. At this point, therefore, Strauss stopped short of the position enunciated by Bruno Bauer in 1840, not to speak now of the even more radical position represented by the latter's denial even of the historicity of Jesus in 1850.

Strauss, of course, did not regard his attack upon the testimony of the gospels as an attack upon religion or even upon Christianity. For on the basis of his idealistic philosophy he sharply separated religion and history. Religious ideas, he said, are real and have permanent validity quite apart from the changing and inadequate historical forms which they may assume. Consequently, while the idea of the God-man is the highest idea conceived by human thought, it is not dependent upon, and cannot be perfectly expressed in, its external representation in the history of Jesus. On this view, accordingly, no amount of historical skepticism can destroy the ideal or real elements of religion.

Turning now to the latter half of the nineteenth century, I shall recall certain important developments which provided the immediate background for the developments of the present century. In general it may be observed that, as the critical conclusions of Baur proved to be untenable, a more sober criticism came to the fore, and that a new regard for the significance of history became evident as new philosophical and theological developments broke the spell of Hegelianism. My concern here is principally with the rise of the Liberal Theology and the emergence of the Marcan Hypothesis in their significance for the study of the life of Jesus. Christian Hermann Weisse, whose work on Gospel History appeared in 1838,[5] was a forerunner of the new approach to the study

---

[5] *Die evangelische Geschichte kritisch und philosophisch bearbeitet.*

of the life of Jesus both by his non-eschatological interpretation of the messianic consciousness and by his argument for the priority of Mark. However, it was not until the epochal second edition of Ritschl's *Die Entstehung der altkatholische Kirche* appeared in 1857, and Holtzmann's *Die synoptischen Evangelien* in 1863, that the new movement really was under way.

The Marcan Hypothesis, which was developed especially by Holtzmann as an important aspect of the two-document theory of synoptic criticism, involved not merely the acceptance of Weisse's conclusion as to the priority of Mark, but also a distinctive judgment as to the general trustworthiness of this gospel. Mark was elevated to a place of high regard at the expense not only of John but of Matthew and Luke as well, the latter two being regarded as possessing little or no historical value independent of Mark, except where they were thought to depend upon a second source which came to be known as Q. Mark, in contrast to the other gospels, was thought to be based very definitely upon historical reminiscence, perhaps that of Peter himself.

On the basis of the outline of Mark the Liberals proceeded with great confidence to compose their Lives of Jesus. Of course, since these Lives presupposed a naturalistic philosophy of history, there were miracles and kindred elements to be laid aside. Another difficulty was found in the fact that Mark hardly provided enough material to satisfy some of the demands of modern biographical study which had come strongly under the influence of psychology and the evolutionary philosophy.[6] Nevertheless, with sovereign self-assurance, the Liberals felt equal to the task of separating the kernel from the husk, and of making "the historical Jesus" psychologically intelligible.

---

[6] Holtzmann, for example, not merely applied the concept of development to the external course of the life of Jesus, going so far as to distinguish seven stages in the Galilean ministry, but also supposed that he could trace the development of Jesus' self-consciousness from that of a prophet to that of Messiah. Cf. *Die synoptischen Evangelien*, pp 479 ff.; *Lehrbuch der neutestamentlichen Theologie*, 2te Aufl., 1911, I, pp 298 ff. Even Strauss forsook the Hegelian approach for the evolutionary in his *Das Leben Jesu fur das deutsche Volk bearbeitet*, 1864 (E. T., *A New Life of Jesus*).

This concern to set forth the life of "the historical Jesus" involved more than a unique estimate of Mark. Factors more distinctly philosophical and theological affected the whole approach in important particulars. Neo-Kantianism had replaced Hegelianism, and with it came, especially through the theology of the Ritschlian School, a new conception of the relation between religion and history. Along with a fundamental theological agnosticism, which ruled out metaphysics and mysticism from religion, there developed a religious evaluation of the purely natural phenomena of history which came to be known as historism. As a corollary of this new approach history came to be interpreted in terms of the influence of great personalities and heroic figures. In this fashion the history of religious personalities and heroes of faith came to be given the value of revelation. In general theocentric Christianity was naturalized as a religion of human experience.

The brilliant lectures which Harnack delivered at the University of Berlin during the winter semester, 1899–1900, published in English under the title, *What is Christianity?*, represent a classical expression of this Liberal point of view. Jesus is presented first and foremost as a great religious personality, whose message, to use Harnack's own words, "may be reduced to these two heads — God as the Father, and the human soul so ennobled that it can and does unite with him", a message which as it was realized in His own consciousness somehow became the basis of a call to "communicate this knowledge of God to others by word and deed".[7] In typically Liberal fashion Harnack, while affirming the historicity of the messianic consciousness, relegated it to the periphery of Jesus' estimate of Himself. It was not essential to Jesus so far as the consciousness of His relation to the Father was concerned. Rather it was merely a formal concept which He took over in order to make His sense of vocation intelligible in terms of the contemporary messianic hope, but which must have been uncongenial and even burdensome to Him. The

---

[7] *Das Wesen des Christentums*, pp. 41, 81 (E. T., pp. 63, 128).

difference between the orthodox view of the significance of the history of Christ and the Liberal conception of the influence of the historical Jesus received pointed expression in Harnack's distinction between the Easter message and the Easter faith. The Easter message, the message of the empty tomb and of the bodily resurrection is, according to Harnack, quite untrustworthy, but its rejection need not destroy the Easter faith, the faith that Jesus lives and that there is life eternal. This certainty of eternal life comes "by the vision of Jesus' life and death and by the feeling of his imperishable union with God".[8] Not His unique redemptive work by way of His death and resurrection, then, but the powerful impression of the personality of the historical Jesus is made the basis of the hope of eternal life.

The Liberal view of Christianity probably never received more fascinating or more influential formulation than in Harnack's lectures, and yet one of the severest and most significant attacks upon the Liberal position emerged in the very next year. I have in mind particularly the book of Wrede entitled *Das Messiasgeheimnis in den Evangelien* which appeared in 1901. This work, which Bultmann has called "the most important work in the field of gospel research in the generation now past",[9] introduced a point of view which has been particularly characteristic of this century. Indeed, Bultmann presupposes so fully the conclusions of Wrede, and goes forward so deliberately in his spirit, that it is convenient to join the consideration of Bultmann's approach to the gospels with that of Wrede.

The main concern of Wrede's book is to attack the Liberal view of Mark. The conclusion that Mark is far superior to the other gospels Wrede regarded as quite mistaken. Mark, he held, is essentially a theological construction rather than history, and is only relatively superior even to John. It is evident that a new approach to the study of history came into play here. The extremes of the psychological study of the

[8] *Ibid*, p. 103; cf pp 101 ff. (E T., p 163; cf. pp. 160 ff.).
[9] *Die Erforschung der synoptischen Evangelien*, 2te Aufl., 1930, pp 10 f. (E. T. in *Form Criticism*, by F. C. Grant, p. 22).

life of Christ were exposed by Wrede, who declared that the science concerned with the life of Jesus had become ill with psychological supposition, which he went on to characterize as a kind of historical guessing. He protested vigorously against the method which in arbitrary fashion picks and chooses within an historical tradition instead of viewing the tradition as a whole. His approach, in other words, represented a strong protest against the manner in which men were wont confidently to regard their own modern views as the kernel and all else as the husk.

In the place of the interpretation of the life of Jesus in terms of psychology, there came to be substituted the sociological approach which has been distinctive of the study of history in the twentieth century.[10] Individual personalities retire into the background, and society is made the starting-point of investigation. Now we begin to hear of *Gemeindetheologie, Gemeindedogmatik, Gemeindebildung*, and less and less of the formative influence of Jesus and His disciples. The approach of Wrede received strong confirmation from Wellhausen in his studies on the synoptic gospels, and Bultmann, expressing his hearty approval, credits Wellhausen with the establishment of the principle that "a literary work or a fragment of tradition is a primary source for the historical situation out of which it arose, and is only a secondary source for the historical details concerning which it gives information".[11]

Bultmann not only shares Wrede's opinion that the gospels are not to be taken seriously as historical records of the life of

[10] Cf. Schmidt, K. L., "Die Stellung der Evangelien in der allgemeinen Literaturgeschichte", in *Eucharisterion*, 1923, II, pp. 50–134, especially 89 ff Schmidt says, p 76. "Das Evangelium ist von Haus aus nicht Hochliteratur, sondern Kleinliteratur, nicht individuelle Schriftstellerleistung, sondern Volksbuch, nicht Biographie, sondern Kultlegende". See also Cullmann, "Les récentes Études sur la formation de la tradition évangélique", in *Revue d'Histoire et de Philosophie religieuse*, 1925, p. 573; Dibelius, "Jesus in Contemporary German Theology" in *The Journal of Religion*, XI, 1931, pp. 182 ff.

[11] "The New Approach to the Synoptic Problem" in *The Journal of Religion*, VI, 1926, p 341.

Christ, but goes beyond him in the development of the view which interprets them primarily as sources for our knowledge of early church history. Indeed, he holds that the gospels are so far removed from the historical Jesus that they do not even reflect primarily the attitude toward Jesus of the primitive Palestinian church, but rather the theology of the Hellenistic communities. Bultmann describes the gospels as expansions of the Hellenistic preaching of Christ, which, he holds, was the earliest preaching to set forth Christ as a cult-deity whose death and resurrection are the basis of salvation. The gospels then are expanded cult legends, and their message is that of the Christ-myth. Mark created the gospel type; in Matthew and Luke the mythical side is developed still further as, for example, by the birth narratives, although they also contain more of historical tradition, especially in the records of the teaching of Jesus. John is distinctive in that the mythological construction has completely conquered the historical tradition.[12]

Enough has been said to indicate how on the Wrede-Bultmann view of the gospels they cease to be witnesses to the history of Christ. For the clarification of this approach it is necessary to enquire as to the basis of their judgment. One cannot read very much either of Wrede or of Bultmann without discovering that their historical skepticism with respect to the gospel records is bound up decisively with their negative judgment on the historicity of the messianic consciousness. While both Wrede and Bultmann intimate that they are inclined to doubt its historicity, and actually seem as a matter of course to refer to the creative activity of the early church those elements of the gospel tradition which reflect the disclosure or recognition of the messiahship, actually they define their position with respect to this matter as that of agnosticism. Bultmann, for example, declares that we cannot even make out whether Jesus regarded Himself as the Messiah, and he goes on to say that, if there is darkness on this point, since the conception of messiahship must have

[12] *Die Geschichte der synoptischen Tradition*, 2te Aufl., 1931, pp. 362 ff.

determined decisively the whole being of one who regarded himself as the Messiah, it follows that we can have no knowledge of the historical personality of Jesus at all.[13]

But there is obviously more at work here than this radically negative attitude towards the historicity of the messianic consciousness, decisive as this factor is in their judgment upon the gospels. For, in treating of the testimony of the gospels, one is not concerned with a messiahship in the abstract, but rather with a concrete manifestation in history. One might affirm the historicity of the messianic consciousness in the abstract, and yet hold that the portrait of the Messiah which is drawn in the gospels is far from being true to historical fact. The negative character of the view under consideration appears, indeed, in its true perspective only when it is observed that the Messiah of the gospels is regarded as obviously unhistorical in view of the thoroughly supernatural character of His person. In modern criticism generally the "historical" Jesus is synonymous with a merely human Jesus, but the distinctiveness of the new view over against the Liberal constructions lies in its clear apprehension of the fact that the gospels consistently present Him as one who cannot be explained in terms of human categories.

Wrede says, for example, that the theological character of the messianic secret becomes wholly clear only when we ask how Mark regarded the object of secrecy, and that the briefest, and for us the most important, answer to this question is that it is conceived in a thoroughly supernatural fashion.[14] In other words, the fully "theological", that is, unhistorical, character of Mark's presentation of the Messiah appears not only in the fact that Jesus does not appear to seek to disclose the messiahship openly, but also in that the messiahship is conceived in such transcendent fashion that it can become known only by way of revelation. In view of Bultmann's hearty approval of Wrede's argument, one hardly need point out his agreement with Wrede in this matter. His fundamentally antisupernaturalistic approach will appear in other ways as this discussion proceeds.

[13] *Jesus*, 1926, pp. 12 f.
[14] *Das Messiasgeheimnis*, pp. 71 ff.; cf. pp. 32, 47, 48.

II

FORMGESCHICHTE. EFFORT TO RECOVER HISTORICAL
TRADITION BEHIND THE GOSPELS.

If then the position of Wrede and Bultmann involves the judgment that the gospels cannot be taken seriously as witnesses to the history of Christ, being, rather, direct witnesses only to the history of early Christianity, it is but a short step to the conclusion that the historicity of Christ cannot be substantiated at all. Yet Wrede and Bultmann do not take this step. Although their skepticism exceeds that of Strauss, as their negative conclusion on the messianic consciousness recalls, they stop short of the conclusion of Bruno Bauer and the more recent representatives of the mythical school. Reflecting on the denial by the latter of the historicity of Jesus, Bultmann declares (too lightly on his own premises) that this position is not worth refutation.[15] It appears then, in spite of the strong reaction of Wrede and Bultmann against the Liberal method of criticism, that they are still on Liberal ground in the judgment that there is a primary stratum of history embedded in the gospels which it is the business of criticism to recover. So Wrede, although he protested in an effective manner against the arbitrary separation of the kernel from the husk which was characteristic of the Liberal approach, and even maintained that Paul was the second founder of Christianity, nevertheless confidently asserted that Jesus' whole concern was with "an ethical imperative born out of the highest religious individualism".[16] And Bultmann frankly asserts that the kernel must be separated from the husk.[17] It is exactly at this point however that Bultmann's advance upon Wrede comes into view. For he maintains that now at long last objective criteria have been discovered whereby the later strata of the gospel tradition may be eliminated and the primary stratum of historical

---

[15] *Jesus*, p. 16.

[16] *Ueber Aufgabe und Methode der sogenannten Neutestamentliche Theologie*, 1897, p. 67; *Paulus*, 1904, p. 104 (E. T., *Paul*, 1908, p. 179).

[17] "Jesus und Paulus", in *Jesus Christus im Zeugnis der Heiligen Schrift und der Kirche*, 1936, p. 72.

fact may be recovered. These objective criteria are thought to be provided by the method known as form-criticism.

Before Bultmann's distinctive interpretation of this supposed primary stratum is considered, it is imperative to examine the process by which it has been reached, and test its supposed objectivity. It will not be possible, of course, to present here a very thorough exposition of *Formgeschichte* nor to criticize it in any really adequate fashion. But I shall aim to deal with its presuppositions, principles, and application only in so far as is necessary to clarify Bultmann's approach to the history of Jesus.[18]

In the remarkable development of the application of this method to the study of the gospels which followed the war, Bultmann has had a prominent place. His greatest work — *Die Geschichte der synoptischen Tradition* — belongs to that small group of writings devoted to this subject which, appearing practically simultaneously, at once arrested the attention of students of the New Testament. Along with Martin Dibelius he has been a leading expositor and defender of the method, and no one has approached him in the thoroughness with which he has applied it to the study of the synoptic gospels.

Its sudden appearance after the war gives it the appearance of novelty, but it is hardly a "wonder child" for there is much in the preceding developments that accounts for its origin. It is not necessary to trace here, as Fascher has done, the history of criticism which has explained the agreement of the gospels as due to the influence of oral tradition, or has set up stylistic and other formal criteria as the basis of historical judgments. The most important consideration here is that form-criticism is not so much an independent method of criticism as a special approach within the broader method

---

[18] Bultmann's exposition of *Formgeschichte* is found in the books and article dealing with the synoptic gospels which have been mentioned and in the article "Evangelien, gattungsgeschichtlich" in *Religion in Geschichte und Gegenwart*, 2te Aufl,. II, coll 418 ff. Notable criticisms of the method are found in Fascher, *Die formgeschichtliche Methode*, 1924; Kohler, *Das formgeschichtliche Problem des Neuen Testaments*, 1927; Easton, *The Gospel before the Gospels*, 1928; Taylor, *The Formation of the Gospel Tradition*, 1933; Grosheide, *Hermeneutiek*, 1929.

known as the *religionsgeschichtliche Methode*. Bultmann's treatment of the contents of the synoptic gospels is essentially an application of the method which Hermann Gunkel applied to Genesis in his epochal commentary which was first published in 1901.[19] The high claims of the method must be judged in the light of its *religionsgeschichtliche* presuppositions.

Some of the implications of these presuppositions will appear as I proceed to examine critically the essential elements of form-criticism particularly as they appear in Bultmann's writings. In its effort to recover the primary stratum of the gospel tradition, this method proceeds in three distinct stages: a preliminary stage in which the stories and sayings are isolated from their contexts in the gospels, a second in which the isolated units are subjected to internal criticism with a view to the recovery of their supposed original form in the oral tradition, and a final stage in which, through the application of external criticism, units that supposedly reflect situations that arose after the death of Jesus are eliminated as anachronistic. Those that remain after this process of reduction and elimination are received as authentic witnesses to the purpose of Jesus.

The preliminary requirement is that the gospel material be broken up into small units by setting aside the framework in which they are found in the gospels. This requirement is

[19] In Gunkel's commentary there appeared the very features that characterize the current study of the gospels: acceptance of the principal conclusions of the literary criticism of the previous generation; classification and evaluation of contents according to form, rejection of the stories as history, with the implication that the "authors" were not responsible historians but mere collectors and editors Gunkel's influence upon the whole development was also very marked in the series of studies known as *Forschungen zur Religion und Literatur des Alten und Neuen Testaments*, 1903 ff., which, in association first with Bousset and later with Bultmann, he sponsored and edited, and through the little book, *Zum religionsgeschichtlichen Verstandnis des Neuen Testaments*, 1903. A detail which confirms the continuity of development from Gunkel to Bultmann is found in the latter's appeal, *Geschichte der synoptischen Tradition*, p 310, in support of his interpretation of the account of the appearance of the risen Lord to Cleopas and his companion as legendary, to Gunkel's statement that this narrative of the appearance of deity might, so far as its style is concerned, have appeared in Genesis.

widely regarded as having been fulfilled by Karl Ludwig Schmidt in his influential book, *Der Rahmen der Geschichte Jesu*, which appeared in 1919. On the basis of a detailed examination of the chronological and topographical references in the gospels, he concluded not only that they do not offer a satisfactory basis for reconstructing the course of the life of Jesus but even inferred that these data, with the exception of the framework of the passion narratives, are almost exclusively the inventions of Mark and the other evangelists. Bultmann presupposes this study of Schmidt, and even goes beyond him in his skepticism as to the reliability of the evangelists' references to time and place. Bultmann holds, for example, that the passion narratives too must be broken up, and that they presuppose nothing more than an old, very brief, report of the arrest, judgment by the Sanhedrin and by Pilate, the removal to the cross, and the crucifixion and death.[20]

The Liberals, it will be recalled, took the order of events in Mark as providing a trustworthy outline of the life of the historical Jesus, and composed their biographical studies accordingly. In so far as Schmidt has shown that the materials in Mark are often loosely joined and that the interest in chronology is not very marked, he has offered an important criticism of the Liberal Jesus. And, in entire agreement with this observation, Schmidt has shown more fully in another significant study on the place of the gospels in the general history of literature that the gospels are not formal historical or biographical studies, written in imitation of literary models, but are essentially non-literary in character and have in view a popular audience.[21] However, these observations of Schmidt as to the popular character of the gospels are hardly to be regarded as new discoveries. Professor W. P. Armstrong, in his inaugural address of nearly thirty-five years ago, concluded on the basis of a survey of the witness of the gospels that they "are manifestly not intended to be biographies or

[20] *Geschichte usw.*, pp 301 f.; cf. 347 ff.
[21] See note 10.

to furnish us with a scientific life of Jesus. They are rather witnesses to the life and work of Jesus, chiefly during His public ministry".[22]

While therefore one may recognize elements of merit in Schmidt's approach, it is necessary to oppose the particular form it assumes when it identifies lack of concern for scientific historical form with indifference to historical fact. It by no means follows from the popular form of the gospels that the evangelists were not particularly concerned to limit their materials to what had actually happened. Support for this supposed indifference to history is often sought in the eschatological outlook of the early Christians which is thought to have centered their attention only upon the future. Aside from the one-sidedness with which this theory is usually formulated, it is open to the serious objection that it misconceives the mutual relations of history and eschatology. For it was the history of Christ that made the disciples concerned with His return, and the significance of His return was understood only in the light of the estimate of His historical mission. I Thessalonians, for example, reflects the early interest in eschatology, but it is significant that the Christ whose coming was awaited from heaven was the Jesus whose death and resurrection constituted Him as Saviour from the wrath to come.[23]

Moreover, the criticism of the framework of the gospels involves an approach to the question of the relations of the gospels which is very unsatisfactory. Form-criticism has again directed attention to the fact that the gospels presuppose a period of oral teaching and preaching, first on the part of Jesus and afterward on the part of his disciples, but the new method has failed lamentably to estimate the decisive significance of this fact. Fascher pointed out that this recognition of the period of oral transmission is irreconcilable with the old point of view in synoptic criticism which tended to

[22] "The Witness of the Gospels", in *The Princeton Theological Review*, II, 1904, p. 47.
[23] I Thess. 1:9 f., 2:15; 4:14, 5:9.

multiply hypothetical documents in the interest of reaching the earliest witnesses to the life of Christ.[24] But the form-critics generally are still so enamoured of the view which reduces the evangelists Matthew and Luke to mere editors of documents that little or no effort is made to estimate their position in the stream of oral transmission. If, instead of being mere editors of Mark and other written sources, Matthew and Luke themselves were active agents in the oral transmission of the Christian message, their differences from Mark may be at least partially accounted for as due to the variety within the oral tradition, and this variety, in turn, may be traced to the variety in the instruction and acts of Jesus. The variety in the teaching ministry of Jesus has recently been recognized in a salutary manner by Burton Scott Easton, a Liberal critic of form-criticism. Reflecting upon the widespread and constant activity of Jesus, he remarks that "we must think of hundreds of instructions delivered in dozens of places. So there must have been an almost infinite repetition of material."[25] Furthermore, Easton observes that, while many of the sayings and parables would have been repeated in the same form, other sayings and parables would have received different form and different grouping on different occasions.[26] Failing to learn the lessons which should have been learned through reflection upon the fact of the early oral transmission of the gospel materials, the form-critics continue to follow the old method of setting gospel over against gospel and account over against account. A sound historical judgment on the diversity within the ministry of Jesus is essential to the interpretation of the contents of the gospels in their mutual relations. The harmony of the gospels

[24] *Op. cit.*, pp. 4 ff., 232 f. Grobel, *Formgeschichte und Synoptische Quellenanalyse*, 1937, pp. 23 f , also calls attention to the sharp differences between the approach of the old source criticism and that of *Formgeschichte*. Grosheide, "The Synoptic Problem", in *The Evangelical Quarterly*, III, 1931, pp. 57 ff. and Greijdanus, "De Boeken van het Nieuwe Testament", in *Bijbelsch Handboek*, II, 1935, pp 95 ff. have recently demanded that the factor of oral tradition be taken seriously in dealing with the origin of the synoptic gospels.
[25] *Op. cit* , p. 39.
[26] *Ibid* , pp 122 f.

does not depend ultimately upon one's ability to arrange all of their contents in orderly succession in a synopsis, but rather upon the unity which they possess as trustworthy witnesses to Christ. On this view the several gospels do not present diverse frameworks for the life of Christ, but each is a witness to certain aspects of the single historical framework of Christ's life which has not been completely preserved. Instead therefore of talk of shattering the framework of the life of Christ, there is need of a recognition of the limits of historical study.[27]

The second stage of the form-critical process is concerned with the internal criticism of the isolated units of tradition. If the evangelists are conceived of as writers who manipulated the tradition of the life of Christ in the interest of their own theological preconceptions, and assembled the separate stories and sayings into a chronological and topographical framework largely of their own invention, it would indeed be a matter for surprise if these units were thought of as having themselves escaped manipulation. As a matter of fact the form-critic claims that he has in his hands the necessary tests for the discovery and elimination of editorial accretions as well as such modifications as had arisen before the stories and sayings reached the hands of the editors. Lest we should suppose that Bultmann is unaware of the boldness of his self-appointed task of tracing the history of the synoptic tradition from the point of its origin to that of its inclusion in the gospels, he admits at the very start that this is a very difficult task and ought to proceed with great caution.[28] Having disarmed us in this fashion, he proceeds confidently to his goal.

The confidence with which he operates is bound up with his acceptance of certain supposedly well-established laws of style which are thought to apply to the development of tradition. In part they may be learned by observing the

[27] For a criticism of certain details of Schmidt's argument cf. Dodd, "The Framework of the Gospel Narrative", in *The Expository Times*, XLIII, 1932, pp. 396 ff. See also Burkitt, *Jesus Christ*, 1932, pp. 69 ff.

[28] *Erforschung usw.*, p. 15; "The New Approach to the Synoptic Problem", p. 344.

manner in which Matthew and Luke are thought to expand upon Mark, and the apocryphal gospels upon the canonical gospels; they may also be learned by taking note of the style of popular literature in the Jewish and Hellenistic world. In accordance with these laws, it is maintained that the various types of traditional discourse, whether parables, apothegms, legends, or the like, are marked by a stereotyped form which permits one to test whether any type has been altered. Each unit is thought of as being complete in itself, rounded off stylistically, self-explanatory, and brief, expressing in simple fashion a single idea or event. The presence of specific details, like the names of the individuals involved in any narrative, is taken as a sign of secondary development. Accordingly, the very elements which by their vividness and concreteness and specific character have often been thought to confirm authenticity are on this approach regarded as evidences of free handling and corruption of the tradition. And since each unit must be complete in itself, any element which intimates a connection with any other saying or event or with a larger historical background is eliminated. The result is that the traditionally primary requirement of exegesis that a text be interpreted in the light of its context appears to be abandoned for the principle that its first task is to trim away the context in order that the text may appear in all of its perspicuity!

One or two examples chosen from Bultmann may serve to illustrate the manner in which formal criteria are made the basis of important inferences. The parables generally are thought to be far simpler than the evangelists supposed, and their interpretations, as in Mark 4, for example, are thought to have come from a time when their original perspicuous meaning had been forgotten. In this connection the style of the rabbinical parables is set up as a standard for the modification of their form in the gospels. Other parables which contain predictive elements are judged to have been allegorized in the process of transmission. So Mark 2:19 is declared to be properly parabolic in its declaration that the sons of the bridechamber are not able to fast while the bridegroom is with them. Yet when in the next verse Mark reports that Jesus adds, "But the days shall come when the bridegroom shall be taken away from them, and then they will fast in that day", Bultmann declares that this is an allegorical addition.[29]

Another illustration of a rather different kind is found in Bultmann's elimination of Mark 16:7.[30] This verse, which tells of the command of the angel to the women to remind the disciples of Jesus' prediction that He would precede them into Galilee, is rejected by Bultmann as not belonging to the story of the empty tomb. Verse 8, which describes the women's flight from the tomb, and contains the report that they told nothing to anyone, is said to follow properly upon verse 6. On this view the reference to the women's silence was meant to account for the (alleged) fact that the story remained unknown for a long time. In other words, Bultmann believes that the report of the empty tomb originated long after the death of Jesus, and the silence of the women referred to in verse 8 was meant to cover up its late origin. Indeed, Bultmann does not seek to rest his judgment concerning verse 7 wholly on its inclusion in the story of the empty tomb. He admits that there is an historical factor too. This verse is secondary also, he affirms, because it presupposes the disciples' presence in Jerusalem on Easter Sunday which is in conflict with the Galilean Hypothesis which he believes to be well-established. I shall have occasion in a later connection to comment upon the strength of the support which Bultmann finds for this hypothesis. Here let me note further only the conclusion of Bultmann that Mark 16:7 (like Mark 14:28) represents an artificial effort of the evangelist, who has suppressed the flight of the disciples to Galilee, to get the disciples to Galilee in accordance with the oldest tradition!

Even this very brief survey of the manner in which Bultmann applies formal criteria in the internal criticism of the separate stories and sayings indicates that the new method of criticism is hardly less open to the charge of being subjective and arbitrary in its effort to eliminate supposedly late strata of tradition than was the old Liberal approach.

---

[29] *Erforschung usw*, pp. 25 f. Jülicher's important work, *Die Gleichnisreden Jesu*, has been of great influence in this connection.
[30] *Geschichte usw*, pp. 308 ff.

Wrede's incisive attack upon the current literary criticism for its over-refinements and divisiveness, the boldness with which it affirmed that a writer could not have said this but could have said that, has apparently been forgotten by his disciple.[31] The radical criticism of today does not serve nearly so well as that of a generation ago to clarify the issues that are at stake, and therefore Bultmann's approach must be judged, in comparison with that of Wrede, to represent retrogression rather than progress.

The central point at issue is the validity of the laws of transmission which have been appealed to, and, on the assumption of their validity in general, that of their applicability to the contents of the gospels. It is apparent at once that the view of the uniformity of the laws of development as here conceived is a corollary of the sociological conception of history. This point is expressed by Schmidt, in connection with his statement that popular tradition has its own laws of style, in the following words: "Style is not an aesthetic fad but a sociological fact".[32] But this view of history is quite untenable in its effort to confine the varied and complex manifestations of life within the limits of rigid evolutionary laws. In its reaction from the bald individualism of the Liberal point of view, it has gone to the extreme where it does not even seriously raise the question whether historic individuals standing in a concrete situation may not have been responsible for creating new forms of expression or adapting old ones. One must challenge therefore the assumption that tradition develops in such inflexible fashion that one can define the precise limits of the original form of a saying or narrative.

The view is very patently at fault when its conclusions as to the development of folk lore and sagas are invoked for the elucidation of the origin and early development of Christianity. For it immediately proceeds to beg the question which is at issue between the positions of thoroughgoing skepticism and historic Christianity. One can rule out the decisive

---

[31] *Ueber Aufgabe und Methode usw*, pp. 26 ff.

[32] "Formgeschichte", in *Religion in Geschichte und Gegenwart*, 2te Aufl., II, col. 639.

determination of the form of the tradition by what Jesus Himself did and taught only by arriving beforehand at the conclusion that Jesus never existed, or that He was so much a child of His time that one only needs to understand His environment to tell what He could have done and said, and what He could not have done and said. Fascher is right, therefore, in observing that the laws of popular tradition are not applicable to a sphere where the matter outweighs the form, as in his further conclusion that for Bultmann the decisive factors are not formal considerations but his own historical judgments.[33] Far from basing his skepticism with respect to the history of Christ on a more general historical agnosticism, he grounds it specifically in his unlimited confidence in his ability, on the basis of his knowledge of the times in which Christ lived and his other historical knowledge, to decide what was possible for Christ and what was not possible.

The final stage of the *formgeschichtliche* process is the most decisive one. Although the consequences of the internal criticism of the units of tradition are serious, it is only when the third step is taken that the testimony of the gospels to Christ is reduced in wholesale fashion, and it is only then that the method is seen in all of its radical implications. The observation that the method sets up the revolutionary hermeneutical principle that the context in which a text appears must first be set aside needs to be qualified here in an important particular. After all there can be no interpretation without relation to a context. What the form-critic is concerned with above all is the substitution of a new historical context which, on the assumption that all or most of the contents of the gospels cannot be accepted as testimony to the life of Christ, will account for the origin and character of these contents. Obviously, this calls for a reconstruction of the origin and early history of Christianity, and it is especially in this stage that the *religionsgeschichtliche Methode* comes into play. The reconstruction might conceivably develop along more radical or less radical lines, but however mild the reconstruction might be, nothing shows more unmistakably

[33] *Op. cit.*, pp. 206 f.

how thoroughly the conclusions reached by the form-critical method are bound up with historical judgments. I am not urging against the form-critics the objection that they combine criticism of the content with criticism of the form but only that they claim to have found in the study of the form of the material of tradition objective criteria for separating the unhistorical from the historical.

Bultmann's reconstruction of the history of early Christianity is not mildly radical. He presupposes the correctness, at least in its main outline, of the view of early Christianity presented in Bousset's famous work, *Kyrios Christos*. Bousset's view has been the subject of so much discussion and criticism since it was first published twenty-five years ago that I need reflect upon it only in its bearing upon the subject under discussion.[34] It was distinctive of Bousset's effort to account for the origin and development of Christianity on thoroughly naturalistic presuppositions that he separated Paul from Jesus by two sharply-delineated stages of development, namely, Palestinian Christianity and Hellenistic Christianity, and it is exactly this characteristic that makes the hypothesis so useful to the form critic. For clearly only a theory which breaks up early Christian history into highly distinctive segments can provide a basis for the discovery of distinctive strata in the gospel tradition. Just as the antitheses set up by the Tübingen School provided a construction of history on the basis of which new dates were assigned to the writings of the New Testament, so Bousset's construction offers Bultmann a new scheme by which the material which the gospels refer to the life of Christ in the days of His flesh is assigned to new situations whether in the primitive church at Jerusalem or in Hellenistic churches.

This sharp distinction between Palestinian and Hellenistic Christianity, which is so indispensable to Bultmann as a

---

[34] For important discussions and criticisms of Bousset's view see especially Vos, "The Kyrios Christos Controversy", in *The Princeton Theological Review*, XV, 1917, pp 21 ff.; the same author, *The Self-Disclosure of Jesus*, 1926, pp. 117 ff ; Machen, *The Origin of Paul's Religion*, 1921, pp. 295 ff.; von Dobschütz, "Kyrios 'Iesous", in *Zeitschrift für die neutestamentliche Wissenschaft*, XXX, 1931, Heft 2.

form-critic, is based not only upon violent and arbitrary handling of the evidence of the writings of the New Testament, but also upon many bold assumptions as to the place of Christianity in the religious world of the time. Bultmann, I believe, weakens this thesis in no small measure in his admission that not very much is known about the relation of the Palestinian world of thought to that of its wider environment. Furthermore, he virtually gives up the position which isolates Judaism from the religious world about it, and isolates Hellenism from Judaism, when, on the one hand, he maintains that Palestinian Judaism may have been influenced by oriental mysticism in important particulars, and, on the other hand, calls attention to the importance of a Hellenism that had come under the influence of Judaism.[35] One cannot both include Judaism within the sweep of religious syncretism and isolate it in any clear-cut fashion. Nevertheless, Bultmann makes the sharp distinction between the Palestinian world and the Greek world, and between Palestinian Christianity and Hellenistic Christianity, the basis for rejecting the authenticity of a great body of the material of the gospel tradition.

Accepting Bousset's characterization of Hellenistic Christianity as a religion of the cult, in the center of which stood Jesus Christ as the Lord who communicated His heavenly powers in the worship and sacraments of the community, Bultmann proceeds to eliminate, first of all, all that reflects this point of view. His view now joins to the judgment that the gospels themselves were edited from the point of view of the faith of the Hellenistic communities the further judgment that much of the material in the gospels originated outside of the Palestinian scene.[36] In this Hellenistic stratum Bultmann includes particularly those elements which view Jesus as the divine Saviour — the birth narratives, most of the miracle stories, the resurrection narratives in their present form, and most of His sayings about Himself, including Mark 10:45, Luke 19:10, and Matthew 11:27. The supper sayings he

---

[35] *Geschichte usw*, p. 330; *Erforschung usw.*, pp 8 ff ; "The New Approach to the Synoptic Problem", pp. 361 f

[36] Cf. *Geschichte usw.*, pp. 333 f.; *Jesus*, pp. 195 ff.

regards as liturgical formulations from the Hellenistic celebration of the Eucharist. It appears then that the very stories about Jesus and the teachings of Jesus which most clearly present Him as Saviour and Lord are judged to have originated at the farthest possible remove from the historic scene in which Jesus lived and moved.

Significant as Bultmann's separation of the supposedly Hellenistic stratum from the gospel tradition is, it is only when he sets up an antithesis within the Palestinian tradition between Jesus and the Palestinian community that his skepticism comes to its sharpest expression. In a word it may be said that while his conception of Hellenistic Christianity serves as a criterion to eliminate some of the teachings of Jesus and most of the historical narratives, his view of the primitive Palestinian church is decisive in the rejection of the rest of the history and nearly all of the teaching. Like Bousset, Bultmann regards the piety of the early church as distinctly eschatological — it did not worship Christ as present Lord but lived in the expectation of His return as Son of Man on the clouds. Its life moved wholly within the limits of Jewish piety, but through its messianic belief had come into conflict with the Jewish leaders. In this situation its needs were many: polemic, apologetic, missionary, disciplinary. On the basis of this conception of the early church Bultmann feels free to judge that all of the material in the gospels that reflects its distinctive view of Jesus, and may be explained as having originated to meet the needs of the early church, is to be explained as the product of the community. I shall not endeavor to set forth in detail how on these principles the contents of the gospels are reduced until only a few sayings are left to be assigned to the primary stratum of tradition. However, since this process obviously presupposes his negative judgment on the messianic consciousness, as well as the view that Jesus cannot have planned for the establishment of the church, there is probably no passage which serves so well to illustrate his method as his treatment of the confession of Peter and Peter's place in the church of Christ as recorded by Matthew.

Briefly stated the narrative of Peter's confession and the response of Jesus are regarded by Bultmann as a story that in its original form described an appearance of the risen Christ to Peter.[37] Wellhausen had expressed the same judgment with respect to the narrative of the transfiguration after Wrede had found in it the key to his interpretation of the messiahship in Mark, and Bultmann feels that his own observations on the earlier scene in Matthew represent an important confirmation of Wrede's hypothesis. Bultmann maintains the Galilean Hypothesis in the extreme form that does not allow belief in the messianic consciousness as the psychological presupposition for the subjective experiences of the disciples, but, on the contrary, makes their belief in Jesus as the Messiah dependent upon a subjective experience of Peter in Galilee.[38] In the face of the complete absence of evidence for this hypothesis, Bultmann is forced to conclude that legends have practically covered over the original, fundamental, and decisive experience which, according to the hypothesis, Peter had. Nevertheless, he confidently affirms his belief that there was such an original experience on the basis of Peter's prominent place in the transfiguration narrative, and in the narrative which centers in Peter's confession![39] In this scene from Matthew 16 Bultmann everywhere finds evidence of the creative influence of the Palestinian church which is conscious that its belief in the messiahship is the mark which distinguishes it from the Jewish people, and here gives its testimony to its belief that its messianic faith has taken its rise from Peter's Easter experience. Nothing could show more strikingly than Bultmann's treatment of Peter's confession how radically the early church is thought to have transformed fact into fiction in the interest of finding support for its Christology in the teaching of Jesus.

[37] "Die Frage nach dem messianische Bewusstsein Jesu und das Petrus-Bekenntnis", in *Zeitschrift fur die neutestamentliche Wissenschaft*, XIX, 1920, pp. 165 ff.; *Geschichte usw.*, pp. 275 ff. An important survey of the modern discussion of this pericope is found in Linton, *Das Problem der Urkirche in der neueren Forschung*, 1932, pp. 157 ff

[38] In view of the fact that this form of the Galilean Hypothesis shares with the common Liberal form the view that the original "Easter experience" was altogether subjective in character, it does not appear that its advocates are in a good position to disclaim all interest in psychological explanations.

[39] *Geschichte usw.*, pp. 314 (cf. n. 1); 332.

But how is Bultmann so sure that this narrative, which Matthew presents as describing what took place before the last journey to Jerusalem, actually originated in the early church after the death of Jesus? There is much here that Bultmann finds incredible as descriptive of the lifetime of Jesus: the discussion as to who Jesus is that is presupposed, the esoteric character of Peter's knowledge, the distinctiveness of the circle of disciples from the rest of the Jews. And everywhere Bultmann finds the situation of the Palestinian church reflected. The confidence with reference to the future of the church is said to reflect the eschatological consciousness of the Palestinian community as it awaited the end. The provision for binding and loosing owes its origin to the need which developed for disciplinary ordinances. The prominence of Peter is in view of the rôle which he played in the primitive church, and the benediction which follows upon Peter's confession in Matthew 16:17 expresses the church's grateful recollection of the fundamental significance which Peter's vision of Christ had for the establishment of the church in its distinctive messianic belief.

Once again it appears how completely the new method of criticism has come under the influence of the sociological approach to history. Everything turns so much around the question whether tradition originated in Hellenistic communities or in the Palestinian that the question is hardly put seriously whether the content and form of the gospel tradition may not have been decisively determined by the impact of the person and message of Jesus upon the historical situation in which He lived. The early church, moreover, is conceived of in a fashion that practically isolates it not only from the life of Christ but even from those who had been in intimate association with Him. It is allowed that Peter was mainly responsible for the messianic faith, but even then Peter is separated from his own historical association with Jesus, and in general no account is taken of the way in which those who had been in association with Jesus would have decisively determined, by their preaching and teaching, the content and form of the tradition. This construction, accordingly, does not allow at all for continuity through the influence of the eyewitnesses of Jesus' life. On this point Vincent Taylor has aptly said. "If the form-critics are right the disciples must have been translated to heaven immediately after the resurrection".[40] It becomes evident that Bultmann is struggling with the question how Christianity as belief in a transcendent Messiah and divine Saviour can be accounted for on the supposition that Jesus was a mere man. When he maintains the historicity of Jesus and recognizes him as a great teacher, and yet cuts off Christianity from Christ's history by a wall of ignorance or indifference, he fails miserably to answer this question. Only the supernatural Christ of the gospels can account for the origin of supernatural Christianity.

III

THE MESSAGE OF JESUS. RELATION TO HISTORICAL SKEPTICISM.

Finally, I turn to a brief consideration of Bultmann's conception of Jesus, in which I shall seek to show how his positive theological estimate of the message of Jesus is bound up with his historical skepticism. Although the gospels are thought not to give any direct information concerning Christ, and His life and personality are judged to be past recovery, nevertheless there remain, after the process of form criticism has reached its goal, certain elements which are distinctive from Jewish piety, and cannot be explained as originating from specifically Christian motives. This earliest stratum, which consists of a few sayings, is to be referred according to overwhelming probability, Bultmann says, to Jesus Himself, although he goes on to say that he has no quarrel with any who may wish to take "Jesus" as an abbreviated designation for the historical phenomenon.[41] While then Bultmann's absorption with the community does not land him in absolute skepticism, he is anxious that we shall not suppose that he is unhappy that the historical remnants are so meager. He is not the least bit uncomfortable in his radical skepticism. Indeed, he expresses his amusement at the suggestions that

[40] *Op. cit.*, p 41.
[41] *Erforschung usw.*, pp. 32 f.; *Jesus*, pp. 12 ff.

in his discomfort he has become busy in his book, *Jesus*, saving something out of the general conflagration, or has taken his flight to Barth and Gogarten for the same reason. So far as he is concerned he is quite ready, he says, to let the whole structure burn down quietly, since ultimately what are burned are the fanciful pictures of the *Leben-Jesu-Theologie*, or what he is pleased to call ὁ Χριστὸς κατὰ σάρκα, a matter concerning which, he declares, he has no curiosity at all.[42]

The earliest stratum tells, according to Bultmann, of what Jesus willed, and this knowledge he considers far more important than the lost knowledge of Jesus' life and personality. What Jesus willed may be learned from a few sayings which by their originality and self-consistency approve themselves as making up the message of Jesus. His little book on Jesus is devoted almost exclusively to the exposition of this message of Jesus, and it is with this exposition that I shall be principally concerned here. Naturally, this is not a message concerned with Jesus Himself; it is not the good news of His coming as the Messiah. It allows us to infer with respect to Jesus, since it is distinctly eschatological and ethical, only that He was a prophet and rabbi. Now, however, in spite of this radical criticism, a measure of sympathy is evoked by what appears to be a definitely theocentric point of view, for Bultmann sums up the proclamation of Jesus under the three heads: the coming of the rule of God, the will of God, and God as the Remote and the Near. In other words, there seems to be a return to the Calvinistic perspective by way of insistence upon the sovereignty of God, the requirement of obedience to His will, and the need of the sinner for His grace. That this appearance does not correspond with reality will become evident as I proceed briefly to examine these three divisions in turn.

It is not surprising that Bultmann begins by speaking of Jesus' proclamation of the coming of the rule of God, for he holds, in common with the interpretation of the gospels which came into vogue particularly through the influence of

---

[42] "Zur Frage der Christologie", in *Glauben und Verstehen*, Gesammelte Aufsatze, 1933, pp. 100 f.

Albert Schweitzer, that the most distinctive and original strain in the gospels is the eschatological. The words, "Repent, for the kingdom of God is at hand", express Jesus' consciousness of the imminence of the great hour of crisis and decision. This kingdom, Bultmann tells us, is not a relative or gradual transformation of things as they are, but is supernatural, miraculous, "wholly other", wholly future.[43] So as man is confronted with it, it calls for repentance and obedience. This interpretation of the kingdom, in so far as it stands in opposition to the Liberal naturalizing and humanizing interpretation is refreshing, but before one concludes that there is a return here to sober exegesis of the gospels, certain clarifying statements of Bultmann must be noted. That Bultmann does not understand the qualifications of the kingdom as supernatural, miraculous, and the like, in the sense that these terms ordinarily have is apparent when, for example, he says: "The future kingdom of God is not something which shall come in the course of time..."[44] The kingdom of God, he maintains, is not a condition or possession or state which is realized in history or as the goal of history. It is not a future something which can ever become a present something; the future deliverance by God never arrives as a state of rest and salvation. Its significance is that it remains future and confronts man as the last hour, compelling him to face the great either-or of life.[45]

A remarkable feature of this exposition of the kingdom remains to be mentioned. Bultmann admits that Jesus Himself must have expected a violent eschatological drama, including the coming of the Son of Man, resurrection of the dead, judgment, and the end of the world. But such events are to be interpreted as "contemporary mythology" along with the conception of Satan fighting against the hosts of the Lord. Jesus shared these notions with His contemporaries; they are the outward expression for His real meaning.[46]

---

[43] *Jesus*, pp 36 ff.: "etwas Wunderbares", "eine ubernaturliche, übergeschichtliche Grosse".
[44] *Ibid.*, p. 49.
[45] *Ibid.*, pp. 49 ff., 40.
[46] *Ibid.*, pp. 38, 53 f.

"The real significance of the 'Kingdom of God' for the message of Jesus", Bultmann concludes, "lies in any case not in the dramatic events associated with its coming ... It does not interest Jesus at all as a condition, but rather as the transcendent event, which signifies for man the great either-or, which compels man to decision".[47] It is perfectly clear then that Bultmann's interpretation of the kingdom as future and miraculous by no means involves departure from the naturalistic interpretation of history which is largely responsible for his historical skepticism.

Two particularly vulnerable points in Bultmann's construction of the eschatological message of Jesus may be noted. The first concerns its authenticity, the second its interpretation. On his own premises how can he be sure that the message of the coming of the kingdom belonged to the earliest stratum of tradition? If that is most unmistakably authentic which cannot be explained as expressing the point of view of the early church, and if it was exactly the eschatological outlook that controlled the piety of the Palestinian community, why does not Bultmann associate these eschatological ideas with the messianic faith of the early church? If the piety of the early church was messianic to the core, if it believed that its acknowledgement of Jesus as the messianic Son of Man constituted it as the holy remnant of Israel, living in the last days before His parousia, as Bultmann seems to maintain, it is not clear why Jesus must be held responsible for the message of the imminent coming of the kingdom of God and not for the indentification of Himself with the Son of Man.[48]

[47] *Ibid.*, p. 40.
[48] Bultmann accepts as historical a few sayings concerning the Son of Man where he thinks Jesus distinguishes between Himself and the Son of Man as, for example, in Mark 8:38 and Luke 12:8. Cf. "Reich-Gottes und Menschensohn", in *Theologische Rundschau*, 1937, pp. 20 f., 25 f.; *The New Approach to the Synoptic Problem*, p. 359. But this involves not merely the rejection of most of the references to the Son of Man, on quite inadequate grounds, as, for example, the predications of suffering, death and resurrection as *vaticinia ex eventu*, but also demands a highly unsatisfactory interpretation of the passages which are appealed to. For, while the passages express a contrast between the present and the future, and possibly imply also a contrast between a present state of humiliation and

It is especially against Bultmann's interpretation of the eschatological message that earnest protest must be made. I mention first the fact that Bultmann follows Schweitzer in his one-sided interpretation of the kingdom as only future, as for example when he translates Luke 17:21 ("The kingdom of God is in your midst") with future reference by the interpolation of the phrase "mit einem Schlage", that is, "suddenly".[49] Another objection is to the fact that, following Wellhausen, he unjustifiably refers Mark 13 to the influence of Jewish apocalyptic upon the early church, such elimination of reflection upon the details of the future being significant for Bultmann's denial that the kingdom is conceived of by Jesus as coming to future realization.[50] However unfounded these conclusions are, for pure arbitrariness they do not approach the indefensible process by which he concludes that certain elements of Jesus' teaching are merely contemporary mythology, shared by Jesus with his contemporaries, *but do not express his real interest.* One recalls the criticism of the Liberal approach to the gospels for its arbitrary separation of the kernel from the husk by a rationalizing and modernizing exegesis, and wonders whether there is not here another instance of the mote and the beam. For Bultmann's rejection of what Jesus said in favor of His "real interest" is not less modernizing and arbitrary than the Liberal criticism.

The second head under which the proclamation of Jesus is viewed is the will of God.[51] Bultmann is inclined to recognize the authenticity of sayings like the antitheses of Matthew 5, introduced by the words, "But I say unto you", and the

a future state of glory, they clearly rule out any contrast in dignity between Jesus who speaks in the first person and the Son of Man. To find such a contrast is to make the greater subject to the lesser, for the eschatological acknowledgement or rejection of men is made to depend upon their relation to Jesus, who, on Bultmann's view, was merely a prophet and rabbi even in His own estimation. It is noteworthy that in these passages Jesus makes eternal destiny to depend on their attitude towards Him, and they are therefore among the most important witnesses to His transcendent messianic consciousness.

[49] *Jesus*, p. 39; cf. *Geschichte usw.*, pp. 24, 128.
[50] *Geschichte usw.*, p. 129; "The New Approach to the Synoptic Problem", p. 358.
[51] *Jesus*, pp. 55–122.

sayings concerning almsgiving, prayer and fasting in Matthew 6 — in short, all sayings which are in conflict with the prevailing legalism. The legalism which Bultmann sets over against the teaching of Jesus is not confined to Judaism, for he believes that the early church did not understand these sayings of Jesus, being itself legalistic in its tendency. Consequently, the origin of much of the ethical teaching which the evangelists attribute to Jesus must be sought in the early church. With some confidence, however, he holds that some sayings may be referred to Jesus, or at least to the influence of His spirit in the early church.[52]

I shall not attempt a critical exposition of Bultmann's conception of the ethics of Jesus, however illuminating that might be for the general estimate of his theology. It is necessary to limit my observations here to a single aspect of the subject which may clarify the central question of the significance of the history of Christ, namely, the place which is assigned to the authority of God. In view of Bultmann's general skepticism and indifference to the person of Christ, one can expect very little that is distinctively Christian at this point. Nevertheless, there is much in his exposition that gives exactly the opposite impression. His sharp polemic against idealistic or humanitarian ethics for placing the norm of conduct in man rather than in God appears to place him on solid ground. Furthermore, he insists that ethics is concerned with obedience to God's authority, a radical and complete obedience to God's will. In so far as the will of God determines our conduct towards others, it may be designated as the commandment of love. "In love", he says, "man's soul does not attain to an infinite value nor does he receive thereby a share in the essence of God; but love is simply the requirement of obedience, and shows how this obedience can and ought to be practised in the concrete life-situation in which man is united with man".[53] As requiring obedience to God's commandments, the ethics of Jesus appear to be theocentric in character, but, to avoid a premature judgment, it is necessary to enquire where, according to Bultmann, the

---

[52] *Erforschung usw.*, pp 31 f.; "The New Approach etc", p. 357.
[53] *Jesus*, p. 104; cf pp. 102 ff.

commandments of God are to be learned. Through this enquiry as to the content of the will of God his precise meaning may remain somewhat obscure, but fortunately he does not leave us in any doubt as to what he does not understand by it.

First of all, the will of God is not to be identified with the Scriptures as the rule of faith and practice. This conclusion is not surprising in view of his radical criticism of the gospels. It also agrees fully with his typically *religionsgeschichtliche* view of the Old Testament as a source for the reconstruction of the religion of Israel and of the New Testament as a source for the understanding of early Christianity.[54] Most of the appeals to the Old Testament have been placed in the mouth of Jesus by the evangelists; they represent not the attitude of Jesus but that of the early church which, in the exigencies created by its controversies with the Jews, sought to defend its beliefs and practices in this fashion. Yet Bultmann maintains that as a matter of course Jesus must have accepted the authority of the Old Testament! This apparent contradiction he seeks to resolve by a distinction between absolute authority and formal authority. The Jews received the Old Testament as a formal authority, Bultmann holds, but it was distinctive of Jesus' attitude towards the Old Testament that He interpreted it in the interest of separating the essential from the non-essential. This estimate of Jesus' attitude towards the formal authority of the Old Testament is not especially new, indeed, it is characteristically Liberal; but the judgment that the absolute authority of the Scriptures is not impaired by the denial of their formal authority could be made, I suppose, only by a representative of the theology of paradox. At any rate it is clear that Bultmann interprets obedience to the will of God as implying the right to determine for one's self what the content of His will is on any particular occasion.

Bultmann's point of view becomes somewhat clearer, and is marked off more pointedly from the Liberal view, when he considers the authority of God's commandments in relation

---

[54] Cf. "Die Bedeutung des Alten Testaments fur den christlichen Glauben", in *Glauben und Verstehen*, pp. 313 ff.

to Jesus' ethical message. We are not to suppose that the formal authority of the Old Testament is set aside in the interest of setting up the formal authority of Jesus' own teaching. He tells us that we are not to do anything because Jesus commanded it any more than because the Bible commands it. Obedience to God, he says, is not conceived radically if authority is appealed to in this fashion. There is no external authority for determining what God's will is; the content of any command is a matter of indifference. Man must ultimately decide for himself what is demanded in any given situation.[55]

The conclusion is at hand that the will of God in Bultmann's language has nothing to do with the historical revelation of God, and once again his historical skepticism is shown not to embarrass his theology simply because his theology moves in a sphere of thought into which history cannot gain admittance. In insisting upon the contemporaneity of revelation as opposed to the historical character of the revelation of the Bible,[56] Bultmann takes his stand with mysticism rather than with historic Christianity. This judgment is not contradicted in the least by the fact that Bultmann constantly polemicizes against mysticism, for he has in view a mysticism which interprets religion solely in terms of inner contemplation and union with the divine, not mysticism in its fundamental antipathy to historical revelation and historical redemption.[57]

---

[55] Cf. *Jesus*, pp. 82-92, 73: "Was Gottes Wille ist, wird also nicht von einer äusseren Autoritat gesagt, so dass der Inhalt des Gebotenen gleichgultig ware, sondern es wird dem Menschen zugetraut und zugemutet, selbst zu sehen, was von ihm gefordert ist "

[56] "Zur Frage der Christologie", in *Glauben und Verstehen*, p. 89: "In der alten Orthodoxie ist Offenbarung die 'ubernaturliche' Lehre, durch ihren merkwurdigen Ursprung als Offenbarung qualifiziert, aber im ubrigen eine Lehre, die wie anderes Wissen verwahrt und weitergegeben werden kann. Der Begriff der Offenbarung ist also um das ihm wesentliche Moment der Gegenwartigkeit beraubt."

[57] At this point it is well to consider Bultmann's conception of the relation of the eschatological elements in Jesus' message to the ethical. Cf. *Jesus*, pp. 11 ff. Bultmann rightly criticizes all views which seek to solve the problem by the denial of the historicity of one or of the other element as well as the solution of Schweitzer, but he himself finds unity at the

After his exposition of Jesus' proclamation concerning the rule and will of God, Bultmann seems to point even more emphatically to the theocentric character of Jesus' message in the formulation: the proclamation of God as the Remote and Near.[58] The question arises as one ponders the rule and will of God how man who has rejected God's claim and is disobedient to His will can acknowledge God as his own God and obey Him. The answer given is that the remote God must also be recognized as near, that is, the Judge who condemns man as a sinner must be recognized as coming graciously to him with a word of forgiveness. Does Bultmann mean to say that the divine Creator and Judge is also the divine Saviour of men? Many of his expressions taken in isolation might seem to point to that conclusion, and they explain in part how many have come to acclaim the theological movement of which he is a representative as a return to the God of Calvin, the God of sovereign grace. It is to the credit of Bultmann that he does not leave us in uncertainty as to his meaning.

That he does not really maintain the transcendence of God, in spite of the characterization of God as the Wholly Other and the Remote, appears from his conception of the relation of God to nature. In this connection he is wont to speak of God as pre-eminently the creating Will, and in a manner that is reminiscent of Calvinism makes much of the creation concept. However, it soon becomes evident that Bultmann does not mean to affirm the Scriptural doctrine of creation, nor even the doctrine that the created world is completely dependent upon God. In speaking of dependence upon the creator he has in mind a distinctly religious relationship only, religious in the sense which presupposes the sin of man. There is, in other words, no account taken of the fall as involving a radical change in man's relation to God. By

expense of "de-eschatologizing" the eschatological message, and so virtually removes the problem by identifying the two elements. "Indem also die Botschaft vom Kommen der Gottesherrschaft wie vom Willen Gottes den Menschen hinweisen auf sein Jetzt als letzte Stunde im Sinne der Stunde der Entscheidung, bilden beide eine Einheit, ja sie fordern einander gegenseitig" (p. 121).

[58] *Jesus*, pp. 123-200.

identifying man's dependence upon God as a creature with man's separateness from God as a sinner, in one blow both the Christian doctrine of creation and the Christian doctrine of sin are emptied of their specific meaning.

His view of God's relation to the world comes to striking expression in his conception of miracle. The uniformity of nature, he maintains, excludes the possibility of miracle (*Mirakel*) in the sense of that which is above nature or contrary to nature. Yet he affirms that belief in God and belief in miracle (*Wunder*) are the same. If miracle is defined he declares as "an act of the divine will outside of my control", it serves to express the paradox that the remote God is near.[59] To talk about miracle (*Wunder*) is to talk about self, that is, that God becomes visible in my life by way of revelation of His grace. Accordingly Bultmann is as hostile to the thought of a Christian *Weltanschauung* which would allow for real miracles in history as he is to a Christian philosophy of history which allows for actual historical revelation.[60] When one has to do with nature, then, there can be no talk of revelation, for then revelation would cease to be momentary and direct.

To all of this the reply must be given that, if God is truly sovereign, nature must be dependent upon His will, and His disclosures concerning the meaning of nature, and the accomplishment of His purposes, by natural means or by supernatural means, must be received as a witness to His rule over all things.

Bultmann's conception of transcendence appears in its clearest light when he relates the remoteness of God to His nearness, His sovereignty to His grace. In thinking of God as the Wholly Other, we are not to think of His transcendence as ontological, Bultmann warns. God is not a higher nature.[61] The distinctive feature of Jesus' teaching about God, he tells us, is that He always saw the remoteness of God in unity

---

[59] *Ibid*, pp 158 ff.; cf. "Zur Frage des Wunders", in *Glauben und Verstehen*, pp. 214–228.

[60] Cf "Zur Frage des Wunders", p. 228: "Der christliche Gottesglaube ist keine Weltanschauung, sondern wird immer im Augenblick gewonnen, und er spricht: 'Herr, Ich glaube; hilf meinem Unglauben' (Mark. 9, 24)".

[61] Cf. *Jesus*, pp 138 ff.

with His nearness. We must accept the paradox that the remote, future God is at the same time, precisely because He is the remote, future God, also the God of the present.[62] The remoteness of God is only His remoteness from the sinner. God's nearness is only His nearness when He comes to man to claim Him, offering the grace of forgiveness, and only as man fails to hear God's demand, does he himself transform God's nearness into remoteness.[63] In this fashion Bultmann thinks that both sin and grace are conceived radically, for man grasps God at once both as the Wholly Other and as the God who judges and forgives in the present. God therefore does not deal with man as possessing a corrupt nature but only as disobedient and remote from Him through His denial of the claim of God. God comes to man as he is and man as he is acknowledges God. Man is quite free and able to respond to the demands of God. It does not surprise us that on this pelagianizing view of sin Bultmann denies the need of the change of man's nature and of redemption by the death and resurrection of Christ.[64]

Again it is evident that Bultmann does not really maintain the sovereignty of God. If God's transcendence is always in unity with His nearness, His grace becomes a corollary of His sovereignty. But then grace is no longer grace since it is no longer free, and all real possibility of grace is gone since God is no longer sovereign.

A question that arises as one considers this exposition of the message of Jesus on the background of the radical skepticism concerning His person is exactly what place is left for Jesus in the determination of a man's relation to God. The answer of Bultmann is plain. Jesus was the bearer of the word, the message which confronts man with God. He has no other significance, and so, on this view, He is not in the

[62] *Ibid.*, p. 147: "es kann sich nur darum handeln, die Paradoxie zu begreifen, dass der ferne, zukunftige Gott zugleich, ja gerade *indem* er der ferne, zukunftige ist, auch der Gott der Gegenwart ist".

[63] *Ibid.*, pp. 179 f.: "Die Ferne Gottes fur den Menschen hat den gleichen Ursprung wie den Nahe Gottes, namlich den, dass der Mensch Gott gehort, dass Gott seinen Anspruch auf ihn erhebt. Indem der Mensch diesen Anspruch uberhort, macht er selbst aus der Nahe Gottes die Ferne".

[64] *Ibid.*, pp. 181 ff., 195 ff.

least indispensable today. For the validity and authority of His message are not acquired from His proclamation of it. Bultmann here easily outdoes the Liberals. Although Harnack described the gospel as Jesus proclaimed it as having to do only with the Father and not with the Son, yet on the Liberal view the life of Jesus through His realization of His message was looked upon as the real foundation of Christianity. For Bultmann the gospel as Jesus proclaimed it has to do only with the God who is Remote and Near and not with the Son, and that is taken seriously to mean that the history and personality of Jesus are of no concern whatever. On this view Jesus is not the founder of historic Christianity and the religion which is attached to His message is a Christless religion.[65]

The point does not have to be labored that the theological point of view I have been considering is not Calvinism. I think I need not prove that this is not Christianity. For Bultmann's differences from Calvinism are not of the kind that have come to expression within the Christianity of the evangelical creeds; his views of the world, of history, of revelation, of salvation are "wholly other"; his God is not the sovereign Creator, Ruler, Saviour whom the Bible reveals.

[65] In "Jesus und Paulus" (see note 17) and in "Die Bedeutung des geschichtlichen Jesus fur die Theologie des Paulus", in *Glauben und Verstehen*, pp. 188–213, Bultmann compares the teaching of Jesus with that of Paul, and finds them in essential agreement on their view of God, the world, and eschatology. He seems to hold that the principal difference is that Jesus looked to the future for the coming of the rule of God while Paul looked back upon decisive events as having ushered in the new world. These discussions are worthy of separate consideration and criticism. However, I cannot refrain from protesting against the arbitrary, modernizing exegesis which allows him to set aside Paul's redemptive interpretation of the cross and resurrection of Christ as theological and mythological in the interest of recovering the fundamental ideas behind the contemporaneous forms of expression. By way of the interpretation that "der Glaube an Kreuz und Auferstehung ist deshalb nicht die Annahme von unvernunftig-mythologischen Lehren, sondern er ist zuerst die Beugung unter Gottes Gericht, der Verzicht auf alles Ruhmen", ("Jesus und Paulus", p. 87), Bultmann makes Paul mean virtually the same thing as his reconstructed Jesus To say the least Bultmann has ceased to be a historian when he seeks to find the kernel of the theology of crisis beneath the "husk" of Paul's doctrine of historical redemption.

Indeed, Bultmann would be the last to claim the Genevan reformer or any other spokesman for orthodoxy as his spiritual father. Instead, as his theological essays indicate clearly, he is conscious of standing in the stream of modern theology, a theology specifically that has been emerging from the Liberal theology of the nineteenth century, not through a return to orthodoxy or a fusion with orthodoxy, but by way of correction and modification of the old Liberalism in the light of new philosophical and historical principles.[66] It is a point of view which seems to be concerned above all to separate religion from everything that might connect it with this present world-order; it seeks to sever Christianity from its roots in creation and history, and herein has a definite affinity with second century Gnosticism. The antithesis between the Easter message and the Easter faith is applied more seriously and consistently than by the Liberals. For although he does not accept the fact of creation, the historicity of the miracles of Christ, revelation and redemption in any objective sense, nor the consummation of history through Christ's return, and is sure that as facts they could have no significance for faith, he nevertheless affirms creation, miracle, revelation, salvation, and eschatology in setting forth the doctrine of God. As he relates these concepts to religion they are, therefore, merely ideological.

That Christianity stands or falls with the historicity of certain foundational events was preeminently the message which Dr. Machen proclaimed to this generation. Not that he advocated a lowest common denominator or an attenuated Christianity. He was an apologist not for a reduced

[66] Cf. especially the essays in *Glauben und Verstehen* where his consistent opposition to orthodoxy and his affinity with the theology of crisis come to clear expression. The opening sentence from the first essay, entitled "Die liberale Theologie und die jungste theologische Bewegung", p. 1, reads as follows: "In der Polemik der jungsten theologischen Bewegung, die wesentlich durch die Namen Barth und Gogarten bezeichnet ist, gegen die sogenannte liberale Theologie handelt es sich nicht um Abfall von der eigenen Vergangenheit, sondern um Auseinandersetzung mit ihr; nicht um Erneuerung der Orthodoxie, sonder um Besinnung auf die Konsequenzen, die sich aus der durch die liberale Theologie bestimmten Situation ergeben". Bultmann's affinity with Herrmann is also noteworthy. For his estimate of Herrmann's point of view, see especially pp. 106 f.

Christianity but for the Christianity of the whole Bible, Christianity in all of its fulness, uniqueness, and intolerance of compromise with human systems of thought. But no one surpassed him, I think, in his awareness of the fact that Christianity, and not merely certain older formulations of Christianity, was at stake in the modern attack upon its historical foundations; and no one has been quite so unwearied and effective in giving expression to the exclusiveness of Christianity as a religion of redemption that is both supernatural and historical. To the exposition and defense of this Christianity he gave his life,— as we well may. I shall conclude by recalling a few pertinent words from his pen: "All the ideas of Christianity might be discovered in some other religion, yet there would be in that other religion no Christianity. For Christianity depends, not upon a complex of ideas, but upon the narration of an event. Without that event, the world, in the Christian view, is altogether dark, and humanity is lost under the guilt of sin. There can be no salvation by the discovery of eternal truth, for eternal truth brings naught but despair, because of sin. But a new face has been put upon life by the blessed thing that God did when He offered up His only begotten Son".[67]

---

[67] *Christianity and Liberalism*, 1923, p. 70.

CHAPTER VI

MARTIN DIBELIUS
AND THE RELATION OF
HISTORY AND FAITH

AS ONE critical school has followed another across the constantly shifting theological scene, however distinctive its fundamental principles and basic elements, each has been preoccupied with the problem of the relation of history and faith. The common absorption with this problem may be explained most satisfactorily perhaps by the observation that those who have come to reject the gospel story concerning Jesus Christ rarely have been able to break completely with Christianity or to leave Jesus entirely out of account in the formulation of their religious faith.

Even some of the most drastic efforts to destroy confidence in the evangelical records have gone hand in hand with an avowed concern to honor Jesus and to defend the Christian religion. So David Friedrich Strauss, to choose a conspicuous example, in spite of the pervasiveness and severity of his criticism of the contents of the gospels, maintained, on the basis of the presuppositions of Hegelian Idealism, that the true foundation of Christianity remained unimpaired since the concern of religion is only that the *idea* of the God-man should be realized in every personality as the ultimate goal of humanity, and that this idea of the God-man, in the nature of the case, could not be realized perfectly on the historical plane. The validity of the idea could not depend, he maintained, on its external representation, not even in the history of Jesus, and consequently no amount of historical criticism could possibly destroy the idea which constitutes the real element of Christianity.

While the Hegelian interpretation represented an almost complete devaluation of history, the movement inspired by the theology of Albrecht Ritschl seemed once more to restore history to a place of honor. Indeed, its positive evaluation of history was so basic to its whole approach that it came to be known as historism. Historism to be sure was far from maintaining a high judgment of the trustworthiness of the gospels, for this school, in spite of its moderateness as compared with the Tübingen School, likewise undertook, because of the demands of its consistent naturalism and its distinctive interpretation of history, a thorough-going reconstruction of the story told by the gospels, a reconstruction which took form characteristically in the numerous Liberal lives of Jesus. Its distinctive judgment upon history is observed in its readiness to attribute to a certain phase of history which, according to its own judgment, was purely human in character, the evaluation of "revelation", and to the purely human "historical Jesus", whom it confidently claimed it could recover from the records by historical criticism, the evaluation of "God".

Although the Ritschlian view of Christianity and of religion is still articulate in this country, especially in the pulpits of the Liberal churches, the attack upon it in the present century on historical, theological, and philosophical grounds, has served to disclose both its unscientific character and its barrenness so far as faith is concerned. Its historical reconstruction has been demonstrated to be arbitrary and modernizing, notably because of its failure to deal realistically with the eschatological elements in the gospels, and its evaluation of history has gradually appeared to offer no adequate basis for a faith which requires an absolute object.

The latter criticism has been the burden of the polemic of the Barthian theology, and the positive effort of this new movement to set forth a theology that meets the demand of faith for a transcendent object, a theology of the Word of God that judges us and offers us pardon, has given it, unless all signs fail, epochal significance in the history of modern theology. The fact remains, however, that for the Barthians, likewise, the significance of history for faith has been an acute problem. One reason for this situation is that the Barthian doctrine of the contemporaneity of revelation excludes the belief, which is an integral part of the historic Christian doctrine of Scripture, that the revelation of God in history which looks to the salvation of man came to a close with the inscripturation of the last book of the New Testament Canon. Still another reason why the historical question thrusts itself forward is that, by drawing its leading motif from the Pauline doctrines of sin and grace, this school has given the impression of a relative unconcern for the history of Christ as recorded in the gospels. Indeed, in so far as it has turned its attention to this history, it has betrayed a critical indifference to its truth or even, in the case of some members of the school, a radically agnostic attitude towards the witness of the gospels to Christ.

This article is not concerned directly with the Barthian point of view but rather with the position of the influential critic and theologian Martin Dibelius. The special interest in his views in connection with the question of the relation of history and faith lies in the fact that he appears to mediate between the position of Liberalism, which he characterizes as radical historism, and the position of Barth, which he designates as radical Paulinism. His avowed concern is to avoid the chief fault of each, and thus to join with the Barthians in the effort to recognize the claims of faith while granting to history a secure and indispensable place as the Liberals had done. In his general outlook Dibelius is unquestionably much closer to the Barthians than to the Liberals. The very mildness of his critique of the theology of crisis points to his affinity with that school, and there is much in the details of his interpretation of the message of Jesus as well as in his general theological perspective that confirms the same conclusion. At the same time, in pleading the claims of history he seems not to have divorced himself completely from the Liberal approach. In any case, it is eminently worth the effort to study his views, and to raise the question whether in seeking to mediate between these schools he has really overcome their weaknesses or has perhaps acquired deficiencies from both sides.

The position of Dibelius merits consideration, moreover, because of the singular influence which he has for some time enjoyed in the English-speaking world, both through his direct personal contacts as a lecturer and as a participant in international ecclesiastical conferences and councils and by means of the circulation of many of his recent writings in

English dress. His most significant contributions to *Formgeschichte*, which are important for the subject under consideration in this article chiefly for their bearing upon his interpretation of the history of Jesus, have been made available for those who do not read German in *From Tradition to Gospel*[1] and *The Message of Jesus Christ*.[2] The same subject is treated more briefly in connection with the broader questions of Introduction in *A Fresh Approach to the New Testament and Early Christian Literature*.[3] So far his theological interpretations have not received the same attention from English and American publishers, a small work entitled *Gospel Criticism and Christology*,[4] consisting of lectures delivered in London, and an article on the subject "Jesus in Contemporary German Theology",[5] making up the chief items. Works in German, which are of considerable value for the understanding of his position as a whole, are *Evangelium und Welt*[6] and *Jesus*.[7]

I. Interpretation of the History of Jesus

The problem of the relation of history and faith is formulated by Dibelius in terms of the distinction between the historical and the supra-historical, and this formulation suggests the need of a survey of his interpretation of the gospel history as an important aspect of the consideration of the problem as a whole. Fortunately, such a survey need not be presented in great detail in view of the fact that on the crucial question of the historicity of the messianic consciousness of Jesus

---

[1] London: Ivor Nicholson and Watson. 1934. 311 pp Translated from the revised second edition of *Die Formgeschichte des Evangeliums* of 1933, the first edition of which appeared in 1919.

[2] New York. Scribners. 1939 192 pp Translated from *Die Botschaft von Jesus Christus* which was published in 1935

[3] New York: Scribners. 1936 280 pp A translation of *Geschichte der urchristlichen Literatur* which was published in 1926

[4] London: Ivor Nicholson and Watson. 1935. 104 pp.

[5] *The Journal of Religion*, 1931, pp 179 ff.

[6] Gottingen· Vandenhoeck und Ruprecht 1929. 176 pp. A first edition of this work appeared in 1925 under the title *Geschichtliche und ubergeschichtliche Religion im Christentum*

[7] Berlin: de Gruyter. 1939 134 pp (Sammlung Goschen, Band 1130).

Dibelius takes the side of the affirmative, and by concentrating upon his view of the person of Christ the question of historical interpretation as well as that of supra-historical evaluation may be crystallized in the sharpest possible fashion. In the interest of clarifying at the very start the basis for this historical judgment on the messianic consciousness, certain negative considerations should be in view. The relatively high estimate of the trustworthiness of the gospel tradition has nothing to do with his affirmation of the supra-historical plane of reality. Dibelius could not possibly subscribe to the formula *credimus ut intelligamus*. The scientific historical method, as Dibelius conceives of it, calls for an interpretation of the records that proceeds quite independently of the presuppositions of religious faith. The task of the historian and the activity of the man of faith are quite distinct.[8] Hence, when Dibelius affirms the historicity of the messianic consciousness of Jesus, and accepts as substantially reliable not only a considerable portion of the tradition which reports the teachings of Jesus but also many records of His deeds, in contrast to the extreme skepticism of Bultmann, he claims to do so on scientific, as opposed to religious, grounds alone. It hardly needs to be added that for Dibelius the scientific interpretation of history involves a consistent naturalism which will not allow for the historicity of miracles.

Nor is the explanation for his relatively moderate conclusions with respect to the testimony of the gospel records to be found in the sphere of literary criticism, for he shares the radical view of the gospels, associated with the names of Wrede and Wellhausen, which understands them primarily as expressions of the faith of the communities in which they originated rather than as witnesses to the history of Jesus. The gospels on his view presuppose a Christological development which began with the rise of the belief in His resurrection.[9]

[8] Cf. *The Journal of Religion*, 1931, pp 179 f , 204 f., 211; *Evangelium und Welt*, pp. 96 ff ; *Jesus*, p. 126.

[9] For the details of his view of the gospels see especially *A Fresh Approach* etc., pp. 56 ff., 95 ff ; *Jesus*, pp 10 ff., 75 ff., *Gospel Criticism and Christology*, pp. 86 ff.

It is as a representative of the method of form-criticism, however, that Dibelius claims to possess a scientific approach by which the contents of the gospels, having been isolated into small units of tradition and assigned to various strata, may be sifted and reduced until the earliest stratum is recovered.[10] But the question remains how, on a common commitment to historical naturalism and to the form-critical assumptions and method, Dibelius comes to affirm the historicity of the messianic consciousness of Jesus whereas Bultmann ends with thoroughgoing agnosticism. A partial answer to this question is to be found in the observation that Dibelius allows for greater continuity between the teaching of Jesus and the belief of primitive Christianity by recognition of the presence in the early church of eye-witnesses of the ministry of Jesus and of their influence upon the contents of the historical tradition. Although he rejects the traditional view of the gospels which traces their origin directly to eye-witnesses or to those who had contact with them, he does allow that a very high degree of authenticity is to be accredited to the earliest stratum of ecclesiastical tradition concerning Christ. The question emerges whether Dibelius is more conservative than Bultmann because of a sounder, more objective, use of the method or in spite of the radical implications of the method, a question that will receive comment later on.

If our gospel records have been formulated from the point of view of the post-resurrection faith of Christianity, and even the earliest tradition of the primitive church presupposes the same influence of the proclamation of Christ, how is it possible to substantiate the historicity of the messianic consciousness of Jesus? In spite of his radical view of the gospels and of the tradition behind the gospels, which would seem to allow only for agnosticism as to what Jesus thought about Himself, Dibelius is confident that a sifting of the tradition will yield a positive result on this subject.

---

[10] This article deals only incidentally with the form-critical method. For a brief survey and criticism of the method by the present writer, especially as that method is set forth by Bultmann, the reader may consult the November, 1938, issue of this *Journal*, pp 13 ff.

His conclusion is based primarily upon an examination of the course of the history of Christ, and especially its climax in the final issue at Jerusalem, rather than upon a study of the claims of Jesus as they are recorded in the gospels.

Although as a form-critic he rejects the chronological and topographical framework of the gospel history as a whole, he finds it impossible to reject the record of the journey to Jerusalem at the end of Jesus' ministry. This journey, he declares, is the only clear sign of a development in the history of Jesus, and he finds in it the deliberate concern of Jesus to present the message of the kingdom of God for acceptance or rejection by the leaders of the Jewish people.[11] The conflict which resulted from His proclamation of the nearness of the kingdom issued in Jesus' execution, and since Jesus was crucified as a messianic pretender, the message of the coming kingdom as well as His acts must have given the charge against Him a certain justification. But how is Dibelius certain that Jesus' death was bound up with His messianic claims? The proof is not to be sought in the record of the trial, for, according to Dibelius, no great value can be placed upon it. In the last analysis he rests his case upon the record of the superscription, recorded in all four of the gospels, that He was "the king of the Jews", evidence which can be accepted because of the public nature of the execution, as opposed to the privacy of the trial, and because the report must go back eventually to eye-witnesses of the execution like Simon of Cyrene, whose sons Alexander and Rufus were known either by Mark or by an earlier narrator.[12]

The cleansing of the temple, Dibelius is also inclined to think, is best understood as an expression of Jesus' claim to messianic authority. The sovereignty with which Jesus took control of this center of Jewish worship appears to transcend a merely prophetic authority. Possibly, it must be admitted, the success of the cleansing and the failure of the Jewish authorities to interfere may have been due to an exercise of sheer moral authority on Jesus' part, and it would not be

[11] Cf. *Jesus*, pp. 52 f., 79.
[12] Cf. *idem*, pp. 81, 113; *Evangelium und Welt*, pp. 46 f., 73 ff.; *The Journal of Religion*, 1931, p. 200.

necessary to interpret the act as messianic, but even such a singular exercise of moral authority would come close, it is thought, to the claim of messianic validity for His person.[13]

Having come to the conclusion that the climax of the history of Jesus is unintelligible apart from the historicity of his messianic consciousness, Dibelius finds that the positive argument receives a certain cumulative character, and he affirms the trustworthiness of the reports that there was a recognition of His messiahship at Caesarea Philippi and on other occasions.[14]

The positive result of this critical process remains a meagre one, however, unless the particular meaning which Jesus attached to this claim can be ascertained. While the decision in this matter is regarded as a difficult one, in view of the judgment that the tradition concerning Jesus is thought to have undergone a Christological transformation, it is argued that the whole tenor of the tradition excludes the interpretation of the messianic claim as political, notwithstanding the fact that the Roman authorities must have understood his claim as a pretension to royalty. The messianic claim is rather to be understood in terms of the coming of the Son of Man. But now an acute difficulty emerges, for Dibelius has apparently proceeded along two distinct critical paths at once. For, on the one hand, he affirms the judgment of the radicals that the doctrine of the gospels concerning the Son of Man is *Gemeinde Dogmatik*. The theology of the primitive church was fashioned, it is maintained, as this concept was utilized to set forth the expectation of the return in glory of Him who had lived in earthly obscurity, and to solve the riddle of the cross. On the other hand, he is in the position of arguing against the radicals in a fashion that is reminiscent of the Liberals, and essays the delicate task of separating history and theology in the gospel records. He discovers a Christian interpretation in utterances concerning the passion of the Son of Man like Mark 14:41 but maintains that the description of His extreme poverty in Matthew 8:20 may be historical. He allows also that Jesus may have spoken

[13] Cf. *Jesus*, p. 80.
[14] Cf. *idem*, p. 82; cf. pp. 85 f.

of the coming of the Son of Man as in Luke 17:24 and Mark 8:38 without referring to Himself openly, and yet, in spite of the reserve and mystery of His speech and the ambiguity of the Aramaic expression, the reference would have been clear to those who shared this eschatological expectation.[15]

It must be admitted that Dibelius' affirmation of a messianic claim on the part of Jesus in the form that He was the Son of Man has a distinct advantage over the old Liberal view in that there is for him a much closer integration of this claim with the interpretation of the message of Jesus, an integration that is possible because the messiahship and the message concerning the kingdom are both set forth in eschatological terms. On this view the messiahship would not have had to be a burden for Jesus because of an inner conflict with His central purpose. The message of Jesus concerning Himself and His message as a whole are a unity, and all of His words and deeds, related as they are to the central proclamation concerning the kingdom, are put in a distinctive perspective by the fact that the one who speaks and acts does so out of the consciousness that He Himself is to be the ruler in the approaching kingdom. This view, it will be noted, implies that Jesus thought of Himself not as a reigning king but only as the one who had been designated as the future king. This conception of the coming king is also thought to explain the reserve of Jesus with respect to the disclosure of His messiahship and the passivity of His ministry, for the future weal is thought of as coming to realization through no human effort in history but by a catastrophic act of God in bringing history to a close.[16]

In spite of the important difference between the views of the Liberals and of Dibelius which has been noted, there is an element in the total estimate of the significance of the messiahship in which there is striking agreement. This element concerns the place which is assigned to Jesus Himself in the message which He proclaimed. For Harnack "the gospel as Jesus proclaimed it has to do with the Father

---

[15] Cf. *idem*, pp. 75 ff., 83 ff.; *Gospel Criticism and Christology*, pp 47 f.
[16] Cf. *Jesus*, pp. 82 f ; *Evangelium und Welt*, pp. 75 f.

only and not with the Son";[17] and Dibelius agrees in refusing a place in the gospel to Jesus. The reserve of Jesus on the messiahship is appealed to as evidence that He did not place the messianic question in the foreground. Moreover, it is said, He did not make confession of His messiahship a requirement for salvation; what He demanded was that in His deeds men should recognize God's action and that in His appearance they should perceive the nearness of the coming of God in His kingdom.[18] When Jesus, in answer to the disciples of John who inquired whether He was the Messiah, spoke of the wonders which had been wrought, and added, "Blessed is he whosoever findeth no occasion of stumbling in me" (Matthew 11:1-6), the sense, according to Dibelius, is that the kingdom is at hand, and that their belief is to be centered in it, rather than in the Messiah![19] According to this view, therefore, while Jesus is thought of as more than a prophet and even is said to have come with more than human claims and with divine authority and divine power in His message and acts, the purpose of Jesus is not to center attention upon His own person but rather to present the claims of the kingdom of which He in His person, speech and acts was the decisive sign.[20]

In order to set in somewhat clearer perspective the manner in which Dibelius endeavors to subordinate the messiahship to the proclamation of the kingdom, it is necessary to explore briefly his treatment of the data in the gospels which suggest that the kingdom has already come in the very presence and activity of the Messiah. If the kingdom is conceived of exclusively in terms of future realization through the miraculous power of God, the significance of the Messiah might possibly be quite secondary and indeed might seem to tend to disappear altogether. On the other hand, if the kingdom is represented as having been realized, at least in a preliminary fashion, through the activity of the messianic king, it would seem impossible to deny the central place of honor

[17] *Das Wesen des Christentums*, p. 91 (E.T., p. 144).
[18] Cf. *Jesus*, pp. 86 f.
[19] *Ibid*, p. 85; cf. p. 65 and *The Message of Jesus Christ*, pp. 25, 143.
[20] Cf. *Jesus*, p. 87.

to the Messiah. The interpretation of Luke 17:21 and of Matthew 12:28 will serve to illustrate the approach of Dibelius to this question. The words of Jesus in the former passage, "The kingdom of God is in your midst", Dibelius is concerned to assert, cannot in the context of Jesus' teaching mean to express the pure inwardness of the kingdom.[21] While admitting the propriety of this conclusion one must wonder that he does not consider the possibility that the passage teaches that the kingdom had come through the very presence of Christ, although the Pharisees by their failure to recognize Christ and the messianic character of His mission had not realized the fact of its coming. Such an interpretation runs counter to the modern effort to interpret every reference of Jesus to the kingdom as eschatological, an effort that has resulted in many ingenious attempts to remove the difficulty of this passage. The simplest methods of achieving the desired end are to change either the subject or the predicate of the saying. Bultmann has chosen the latter method in his paraphrase of the saying in the interest of giving it future reference.[22] Dibelius takes the former method, achieving harmony with the exclusively eschatological view in the affirmation that Jesus means to say not that the kingdom is in the midst of the Pharisees, but that the *signs* of the kingdom are present. Accordingly, Jesus is opposing the Pharisaic view, which in Mark 13 once again is thought to have found its way into the

[21] *Ibid.*, pp. 62 f. Cf. *Evangelium und Welt*, p 40: "Auch hier ist die Verkurzung der Redeweise —'Reich' statt 'Zeichen fur seine Nahe'— nur von denen misszuverstehen, die sich von der Gewohnung an modernen kirchlichen Sprachgebrauch nicht frei machen konnen. Was abgelehnt wird, ist nicht der Zukunftscharackter des Reiches, sondern die ubliche Technik apokalyptischen Observierens. Das Reich Gottes ist im Kommen, aber nicht aus den Gestirnen, sondern aus eurem Herzen soll euch Gewissheit seiner Nahe werden". The translation of this passage in *Die Botschaft von Jesus Christus*, p. 65, is also illuminating· "Nicht spuren Gottes Reich die es errechnen noch spuren es die sagen: es ist hier — oder: es ist da; denn siehe, Gottes Reich ist zu spüren in eurer Mitte". Here he effects the same result by reading "spuren" into the predicate. See also *From Tradition to Gospel*, p. 162.

[22] Cf. *Jesus*, p. 39: "Die Gottesherrschaft ist (mit einem Schlage) mitten unter euch". Cf. *Die Geschichte der synoptischen Tradition*², p. 128.

Christian church, that the kingdom does not come with observation, and means to say that He Himself with His message and deeds forms the sign of the breaking in of the kingdom.

The proclamation of the coming of the kingdom involved, therefore, the warning of its imminence. The proclamation is by no means merely the announcement that God's rule will be established in glorious fashion at some future time; the urgency and arresting force of the message were due to the fact that God's decisive action was declared to be at the very door. While it is thought of as definitely future, its nearness is conceived of so vividly that it is sometimes even spoken of as in process of coming because of the signs that were present. It is significant that Dibelius finds the essence of Jesus' message in the announcement of the nearness of the kingdom rather than in its strict futurity, for with this concept he associates his view, which will require further consideration at a later point, that the message does not center attention upon the realization of promises of God in the future but, by placing us *zwischen den Zeiten* of unfulfillment and fulfillment, forces us to decision in the present.[23]

The extraordinary deeds of Christ are interpreted likewise, not as evidence that the king has come and is exercising His rule, at least in a preliminary fashion, but merely as signs of the nearness of the coming kingdom. This viewpoint comes to expression in the interpretation of Matthew 11:1-6 as centering attention upon the kingdom rather than upon the Messiah, as was noted above, and it may also be observed more particularly in connection with his exposition of Matthew 12:28: "If I by the Spirit of God cast out demons, then is the kingdom of God come upon you". Dibelius interprets this passage as meaning, "Then God's kingdom is already made known among you". Evidently recognizing that the rendering is an interpretation rather than a translation (for certainly the language does not state that the exorcism of demons by

---

[23] Cf *Jesus*, p. 58: "Dieses Dasein zwischen 'noch nicht haben' und 'haben' muss man verstehen, wenn man die geschichtliche Stellung des Evangeliums verstehen will". This evaluation of the message will be discussed below.

Christ *informs* them of the imminent coming of the kingdom), Dibelius states that the Greek might be translated, "God's kingdom has reached as far as you", which he sets over against the thought of the actual arrival of the kingdom.[24] Admitting the possibility of this rendering, the question may well be put whether Jesus by these words, rather than merely announcing the *nearness* of the future kingdom, does not pointedly declare the *arrival* of the kingdom in view of the fact that the Messiah, who was anointed by the Lord with His Spirit, now fulfills His messianic functions by the same Spirit.

Ultimately, to be sure, the issue whether Dibelius is correct in his general interpretation of the significance which Jesus attached to His own person, and in particular in his view that His person was subordinated to the proclamation of the nearness of the kingdom of God, is not primarily one of the soundness of his exegesis of isolated passages but of the validity of his historical criticism. For it is the elimination of various elements of the gospel teaching concerning Christ as due to the modification of older tradition or to the creation of new tradition, on the basis of his form-critical method, that most decisively affects his view of Jesus, resulting in the sharp distinction between the messianic consciousness of "the historical Jesus" and the Christology of the gospels. With a view to the further clarification of his conception of the messianic consciousness one must examine his interpretation of the supposedly conflicting tradition. His criticism of many of the miracle stories and of other narratives which he designates as legends is most significant in this connection.

Attention has been directed to the fact that Dibelius accepts as historical certain of the records of extraordinary deeds of Jesus, interpreting them as signs of the coming of the kingdom, but these deeds, whether healings or exorcisms, are distinguished sharply from other miracle stories which are thought to have been imported from the non-Christian

---

[24] *Ibid.*, pp. 65 f ; cf. *Evangelium und Welt*, pp. 39 f., 48; *Die Botschaft von Jesus Christus*, p 75 The renderings in German are as follows: "Dann hat sich Gottes Reich schon bei euch kundgetan" and "Gottes Reich ist bis zu euch gelangt".

world or, at least, to represent in their present form a radical transformation of the historical tradition.[25] The former group is classified under the head of *paradigms* in view of the close connection which they are thought to have sustained with the early Christian preaching. On the basis of the observation that orientals often have extraordinary psychic powers, and with the results of modern psychiatry and a recently developed treatment of neurotics through the use of will-power (*Überwaltigungstherapie*) in mind, he thinks it impossible to deny that Jesus actually performed remarkable cures. Jesus, as distinguished from John the Baptist, possessed, he maintains, a charismatic healing gift, and in its exercise He proved in a practical way the nearness of the kingdom. The latter group of miracle stories, consisting of such narratives as the feeding of the five thousand, the walking on the sea, the marriage at Cana, and the raising of Lazarus, as well as many stories of healings, are designated as *tales* since they are thought to betray secular and literary interests, that is, they are told in lively and graphic form, not from any religious motive, but for their own sake. According to Dibelius these tales present an entirely distinct conception of Jesus from that which is found in the paradigms. "It is not Jesus as the herald of the kingdom of God with His signs, demands, threats and promises, who stands in the centre of these stories, but Jesus the miracle-worker. *The tales deal with Jesus the thaumaturge.*"[26] These stories are not brought into any particular relation to the message of the kingdom but instead were told to draw attention to Jesus Himself. Here then there is no subordination of the activity of the charismatic herald to the message of the kingdom. Not the historical activity of a man who speaks with divine authority and acts with divine power is in the foreground, but the epiphany on earth of a divine being. It appears, therefore, that many stories which represent Jesus as exhibit-

[25] For Dibelius' discussions of paradigms and tales, and the question of miracle in general, see *From Tradition to Gospel*, pp 37 ff., 70 ff.; *The Message of Jesus Christ*, pp 135 ff , 166 ff ; *Jesus*, pp. 50 f , 63 ff.; *Gospel Criticism and Christology*, pp. 34 ff., 63 ff., 83 ff.; *Evangelium und Welt*, pp. 49 ff.

[26] *From Tradition to Gospel*, p. 80.

ing divine authority and divine power, and invite wonder and arouse curiosity as to who He is, are excluded from the historical data that bear upon the understanding of the messianic consciousness.

The other class of narratives which is concerned with the person and life of Christ rather than with the message of the kingdom is that which is designated as *legends*.[27] This class includes the stories concerning the Virgin Mary, the shepherds, Jesus at the age of twelve, the baptism, the temptation and the transfiguration. In calling such narratives legends, Dibelius does not intend to deny outright their historicity, for legends are properly "religious narratives of a saintly man in whose works and fate interest is taken".[28] In the case of Jesus the term is applied to religious stories "in which Jesus brings to light His purity, wisdom, and virtue, or in which the Divine protection and care of Jesus are revealed".[29] A legend does not imply the mythological character of the person whose life is described, nor is any particular incident that is narrated necessarily without historical foundation. Thus the baptism of Jesus by John is assumed by Dibelius to be historical, and he even goes so far as to affirm that it was in connection with the baptism that Jesus must have come to realize His mission, but the story of the baptism as told in Mark 1.9–11 is felt to betray its legendary character in its report of the heavenly sign and voice.[30] Nevertheless, the clear implication of the use of the term, as it applies to the life of Jesus, is that a new motif has entered the tradition in the interest of centering attention upon His life, and that in so far as the tradition acquired a "legendary form" it became unhistorical. Taking the gospel tradition as a whole, but noting Luke as an exception, Dibelius is inclined

---

[27] The materials designated as legends are discussed fully in *From Tradition to Gospel*, pp 104 ff.; *The Message of Jesus Christ*, pp. 174 ff ; *Gospel Criticism and Christology*, pp. 90 ff.

[28] *From Tradition to Gospel*, p. 104.

[29] *Ibid.*, p. 120.

[30] Cf *Gospel Criticism and Christology*, pp. 90 ff.; *Jesus*, pp. 46 f In the later work he is much less certain that the origin of the messianic mission was associated with the baptism On the narrative of the baptism see also *The Message of Jesus Christ*, pp. 183 f.

to the position that it has not come under the influence of the legendary motif in any thoroughgoing fashion; this motif found place in the New Testament only as it were by footnotes, and the fact that not more stories of this kind were included is taken as evidence that the tradition was shaped by the message of the eschatological faith rather than by a faith which was concerned with Him whose life from the beginning to the end was under the divine protection. In view of his judgment that the legends in the gospels, with few exceptions, have to do not with the special virtue and piety of Jesus, but rather with God's particular and wonderful care for His anointed, it might appear that there would be no insuperable objection to accepting the authenticity of such stories. Perhaps Dibelius is indicating his decisive objection to their historicity when he says that "not miracles performed by Jesus, but miracles done to him, form the heart of these legends".[31]

The Passion story is also classified as a legend.[32] In Luke the story is thought to have developed in the form of a personal legend with the interest centering in His heroic virtue, but in Mark it is set forth in the form of a cult-legend. Although from the beginning the Passion story must have been told in a continuous narrative, and it must be rooted in the testimony of eye-witnesses so that, as has been observed above, it may be appealed to as a chief support for the historicity of the messianic consciousness, nevertheless, the story as a whole is viewed as having been fashioned from the point of view of the faith in the risen Saviour. The whole narrative is controlled, it is maintained, by the place which it had together with the resurrection-belief in the preaching of early Christianity. In particular the legendary character is thought to appear in the fact that the disgraceful events of the condemnation and execution of Jesus were set forth to the hearer or reader as the expression of the will of God. To those

[31] *The Message of Jesus Christ*, p. 179. Cf. *From Tradition to Gospel*, pp. 116, 132.

[32] For Dibelius' treatment of the Passion narrative see especially *From Tradition to Gospel*, pp. 105, 178 ff.; *The Message of Jesus Christ*, pp. 130 f , 144 ff ; *Gospel Criticism and Christology*, pp. 19 ff., 57 ff., 79 ff.; *Jesus*, pp. 109 ff., 112 ff.

who acknowledged the risen Lord the evidence that everything shameful and dishonorable that had happened to Jesus happened according to God's will was declared in the Old Testament. "The Old Testament passages on suffering were read as normative sources for the Passion story".[33] This is not to say that none of the incidents were historical, the parting of the garments, for example, being highly probable on general historical grounds. Nevertheless, it was the Old Testament that shaped the whole story, giving it a soteriological perspective. Dibelius, it must be admitted, very effectively demonstrates how fully the Passion narrative is expressed in the language of the Old Testament or motivated by reference to it,[34] but he unfortunately fails to ask whether the reference of the Passion to the will of God as recorded in the Old Testament was necessarily determined by the experience of the early church. May it not have been the result of Jesus' own consciousness of being the Messiah?

II. EVALUATION OF THE CHRISTIAN MESSAGE

Can the historical message of Jesus, the message concerning the nearness of the kingdom of God, as Dibelius understands it, call forth saving faith? Dibelius claims that he can be true to his ideals as a scientific historian and likewise can satisfy the demands of personal faith in answering this question in the affirmative. In order to understand the implications of this position, especially in the perspective of his judgment that the kingdom which Jesus expected failed

[33] *From Tradition to Gospel*, p 188.
[34] Cf. *From Tradition to Gospel*, pp 186 ff His interpretation of Jesus' words, "My God, my God, why hast thou forsaken me?", is notable. "It is certain that they were not meant to signify that Jesus had lost faith in his mission and had succumbed to despair. It is certain that the words of this Psalm on the lips of the dying Jesus signified that he was resigned to God's will. These words conceal no psychological fact; and here again the view taken of them is the expression of an understanding of the story of the Passion based on faith This view holds good whether the words are Christ's own, or have only been attributed to him". *Gospel Criticism and Christology*, p. 59; cf. *From Tradition to Gospel*, pp. 193 f.; *The Message of Jesus Christ*, p. 145.

to come, it is necessary to set forth briefly what the message of Jesus Christ, on his view, really meant.

Jesus' proclamation of the coming of the kingdom was set forth within the framework of threats, promises and demands.[35] The hearer was constantly placed between the threat of judgment to come and the promise of grace, a situation which excluded the possibility of neutrality and demanded a decision either for or against God. Faced with this crisis and desiring to know how to escape the threat and to participate in the promise, he sought to understand God's demands. These demands of Jesus, it is thought, have been grossly misconstrued; they were not meant as a system of ethics of universal validity, nor even as an *Interimsethik* which was to be in force for the short interval before the coming of the kingdom. Jesus was not a lawgiver either for the church or for mankind generally; wherever such an impression is created in the gospels, and Dibelius thinks such an impression is given especially in Matthew, it must be explained as due to the transformation of Jesus' teaching through legalistic and secular influences at work in early Christianity or even as the result of the reference to Jesus of rules and regulations that were developed in the primitive church to meet its special needs.[36]

If the ethical teaching of Jesus is conceived of as claiming external authority, the eschatological character of the message, Dibelius maintains, has not been grasped at all. For Jesus, it is said, was not concerned with how men should live in the

---

[35] Dibelius' evaluation of the message of Christ is found especially in *Jesus*, pp. 88 ff.; *Evangelium und Welt*, pp. 44 ff., 54 ff ; *The Message of Jesus Christ*, pp. 140 ff , 163 f , *Gospel Criticism and Christology*, pp. 38 ff.; *The Journal of Religion*, 1931, pp. 200 ff.

[36] Thus, according to Dibelius, Jesus' word on divorce in Mark 10:9 is misunderstood if it is taken as a divine, universally valid, law, although Matthew is said to have given it such a legalistic interpretation. If the message of Jesus is understood eschatologically as "the shining forth of the new being", and this saying is understood not as a law but as circumscribing the ideal marriage state, there will be the realization of a motive for a new view of marriage. Jesus, then, was not concerned to condemn divorce in the world of His day; the presence of divorce He would have regarded simply as a sign that the old evil world was still present. *Evangelium und Welt*, p. 153; *Jesus*, p. 100.

world but what they should be when the new world dawned. The one thing needful is an attitude of radical obedience, which comes down to a matter not of obedient acts in response to divine laws but of an obedient person in the presence of God. The gospel as Jesus proclaimed it simply calls on men to be prepared for the kingdom, to live not as ascetics or legalists or mystics, but as those who see that all human norms are transcended in the light of the kingdom. Such men will possess true faith which involves a recognition of the message of the kingdom, and a turning to God's messenger and His salvation. It also demands that men come to God with their sin and need in order to receive both forgiveness and help without asking about merit or the lack of it, without comparison or computation.

All or most of this perspective on the message of Jesus is not particularly distinctive of Dibelius. It is quite in the line of the Barthian approach, and there is, therefore, no need of a more detailed exposition here.[37] But Dibelius himself calls attention to a rather singular influence on his views by Johannes Müller, and he finds the main distinction between his own position and that of Bultmann in the fact that Müller, more than Kierkegaard, has affected his point of view.[38] This distinctive element finds notable expression in the fact that Dibelius characterizes the man who responds to the message of the kingdom as "a new being". This *neue Dasein* could not in the nature of the case be described by Jesus; it

[37] Bultmann's view of the message of Jesus was set forth by the present writer in the November, 1938 issue of this *Journal*, pp. 29 ff

[38] Cf. *The Journal of Religion*, 1931, p. 203. Windisch, *Der Sinn der Bergpredigt*, p. 25, states that Muller, rejecting the universal validity and practicability of the teaching of the Sermon on the Mount, called for a living understanding of it, and that he maintained that this understanding was to be found "in der Einsicht, dass uns die Bergpredigt das neue Menschenwesen beschreibt, das in uns erstehen muss, sein Werden und die Gesetze seiner Entfaltung, und das wir die Rede nur insoweit begreifen, als wir dies neue Sein in uns selbst haben und spuren". In criticism Windisch states that Muller "ist der Typus des modernen Menschen der Vorkriegszeit, der eine neue religiöse Gnosis gefunden und diese nun folgerichtig in den alten Text der Bibel hineinliest". An illuminating review of Muller's recent autobiography appeared in *Theologische Literaturzeitung*, 1939, Nr. 10, coll. 379 ff.

could only be circumscribed, for man is ever in new life-situations which demand new decisions. And since Jesus' teaching was intended only as a sign of the kingdom, and not as permanently binding law for the kingdom, it cannot be analyzed or described. The new being is not a new condition or a new nature, but simply a new readiness to hear and to obey. "The message of the kingdom does not make man better, but it seizes his whole being and changes him. And what he then says or does is said or done with a view to the kingdom".[39] The hearer of Jesus does not receive "a new world-view, a new statement of principles, a newly manifested wisdom, but the awakened feeling of the overpowering nearness of God — that is, the nearness of the kingdom of God in the eschatological sense — a feeling that also reshaped, ennobled and expanded other emotions".[40] In a word Dibelius appears to mean that the transforming power of the message of Jesus concerning the kingdom was to be found in the conviction which it gave of the nearness of God, and herein the demands of religious faith are satisfied.

But does faith remain even if the message of Jesus concerning the nearness of the kingdom be thought to have been proved to be in error? Dibelius thinks it does. For ultimately faith is concerned with the supra-historical rather than with the historical order. Certainly, Dibelius says, Jesus expected that the heavenly reality of the kingdom of God was about to become earthly reality; but if the coming of the kingdom meant nothing else but cosmic revolution with great disturbances in the planetary order and catastrophes in the earth, and finally the coming of the Son of Man on the clouds and the final judgment, then the proclamation of the kingdom was a colossal error. But such "apocalyptic" expectations

[39] *Jesus*, p. 99; cf p 101 and *Evangelium und Welt*, pp. 60 ff. Note especially the statement on p. 60 of the latter work: "Alle Forderungen Jesu, ob sie nun als ausfuhrbare Regeln oder als uberspitzte Imperative erscheinen, wollen im Grunde auf das eine Ziel hinaus, dieses neue Sein zu erwecken. So sieht jedes Gebot Jesu, das scheinbar alltagliche wie das fremdartig schwierigste, auf dem immer neuzeugenden und alle tragenden Grunde des Endglaubens: Gott ist nahe, nun fallen alle Bedenken und Bedingtheiten, nun ist nur eines not, nun sei, lebe, handle nur im Blick auf dies eine!"

[40] *The Journal of Religion*, 1931, p. 202.

are merely the presuppositions which are connected with the expectation of the kingdom, for that time, indeed, indissolubly connected. As a matter of fact such elements, Dibelius declares, were not prominent in Jesus' teaching, concerned as He constantly was to utilize the preaching of the kingdom in order to give testimony to the absoluteness of God,— the absoluteness of His demand without any reference to the possibility of its fulfillment within human conditions and the absoluteness of His promise without any question as to its possibility of realization! The reality of God in all of its radical earnestness appears in time only in the form of a sign, and the real sign is the appearance of Jesus Himself. Not apocalyptic hopes, then, but the reality of God is the true concern of faith. But eschatology remains significant for faith since the believer stands in the world as having nothing and yet having all; he knows that this Reality exists even though it is not yet present in space and time, and his faith must satisfy itself with the historical sign of the revelation in Jesus the Christ.[41]

The same readiness to admit that faith may be called forth by a message which historical investigation may prove to be in error, and yet be valid faith, may be observed in connection with Dibelius' treatment of the resurrection faith and the resurrection message; indeed, the separation between history and faith comes to even sharper expression here since, on his view, the message of Jesus concerning the kingdom involved an expectation concerning the future that could be proved erroneous only afterward, whereas the proclamation concerning Jesus as the risen Lord is thought to presuppose a completely mistaken notion as to the historical foundation of that faith. Before his solution of the problem is indicated, it will be well to review his criticism of the resurrection narratives.

The history of Jesus with which scientific investigation is concerned ended, Dibelius declares, with His death, but faith proceeds to narrate the resurrection.[42] The story of the

[41] *Jesus*, pp. 124 f ; cf *Evangelium und Welt*, pp. 40 ff.

[42] Cf. *Jesus*, pp. 119 ff.; *Evangelium und Welt*, pp. 78 ff.; *The Message of Jesus Christ*, pp 181 f., *From Tradition to Gospel*, pp. 179, 190 ff.; *Gospel Criticism and Christology*, p. 19.

empty tomb is a legend which developed a considerable time after the beginning of the Christian church. Another example of a legend is found in the narrative of the appearance of Jesus to the disciples on the way to Emmaus. Considered as a whole, his treatment of the resurrection narratives follows the Galilean Hypothesis, and here again his approach has more in common with the old Liberal effort to account for the origin of the belief than with the later radical views. The Easter faith of the primitive church was not produced, he holds, by the Easter stories. These stories are thought to have been a later development, and for evidence he contrasts the agreement of the gospels on the continuity of the Passion narrative with the diversity of the accounts of resurrection appearances. His conclusion is that the Easter stories were produced by the Easter faith.

The problem of the origin of this faith remains, and he finds the presuppositions of this faith in the common belief in the resurrection on the last day, the expectation of the return of the Son of Man from heaven (which would demand that He had gone to heaven), and the promise of future communion with the disciples which was given at the last supper. These presuppositions, he freely admits, cannot account for the origin of the belief in the resurrection of Jesus as an historical fact; at the most they might intimate that Christ would be raised at some future time. Something must have happened to change the disciples from a state of despair to an attitude of faith which found expression in their new activity in the establishment of the church. This "something" is the historical kernel of the Easter faith; what exactly it was we cannot say. Evidently there were visions of Christ, and apparently Peter was the first to enjoy this experience.[43] And it was as the products of this experience that all of the Easter stories recorded in the gospels developed.

[43] Cf. *Jesus*, pp. 120 f. In his earlier work *Evangelium und Welt*, p. 80, he speaks of a psychological factor: "Der Kern des Osterglaubens bilden also jene Visionen und der mit ihnen über die Bewusstseinsschwelle tretende psychologische Vorgang, in dem wir die Wirkung der von Jesus mitgeteilten inneren Kräfte wahrnehmen, den wir aber nicht analysieren können".

In spite of the judgment that the resurrection message as found in the gospels is unhistorical, and that the original experience, which is conceived to have been the cause of the belief in the risen Lord, was merely a subjective vision or series of visions which somehow came to the disciples after they had returned to Galilee, Dibelius affirms the validity of that faith, and even its essential agreement and continuity with the faith which had been aroused by the preaching of Jesus.[44] For the new proclamation of Jesus Christ after His death, however different it may have been in important particulars, was essentially an eschatological message in that the early Christians looked upon the resurrection of Christ as the first act of the great cosmic upheaval that was coming. The pathos of the first Easter faith lies in the fact that they thought the door of the new world had been opened and the hour of its becoming visible had struck. The concrete form of the concept of the Easter faith is bound up with the apocalyptic image of the world. But the rejection of this worldview, and with it of the form which the Easter faith took, does not invalidate that faith any more than the failure of the kingdom to come invalidated the *Endglaube* which Jesus proclaimed; faith which is really faith cannot be destroyed in any such fashion.[45] The Christians of that day were not concerned, he thinks, with the question of the fact of the resurrection of Christ from the grave as such, but only with the question whether the new world was at hand. And the real meaning of the Easter faith was that they could believe in the kingdom of God, that is, in the reality of God and in Jesus' dignity and vindication. Thus the Easter faith, with or without benefit of miracles, may be affirmed today. It is the form in which the belief in the kingdom lived on, symbolizing another and a different kind of world.

[44] Cf. *Evangelium und Welt*, pp. 81 f.; *Jesus*, pp. 124 ff ; *Gospel Criticism and Christology*, p 46

[45] Cf. *Evangelium und Welt*, p. 81: "Der Vorstellungsgehalt des Osterglaubens ist also nicht zu trennen von den apokalyptischen, mit geozentrischer und wunderglaubiger Einstellung unmittelbar zusammenhangenden Weltbild. Aber wie bei Endglauben so gilt es auch hier, dass ein Glaube, der wirklich Glaube ist, mit der Erledigung seines Vorstellungsgehaltes nicht zerstort werden kann".

From this summary it appears that the continuity which Dibelius allows between the message proclaimed by Jesus and the message about Jesus which was preached by the early Christian missionaries is not, in the last analysis, a continuity in history. It may be admitted that a measure of agreement is found in the common concern with the other world, the world of eschatology. But this view of the measure of agreement provides a most slender thread of continuity, especially in view of the sharp contrast which he finds between the place which Jesus ascribed to His own person in His message and the place which the church gave to Him in its proclamation. If the difficulty of subordinating the person of Jesus the Messiah to His proclamation of the kingdom has been shown, how much more difficult it is to give a subordinate place to Him who is set forth as the risen Saviour? Indeed, Dibelius seems to recognize that there is no real historical continuity when he speaks of the Christian message as having adopted the form of a Christ-myth, the story of a divine being who came to earth, died and arose from the dead, and went again to heaven.[46] There can be for Dibelius no continuity between "the historical Jesus" and "the mythical Christ". The continuity that is affirmed is, therefore, in the sphere of faith, the sphere of the supra-historical.

The exposition of this point of view has called attention to the sharp divorce of history and faith which it demands. It is unfortunate, he thinks, that the polarity of history and faith have not been observed in the history of Christianity, and that in the Christian formulation of the doctrine of the person of Christ there has been a union of history and supra-history. Science is concerned with that which is historically conditioned, and faith with the undetermined and unconditioned realm. It remains to be observed, however, that he does not rest his case with the sharp separation of these realms, but goes on to affirm that the two must be seen in their true relationship.

Rejecting the Liberal view which seeks to find the kernel that can satisfy faith within the husk of historical growth as well as the Idealistic approach which endeavors to comprehend

[46] Cf. *idem*, pp. 82 ff.

the idea behind the historical form, Dibelius maintains that the relative character of the historical realm and the unconditioned character of the supra-historical are maintained if the latter is viewed as the background of the former. The realm of the noumenal cannot be apprehended as the phenomenal is; indeed, one's goal should be not to understand this phase of reality but to appropriate its highest values. To make an adequate expression concerning that which is divine is beyond human possibility. Nor can there be any experience of supra-historical life by the process of imitation, for the imitation would remain on the limited, historical plane. Only he who seeks to guide his life and to fashion his world by the supra-historical background of the gospel will realize in his life that new being, which came into the world with Jesus, the being which is marked by the deepest tumult because of God's judgment and by the highest bliss because of God's grace.[47] Christian faith has nothing to do with the acceptance of the history of Christ as true, but is essentially the recognition that that history, in spite of its purely relative character as history, and the record of it in the New Testament, however defective and however burdened with error it may be, comprise a genuine sign of the reality of God upon which one must venture his life. Faith sees in that history the evidence and warrant of God. In this sense, then, human destiny is bound up with history, and there is need of understanding this phase of history as clearly as possible [48] It appears, accordingly, that Dibelius, while denying that faith can properly be directed towards the historical events of Christ's life, ascribes to that phase of history distinct religious significance.

III. Presuppositions and Deficiencies

In this exposition of Dibelius' views of the history of Jesus and of the religious significance of His message, there has not been entirely absent an effort to center attention upon certain weaknesses and inconsistencies in detail which cast grave

---

[47] Cf. *idem*, pp. 170 f.
[48] Cf. *Jesus*, p. 126; *Evangelium und Welt*, pp. 96 ff , *Gospel Criticism and Christology*, p. 100.

doubt upon the success of his whole attempt to overcome the deficiencies of the earlier criticism and to satisfy the demands both of history and of faith. It now remains necessary, however, by way of conclusion, to offer a general criticism which not only will seek to sum up the basic weakness of the historical construction but also will examine briefly the presuppositions of his approach as a whole.

It would be worth while to seek to trace in detail the diverse influences which have affected the position of Dibelius. For clearly there have been many cross-currents of thought that have molded his distinctive critical and religious approach. Although the influence of Wrede and Bousset and Schweitzer has been very marked, there remain signs of the presence of the leaven of the old Liberal historical criticism. He has evidently come strongly under the impression of the theological conceptions which have come to most influential expression in the Barthian theology, but the more or less distinctive views of Herrmann, Otto, and Johannes Müller have also had a notable effect. The diversity is not as great as it might appear, however, for especially in his philosophical presuppositions there is a unity that results from the monumental influence of Immanuel Kant, and rather than to undertake the difficult task of tracing his affinity with various recent thinkers it seems more advantageous to note the decisive bearing of the Kantian presuppositions.

The gulf that is fixed between the historical and the suprahistorical planes of reality, which allows Dibelius to affirm the message of Christ on one level and to deny it on the other, presupposes a Kantian theory of reality and of knowledge from beginning to end. Since one is concerned with God only in the realm where faith makes a supra-historical affirmation, the realm of the undetermined, evidently the phenomenal realm, that is, the plane of nature and history, although it is described as the realm of the conditioned, is not dependent upon God. His rejection of the facts of creation and providence, which are basic to the Christian theistic view of nature and of history, is due simply to the Kantian metaphysics.

If God is somewhere in the background of the phenomenal world but does not govern it, there may be many surprising happenings in history but, obviously, there can be no place for miracles. The order that is determined by an inner necessity cannot possibly be broken into by an exercise of divine power. Jesus could not have been a worker of miracles. He could not have been raised from the dead. He cannot possibly come on the clouds of heaven to usher in a new world in catastrophic fashion. Dibelius characterizes the ancient belief in miracles as a naive, completely uncritical, discovery of God in every action that could not be explained, and he asserts that an apologetic for miracles either rationalizes them by reference to undiscovered laws or takes the view that the law of causality did not invariably apply to the Biblical history, with the result that miracles are preserved but the original faith is lost.[49] Evidently on his view God is subject to the law of causality.

And can he justify his distinction between the orthodox view of miracles today and the belief of Jesus' disciples? Clearly the eschatological faith in a transformed world presupposed something more than a recognition of God's action in that which could not be explained; it involved the belief that God would transform the world in which they lived and bring history as they knew it to a close. Indeed, Dibelius looks upon the Christian belief in miracles generally, and in the resurrection and return of Christ in particular, as involving a distinctive *Weltbild* which must be dissociated from the Christian message if it is to be a message for our day. But this demand simply involves the substitution of a Kantian view of reality for the Christian theistic view of the world. Dibelius may condemn as arbitrary and modernizing the Idealist's rejection of the form in the interest of recovering the idea, and the Liberal's tearing away of the husk with the aim of appropriating the kernel, but is he less arbitrary and modernizing in dispensing with the theistic presuppositions of the Christian message?

It appears also, therefore, that his scientific, historical method is only as neutral and objective as his Kantian presuppositions allow. Man can cease being a man of faith in his historical investigations only if the object of his study is

---

[49] Cf. *Jesus*, p. 68; *Evangelium und Welt*, pp. 49 ff.

not dependent upon the object of his faith. In the last analysis even Dibelius does not completely separate the historical plane from the supra-historical, and if the latter is conceived of as providing the background for the former, it would seem to be inconsistent to regard the historical plane as sufficient unto itself, as determined by its own laws and, consequently, as demanding a scientific approach that sets aside the implications of faith. The connection between the two planes of reality is suspended by such a slender thread, however, that it is his fundamental dualism that controls his method rather than an ultimate unity. Only the Christian theistic view of the world satisfies the demands of our minds for ultimate unity in that it refuses to recognize that any part of nature or of history can be outside of the divine control and knowledge. It cannot regard as scientific, therefore, any historical method which does not take due account of the fact of that divine control and knowledge of the objects of investigation.

The Kantian premises appear with particular clarity in Dibelius' interpretation of religion. Religion, he defines, as an emotional relation to a higher world.[50] Religion as such has no relation to this world, and the consciousness of a mission to transform the world, however inevitable its development may be when a small religious group expands and comes in conflict with the world, represents a defection from religion. Hence Dibelius describes as *secular* any sign of concern for a place or a task in the world, and even uses secularism as a criterion for the reference of some of the gospel materials to the later stages of the development of tradition. This conception of religion, while its distinctive formulation may be a recent development, is essentially Kantian in its sharp separation of the concerns of religion and the issues of this world. It leaves a most disturbing dualism in the center of our life, for it fails to recognize that all of the world belongs to God, and, accordingly, that true religion involves a recognition of the sovereignty of God in every sphere of life.

[50] Cf. *Evangelium und Welt*, p. 21: "Religion ist eben immer — wie ich es in leichter Abwandlung der Wobberminschen Religionstheorie ausdrucken mochte — affectvolle Beziehung zu einer Ueberwelt". His views on religion and the world are set forth in this same work, pp. 15 ff., 98 ff.

On this view of religion it is readily understood why the idea of eschatology is utilized both to set forth the meaning of Jesus' message and the Christian proclamation of the risen Lord, for the other-worldly conception of religion seems to receive pointed expression in the faith in the nearness of a totally different order of affairs with which we as men must reckon most earnestly. Properly speaking, however, eschatology presupposes the theistic conception of history, and when it is not isolated from theism it does not foster an anti-worldly conception of religion. If God is the God of all of history, He who will make the new world of glory must demand that His creatures in the present world, which is also His, recognize and seek to advance the recognition of His sovereignty in all the world. Having denied the theistic presuppositions of eschatology, Dibelius in effect denies outright a place to eschatology in religion. For his evaluation of eschatology, which was noted above in connection with the exposition of the meaning of the message of Jesus, transcendentalizes it out of the historical sphere where alone it has meaning, and rationalizes away its distinctively supernatural character.

Furthermore, it is his Kantian metaphysics and epistemology that exclude the possibility of historical revelation and historical redemption. The basic dualism of the Kantian system is irreconcilable with a specifically historical revelation, and its agnosticism will not allow any real knowledge of the super-phenomenal world. Indeed, since rationality is confined to the phenomenal world, the basic irrationality of the suprahistorical reality does not permit of true description; it may only be circumscribed and perceived in a practical fashion.[51]

[51] Cf *Evangelium und Welt*, p 51· "An die Stelle des alten Wunderglaubens ist fur unser religioses Leben das Erfassen des Irrationalen, des 'ganz Anderen', des Gottlichen getreten, das uns als Moglichkeit in jedem Geschehen nahe tritt, als wirkliche Erfullung dem einen hier, dem andern da geschenkt wird, im Anschluss an Ueberlieferung oder frei von ihr, jedenfalls aber ohne dass wir Gesetz und Regel anzugeben wussten Gott spricht auch heute in wundervollen Zungen, und wir vermogen ihm zu lauschen genau so ohne Bedenken und Vorbehalte, wie die Alten der Sprache des Wunders lauschten Und diese Erkenntnis macht uns auch frei von jeder unkritischen Aengstlichkeit gegenuber antiken Wunderberichten".

Altogether in harmony with this view of religion as having to do with the irrational, Dibelius develops his view of faith as in sharp antithesis with knowledge. For, according to his thought, faith is not a response of the individual living in the midst of history to the divine word spoken in history, but merely the appropriation of the values of the supra-historical reality. Here fundamentally the choice lies between a rational universe and an irrational one. For if any part of reality is irrational, all of it must be irrational. The view of reality as absolutely and thoroughly rational is possible only on the basis of Christian theism. And true knowledge of God is possible because man has been created in His image.

It must be admitted that Dibelius seems to qualify the dualism at this point by relating faith to the knowledge of history when he says, as was observed more fully above, that the history of Christ is a genuine sign of the reality of God upon which we must venture our life. Although this qualification may be viewed as a step back from Barthianism towards the historism of the old Liberal position, it is not clear how it harmonizes with his basic principles nor how it overcomes his own objections to the Liberal view. For it evidently departs from the basic distinction between the realm of history and the realm of religion which has been drawn with an indelible line throughout his writings. And in describing a phase of history, that is thought of as purely relative, as constituting a genuine sign of the reality of God, he virtually ascribes to that history the evaluation of revelation, and so falls back into the error of historism which he has been so much concerned to oppose. The tenuousness of this connection of faith with history and the incongruity of stating, on his principles, that human destiny is bound up with history are observed most pointedly when it is recalled that, according to his judgment, faith that is real faith cannot be destroyed by any proof that the historical message was false, and that he asks us to venture our lives upon a record that is defective and burdened with error on the view that, notwithstanding these faults, the record is a sign of the reality of God![52]

---

[52] On the subject of faith and the truth of the Christian message the reader may profitably consult *What is Faith?* by J. Gresham Machen.

The faith which affords contact with the supra-historical realm has been described as involving such a powerful change in attitude that the man who experiences it may be described as a new being. This language, it should be noted, is not intended to express anything like the orthodox doctrine of salvation. It is not an experience that involves a change of human nature or is grounded in the historical redemption of Christ. On Dibelius' view of history Christ's life and death could not constitute God's action in history for the redemption of His people; and on his view of man there can be no talk of human guilt or of the corruption of human nature. Sin is essentially an aspect of "creaturehood", of man as man; it is a corollary of man's position on the historical plane of existence. So also grace, losing all of its particularity and power to save, becomes a corollary of the nearness of God. It is not surprising, therefore, that "the new being" in Dibelius' construction is not one who has been saved by the sacrifice and Spirit of Christ but one who, through the proclamation of the kingdom, is "seized by the overpowering nearness of God". It appears, therefore, that his view of individual salvation, like the other elements in his interpretation of Christianity, is determined by his philosophical presuppositions or, at least, is the result of a reshaping of the materials of Christian tradition in a modern philosophical mold.

The chief deficiency of Dibelius' historical reconstruction is bound up with the factor that gives it its greatest strength, namely, the affirmation of the historicity of the messianic consciousness of Jesus. It is clearly to his credit that he admits that even the radical reduction of the evangelical tradition by the method of form-criticism does not succeed in discovering an unmessianic stratum, but, unfortunately, the implications of the acknowledgment of the historicity of the claim fall far short of realization. While he does not yield to the Liberal absurdity of interpreting the messianic consciousness as a mere form that does not touch His central thought concerning Himself and as a burden that He would gladly have thrown aside, he does fail to recognize the profound meaning which anyone who claimed messiahship would discover in his own history. If this is true on any meaning of messiahship, how can it fail to be comprehended if the Anointed of the Lord interpreted His significance in terms of the coming of the Son of Man? Surely, this view of messiahship is supernatural to the core. Indeed, Dibelius does somewhat dim the glory of the light which shines about the figure of the Son of Man by giving the whole concept, on inadequate grounds, an exclusively future reference. But even such an expedient does not succeed in reducing the figure to natural limits, a fact which the radicals, in keeping with their characteristically sounder interpretation of the meaning of the gospels, have not failed to recognize.[53] Because of the supreme self-importance which was necessarily involved in the claim to be the Son of Man, it is impossible to subordinate the person of Jesus to the message of the coming kingdom, as Dibelius attempts to do. This judgment is fully borne out by Daniel 7:13 f. where the glorious figure who is in intimate association with the Ancient of Days is given dominion, glory and a kingdom. He is not called to serve the kingdom, as Dibelius' construction would seem to involve, but to be served by the kingdom, and that eternally.[54]

From still another point of view the inadequacy of Dibelius' view of the messiahship may be observed. He makes use of the generally recognized presence of an attitude of passivity on Jesus' part to support his view of the subordination of the messiahship to the coming kingdom. Although Jesus was not an activist in a worldly sense, His passivity is both exaggerated and misunderstood widely. For He did freely acknowledge the recognition of His messiahship, and all of His teaching and activity bore the impress of the messianic authority which He claimed. The passivity which was present was really an expression of the thoroughly theocentric character of His consciousness, and it was because of that fact that He was con-

[53] E. g., Bousset in *Kyrios Christos*, pp. 11 f. and Bultmann in *Die Geschichte der synoptischen Tradition*², p. 145.

[54] The inadequacy of Dibelius' view of the messiahship also appears in connection with his consideration of the reason for the execution of Jesus. While the mere claim to be the Messiah, interpreted politically, might account for the Roman sentence, it does not begin to account for the judgment by the Jewish authorities The basis for their judgment must have been the supernatural character of His messianic claim Cf. Dalman, *Die Worte Jesu*², pp 256 ff (E.T , pp. 312 ff.); Vos, *The Self-Disclosure of Jesus*, pp. 173 ff ; Strack and Billerbeck, *Kommentar usw.*, p. 1017.

cerned to do only God's will in the world, even though that will required Him to endure suffering and humiliation [55]

It is because Dibelius fails to interpret the messianic consciousness as theocentrically constituted that he finds no room for the redemptive significance of the Passion as that is set forth in the record of Jesus' teaching. He would admit, of course, that the gospels represent the suffering and death of Christ as the fulfillment of the will of God as found in the Old Testament, his interpretation of the Passion story from this point of view having been outlined above. But he does not recognize this view of the death of Christ as historical; it has arisen, he thinks, to meet the theological and apologetic needs of the early church. Once the messiahship is accepted as historical, however, the interpretation of the messianic task in terms of the Old Testament should follow as a matter of course. And the manner in which the passivity of Jesus is unfolded in the gospels implies that the messianic task was understood in terms of the divine declarations concerning the Servant of the Lord in Isaiah.[56] The soteriological interpretation of the life and death of Christ need not be referred, therefore, to the developments in the early church. It is an inseparable element of the messianic consciousness of Jesus. Accordingly, the history of Jesus, once He was recognized as the Messiah, immediately became the object of interest and concern not only because of the supernatural claims which He made but also because this history was viewed as fulfilling the will of God concerning the redemption of His people.

Moreover, if the tremendous implications of Jesus' claims are acknowledged, it is no longer necessary to set the Christology of the early church sharply at variance with Jesus' thought concerning Himself. If the disciples after His death could have conceived of the possibility of His resurrection from the dead, it does not appear why the Son of Man, who went to the cross to accomplish God's redemptive purpose

[55] The implications of the theocentric character of the messiahship of Jesus have been admirably stated by Schlatter in *Die Zweifel an der Messianität Jesu*, 1907, cf also Vos, *op cit.*, pp 56 ff, 98 ff

[56] It is a merit of Otto's interpretation in *The Kingdom of God and the Son of Man* that he recognizes that Jesus joined to the Son of Man conception the program of suffering as the Isaianic Servant.

as a ransom for many, might not have expected and taught His victory over the grave. The gospel of the death and resurrection of Christ, while it necessarily waited for the history to be accomplished to receive its complete formulation, by no means represents a conception of the history of Christ that is at variance with His own messianic consciousness. Accordingly, the claim that Jesus did not demand recognition of His messiahship as a requirement for salvation cannot stand because it is contradicted not only by particular passages like the parable of the wicked husbandman but also by the very meaning of the messiahship.[57]

The intrinsic weakness of the literary criticism of Dibelius also appears in a clear light if it is related to his treatment of the messiahship. His fluctuations between the Liberal and the radical points of view have been noted. If the historicity of the messianic consciousness, and of a considerable portion of the rest of the tradition, may be accepted because of the presence of eye-witnesses in the early church, the question arises why their presence was not determinative of the tradition in a more comprehensive fashion. Moreover, if the history of the Messiah was set forth as a sign of the coming of the kingdom, and had an indispensable place in the Christian message, why was there not an immediate need of appeal to those who could attest the truth of this history, and an immediate interest in trustworthy reports of that history; indeed, why should Jesus not have appointed His disciples to provide that attestation of His history?[58] Dibelius is in the

[57] Dibelius refers this parable to the reflection of the early church, *The Message of Jesus Christ*, p. 154.

The tension in Dibelius' reconstruction may be observed in still another matter. If Jesus teaching about Himself is acknowledged at its true value, and is freed from the extreme eschatological interpretation which represents Him as quite mistaken about His central message, it will no longer appear incongruous that Jesus should have given specific teaching for the life of the church. In *Jesus*, p. 49, he speaks of the circle of disciples as forming "die Kerngemeinde des kunftigen Gottesvolks".

[58] Dibelius, *Gospel Criticism and Christology*, pp 82 f., in a fashion that is typical of the form-critical approach, condemns Papias' concern with individuals like Peter and Mark, as opposed to the many preachers who have remained nameless, as representing the first age of Christianity "far too much after the style of a later, more educated and more literary Christianity".

strange position of viewing the gospels as Christological documents of the primitive church which represent a point of view at variance with that of Jesus Himself and yet regarding them as reliable in their main affirmation about Jesus.

As a form-critic he insists that the framework of the gospel records must be rejected on the view that the stories and sayings at first circulated in isolated fashion; yet he appeals to the absence of a framework in the resurrection narratives as evidence of their unhistorical character and supports the messianic consciousness on the assumption of the correctness of the framework of the Passion story. His form-critical method does not offer any really objective criteria to support his positive interpretation of Jesus, for only his own historical presuppositions and his resultant reconstruction of the early history can provide a basis for distinguishing between the message of Jesus and that of the early church. Thus his views of the "tales" and "legends" are decisively determined by his judgment as to what Jesus may have been and what He may not have been. His presuppositions may not allow him to affirm that Jesus performed real miracles and received divine protection, but these elements cannot be eliminated on the ground that they are incongruous with the claim of messiahship. Why should not the transcendent Anointed of the Lord receive His divine protection and why should He not exhibit supernatural power?

Ultimately the choice which the gospels offer is that of believing their testimony or that of rejecting it outright. The issue lies between the radical view which sees that testimony in its unity but frankly rejects it because of its own critical presuppositions and the position of Christian theism which acknowledges the history of Jesus as God's action in history for the salvation of His people. The mediating effort of Dibelius fails to persuade our minds and to set our hearts at rest, and leaves us with an inner conflict between them.

CHAPTER VII

LUTHER AND THE NEW TESTAMENT CANON

IN THIS brief paper, announced in your program as concerned, without further qualification, with the Canon, the inevitability of some substantial limitation of treatment will be recognized. The aspect of the subject to be discussed is "Luther and the New Testament Canon," and my purpose is to evaluate his views largely in terms of his own expressed attitudes towards Hebrews, James, Jude and Revelation. Whether this constitutes a significant approach will have to be judged in the light of what follows.

Fortunately one may assume considerable interest in the person and views of Luther at the present time, for one meets many evidences of an awareness of his religious genius and the profound relevancy of his thinking concerning the gospel of Jesus Christ. The unexpected interest in the Martin Luther film is not without meaning in this connection. The considerable success of Bainton's brilliant biography, *Here I Stand*, is another token. Of less popular but perhaps of profounder historical and theological significance is the fact that particularly since 1917, the anniversary of the posting of the 95 theses, there has been, as Wilhelm Pauck has said, "a veritable Luther Renaissance."[1] Modern theology particularly in Germany has characteristically sought support in the outlook of Luther, but it has been especially since the first World War that Barth and men of his general outlook have claimed spiritual kinship with Luther in setting their views over against the positions of theological orthodoxy which came to be formulated in the creeds of the churches. In that connection Luther's attitude towards the Bible has naturally received close attention, and the great Reformer has been hailed as being, in spite of a biblicism which he shared with his times, the exponent and forerunner of a freer, critical attitude which was the consequence of his unique religious genius and experience.

[1] Wilhelm Pauck, *The Heritage of the Reformation*, (Boston, 1950) p. 14.

Quite apart from such modern developments, however, it would be advisable to take account of Luther's views concerning the Canon. The history of the New Testament Canon in the narrower sense is an aspect of ancient church history, treating as it does the history of the collection of the individual writings into a single work and their recognition as Scripture alongside of Old Testament Scripture. It refuses to remain, however, within such rigid limits. The study of that phase of history involves evaluations, and as such entails judgments concerning the very nature of Christianity.[2]

On the other hand that study of the past embraces the present since we who evaluate it are not unconditioned by the modern life situation. We live in the stream of modern history, and our Christian outlook in particular is not a purely independent response arrived at in isolation from what has gone before and what is taking place round about us. To a large extent, it will be recognized, we continue to formulate our faith, including our attitude toward the Scriptures, in terms of the historic confessions and by appeal to the Reformers. But we as evangelicals who judge that our faith is in substantial agreement with that of Martin Luther nevertheless must recognize a responsibility to take care not to read our own views into his. It ought to be possible to approach him sympathetically and gratefully and yet critically, at least so if as true Protestants we acknowledge a qualitative distinction between the teaching of Scripture and the voice of tradition.

In this paper two matters will come under review. (1) Luther's actual evaluation of the four Books of Scripture writings mentioned, and (2) the criteria he employs in judging them. The latter obviously has broader implications for his total view. But it cannot be studied except on the background of the former, especially since there is not agreement as to whether he accepted the four as canonical.

Among those who would not subscribe to the proposition, at least not without qualification, that Luther excludes the

[2] See my article on "The Authority of the New Testament," in *The Infallible Word*, A Symposium by the members of the Faculty of Westminster Theological Seminary, (Philadelphia, 1946, Grand Rapids, 1953), where this and other questions relating to the canonicity of the New Testament are considered.

four from the Canon, two representative positions may be distinguished. The position of Johannes Leipoldt[3] is rather equivocal. The question whether Luther reckoned the doubtful books as a part of the Canon cannot, he says, be answered "klipp und klar." And in connection with a review of evidence that Luther distinguished between these four and the others, he concludes that Luther did not ascribe full canonicity to them.[4] This suggests that Leipoldt regards Luther as ascribing to them a kind of deutero-canonicity, although he does not use the term in this connection. His classification of the books of Luther's New Testament into three groups at an earlier point of analysis[5] and his assigning of Jude to the third class of "doubtful books"[6] also seems to indicate that he does not regard the four as standing, for Luther, unmistakably outside the collection of New Testament Scripture

A second representative viewpoint is that the four writings, though subjected to much forthright criticism on Luther's part, were nevertheless accepted as canonical. Ronald Bainton is a recent exponent of this point of view. In connection with a broader estimate of Luther's conception of Scripture, he states categorically that Luther "did not venture to reject James from the canon of Scripture."

> If on occasion he could speak of every iota of Holy Writ as sacred, at other times he displayed blithe indifference to minor blemishes, such as an error in quotation from the Old Testament in the New Testament. The Bible for him was not strictly identical with the Word of God...
>
> But when doctrinal matters were involved, the case was different. Luther read the New Testament in the light of the Pauline message that the just shall live by faith and not by works of the law. That this doctrine is not enunciated with equal emphasis throughout the New Testament and appears to be denied in the book of James did not escape Luther, and in his preface to the New Testament of 1522 James was stigmatized as "an epistle of straw." Once Luther remarked that he would give his doctor's beret to

---

[3] Cf. Johannes Leipoldt, *Geschichte des neutestamentlichen Kanons*, (Leipzig, 1908) pp. 62 ff.
[4] Pp. 81, 82
[5] Pp 70 f
[6] P. 74.

anyone who could reconcile James and Paul. Yet he did not venture to reject James from the canon of Scripture, and on occasion earned his own beret by effecting a reconciliation. "Faith," he wrote, "is a living, restless thing. It cannot be inoperative. We are not saved by works; but if there be no works, there must be something amiss with faith." This was simply to put a Pauline construction upon James. The conclusion was a hierarchy of values within the New Testament. First Luther would place the Gospel of John, then the Pauline epistles and First Peter, after them the three other epistles, and in a subordinate place Hebrews, James, Jude and Revelation. He mistrusted Revelation because of its obscurity. "A revelation," said he, "should be revealing."[7]

On this analysis all are therefore canonical (including the Synoptics and Acts, which Bainton inadvertently fails to mention here), and the writings are distinguished in terms of practical worth only.

We turn now to consider the evidence bearing upon the question of Luther's estimate of the four which, as everyone agrees, are distinguished in some respect from the rest. Our attention is arrested, first of all, by the table of contents of his New Testament. The twenty-seven appear there, but only twenty-three, from Matthew to III John, are numbered. Hebrews, James, Jude and Revelation are listed but without numbers.[8] This order also obtains in the text of the New Testament itself. Thus Hebrews loses its accustomed place following the Pastoral Epistles and James its place at the head of the General Epistles. On the other hand, account must be taken of the fact that Luther did not venture to omit these four from his translation. That this action is not tantamount to acceptance as canonical is seen, however, when it is recalled that he also translated the Old Testament apocrypha, which admittedly he rejected as devoid of scriptural authority.

The significance Luther attached to his distinctive order fortunately is not left to speculation. For in the first preface following the twenty-third book, in the preface to Hebrews,

[7] *Here I Stand*, (New York, 1950) pp 331 f. Quoted by permission of the publishers, The Abingdon Press.
[8] Weimar Ausgabe, VI, pp. 12 f.

he comments: "So far we have had the right certain Capital-books. The four which follow have possessed a different regard in former times."[9] Two matters should be noted. (1) His reference to ancient opinion might suggest that, perhaps on the background of the attention centered upon the ancient church by Erasmus and others, he has merely decided to place the "disputed" books (the *antilegomena*) after the acknowledged books. But in that case of course he would have had to draw his line of demarcation considerably earlier. (2) Of greater significance for our understanding of Luther's position is his designation of the twenty-three, including several books disputed in ancient times, as "die rechten, gewissen Hauptbucher." The term *Hauptbucher* (Capital-books) therefore includes all that precede. Since it appears again in later prefaces where the context casts light upon its meaning, it will be important to keep this terminology in view. In the present context, at least, it would be entirely appropriate to think of it as a synonym for canonical books. That they are the "right certain" *Hauptbucher* evidently is expressive of Luther's personal assurance with regard to them rather than a reflection of ancient or contemporaneous opinion.

The designation *Hauptbucher* appears also in connection with his comments on James and Jude. Particularly illuminating is his formulation in connection with his treatment of James when he says: "And herein all truly holy books agree, that they all without exception preach and urge Christ. That, too, is the right touchstone whereby to judge (censure) all, whether they urge Christ or not, since all Scripture manifests Christ. That which does not teach Christ is still not apostolic, even if it were the teaching of St. Peter or St. Paul. Again that which preaches Christ, that were apostolic even if Judas, Annas, Pilate and Herod did it."[10] In this broad characterization there can be no question but that Luther is formulating his fundamental criterion of canonicity as *that which presses home Christ* (was Christum treibet), and that he defines apostolicity in the same terms. It must be stressed here that

---

[9] W. A VII, pp. 344 f : "Bisher haben wir die rechten, gewissen Hauptbucher des Neuen Testaments gehabt. Diese vier nachfolgende aber haben vor Zeiten ein ander Ansehen gehabt."

[10] W. A. VII, pp. 384 f

he is speaking of all *truly holy* books,[11] thus not in terms of their general acknowledgment as canonical in the past or present, but rather as to their essential character according to his personal judgment.

James clearly is excluded from this group. He is not without praise for some of its contents, stating, for example, that it "presses home the law of God" (Gottes Gesetz hart treibet). But he is evidently leading up to his forthright attack upon it. With some exaggeration he says that it "was rejected by the ancients." And he proceeds to show why the contents of the Epistle do not allow him to classify it as apostolic. In brief his indictment takes the form that (1) James "contradicts Paul and all other Scriptures" on the matter of justification and works, and (2) it omits Christ. On the latter he says: "He would teach Christian people, and yet does not once notice the passion, the resurrection, the Spirit of Christ. The writer names Christ a few times, but he teaches nothing of him, and instead speaks of a general faith in God while it is the duty of a true Apostle to preach Christ's sufferings and resurrection and office, and lay the foundation of the same faith. . ."

Commenting further on its lack of apostolicity he says that James so mingles law and works that "I think he was a good pious man, who took certain sayings of the disciples of the apostles, and cast them on paper. Or perhaps they were written down by another from his preaching." And summing up he says: "So I cannot place it in my Bible in the number of true Capital-books (in der Zal der rechten Hauptbucher), but will forbid no one to place and elevate it as he pleases."

In the 1522 preface there was added the sentence: "One man is no man in worldly matters; how then should this single writer all alone hold good against Paul and all other Scripture?" Further confirmation is provided by his evaluation of James, therefore, that the true *Hauptbucher* are for Luther the truly canonical books and the only apostolic books. All others are excluded from this group, and James, as contradicting Paul and all other Scripture, disqualifies itself in the most conspicuous manner. Surely there is nothing to suggest that

[11] 1522: "rechtschaffene heilige Bucher," 1546: "rechtschaffene Bucher"

even a kind of deutero-canonicity is ascribed to James. Luther's only qualification is that he will not sit in judgment upon those who form a different judgment from his own, a qualification introduced seemingly out of an awareness of the uniqueness of his personal evaluation.

With regard to James it appears that he did not modify his judgment in any essential manner in later years. He did indeed not repeat in later editions of his New Testament the characterization of James as "a right strawy epistle compared with the others,"[12] a fact that is usually overlooked by those who seem fond of quoting it as summing up Luther's opinion of James. In any case, in that context he was not discussing canonicity but practical worth, indicating the writings which Christians "should be counselled to read first and foremost." It is in this context that he speaks of "the right and noblest books of the New Testament," a rather different designation from "the right certain *Hauptbucher*" and "the truly holy *Hauptbucher*."

Though Luther chose to drop this statement from the 1530 and 1546 editions, the later scattered criticisms of James are hardly of greater moderation! It was c. 1533 that he made the remark, referred to by Bainton, that, to any one who could harmonize James and Paul, he would be willing to give his doctor's beret, and that he would be willing to be called a fool.[13] And about 1540, he speaks of James' teaching on righteousness by works as "absurd and against Scripture. Some day I will use James to fire my stove."[14] And in 1542: "The Epistle of James we have thrown out from this school [Wittenberg] because it has no value (denn sie soll nichts)."[15]

The harmonization between James and Paul to which Bainton refers when he says that Luther won his own beret is found in a work dating from 1521, thus before his New Testament of 1522 and many years before his reference to the beret! It may therefore reflect his earlier state of opinion when he still received the four as a part of Scripture.[16]

---

[12] Preface to New Testament., 1522, W. A. VI, p. 10.
[13] *Tischreden*, 3292a, W. A. III, p. 253.
[14] *Tischreden*, 5854, W A V, p. 382.
[15] *Tischreden*, 5443, W. A. V, p. 157, cf. 5974, W. A. V, p. 414.
[16] *Evangelium von den zehn Aussatzigen*, W. A. VIII, pp. 361 f.

Luther's comments on Jude are also illuminating, although his objections to it are relatively moderate. No one can deny, he says, that it is an abstract or copy of II Peter. This evaluation seems to be particularly in view when he concludes that "it is an unnecessary epistle to reckon among the *Hauptbucher* which ought to lay the foundation of the faith."[17] Thus confirmation is provided that *Hauptbucher* is the equivalent of canonical works. In this same connection Luther mentions the fact that Jude includes teaching and history nowhere referred to in the Scripture (evidently alluding to the Enoch reference), and states that this consideration moved the ancient fathers "to reject it from the Capital-scripture (aus der Hauptschrift zu werfen)." The use of the term *Hauptschrift* apparently with the same force as *Hauptbucher* affords still further support of the position taken here. And the fact that he says that the ancient fathers rejected it shows that he is not merely disclosing a knowledge of its doubtful or disputed status in earlier times. Though the statement, like that regarding James referred to above, is guilty of exaggeration, the absoluteness with which he speaks allows only for the view that it is being classified as non-canonical.

This rather specialized terminology (*Hauptbucher* and *Hauptschrift*) is not found in the particular comments on Hebrews and Revelation. Rather he employs the term "apostolic," which however has been seen to be the equivalent of canonical. His general judgment with regard to Hebrews is that, in spite of much praise that may be heaped upon it, "one must not place it in all things on a level with the apostolic epistles."[18] In support of this conclusion Luther appeals to Hebrews 2:3 as disproving apostolic authorship. But his principal objection, as in the case of James, is evidently to certain contents of Hebrews, for he affirms that it contradicts the gospels and Paul in its doctrine of repentance.

In 1522 Luther took an outrightly negative attitude toward Revelation, criticizing both its form and content, and declaring: "This book lacks everything that I hold as apostolic or prophetic." He further intimates that the sufficient reason

[17] W. A. VII, p. 387
[18] W. A VII, pp. 344 f.

why his spirit cannot acquiesce in it is that "Christ is not taught or proclaimed therein which after all in all things is the obligation of an apostle."[19] It is true that in the 1530 and 1546 editions he discloses that his difficulties had been substantially removed, and he even finds in this book the message that "through and above all plagues, beasts, evil angels Christ is still near and with his saints, and at last overthrows them."[20] One gathers that if his later evaluation of Revelation had been present from the beginning, he might possibly have resisted his classification of it with James and the rest. Nevertheless, even in the later formulations Luther remains in doubt as to the authorship of Revelation, and this perhaps is indicated as a sufficient reason for perpetuating his distinctive arrangement and evaluation.

On the background of this survey and evaluation one may note, in summary form, Luther's criteria of canonicity. External historical factors may not be altogether discounted. In rejecting the several writings he alludes to their status in the ancient church, and recalls some of the particular criticisms leveled against them in former times. The Erasmian criticism may have been a factor in this regard. That such considerations were not basic to his thinking appears however from two considerations: (1) he accepted II and III John and II Peter without question; and (2) his references to ancient opinion are introduced in such a manner as to suggest that they are intended to lessen the shock generated by his fundamental criticism of their contents.

In connection with his historical evaluations he indicates an interest in apostolicity and appears to identify apostolicity and canonicity. He is not indifferent to the question of apostolic origin, as his comments upon authorship reveal. Nevertheless, apostolic origin can hardly be determinative since he has no difficulty with Mark and Luke. That indeed he basically identifies apostolicity with that which is orthodox, or *was Christum treibet*, is vividly stated in his declaration: "That which does not teach Christ is still not apostolic, even if it were the teaching of Peter or Paul. On the other hand,

---

[19] W. A VII, p. 404
[20] W. A. VII, pp 406 ff.

that which preaches Christ, that were apostolic if even Judas, Annas, Pilate and Herod did it."[21] Even allowing for the rhetorical exaggeration of the statement, it serves to emphasize the essentially theological or dogmatic character of his most basic criterion of canonicity. One should add, however, that apostolicity apparently means that which is ancient as well as orthodox, for Luther's conception of the gospel as the message proclaiming what Christ had done by his death and resurrection excludes the notion that any Christian of later times, say Luther himself as a man of faith, could provide the historic witness and attestation that was required.

Our consideration of apostolicity conveys us therefore from the sphere of tradition to that of internal criticism. And as we have had occasion to note particularly in treating his statements concerning James and Revelation, he affirms emphatically that the real test is that only that is canonical *was Christum treibet.*

It should be observed, however, that he associates intimately with this criterion the further principle that that is not canonical which contradicts Scripture, including of course the gospel of Christ. James and Hebrews particularly are criticized from this point of view. He thus implies that no real contradictions appear within the Scriptures. His rejection of James and the others accordingly is in complete harmony with his declarations that Scripture cannot err; indeed his rejection of them, rather than attesting a rejection of infallibility, is intelligible only on the background of a firm maintenance of the doctrine. If Luther had had as low a view of inspiration as modern writers often ascribe to him, his sharply distinctive treatment of the four would not have been necessary.

That there was no tension or contradiction between Luther's high view of Scripture and his low view of the four writings receives significant confirmation when one observes that both originated in a single concrete situation. As Martin Reu, for example, has shown, prior to c. 1520 Luther's view of Scripture was not particularly distinctive: he held to the inspiration and authority of Scripture but also attached

[21] Preface to James

substantial authority to tradition. Likewise he entertained no particular difficulty so far as the four writings were concerned. But his *sola Scriptura* doctrine came into being in the great crisis years from 1517-1521 and found clear expression in his noble testimony at Worms that his "conscience was captive to the Word."[22]

In that conflict he was fighting to maintain the gospel of justification by faith alone, and this demanded that he condemn the current doctrine and practice of indulgences. It was not enough therefore to support his position by exegesis of Scripture; he had also to repudiate the spokesmen of the Pope who were attacking his position by appeal to tradition. But the very forces which served to crystallize the doctrine of *sola Scriptura* brought other consequences that had not been anticipated. The gospel was contradicted and set at nought by the papal indulgences. But what if some of the writings handed down as part of the New Testament also omitted the gospel and even contradicted it? The only consistent thing was to reject them too, even if they contained many things that he could approve. In the white heat of his life struggle for the faith Luther found the boldness to do that very thing.

Nevertheless, Luther's distinctive approach is not invulnerable. To understand how it came to develop and to examine it sympathetically is not to approve. Luther himself, judging by his readiness to allow others a different judgment, was aware of its individuality and perhaps even of its subjective character.

My basic criticism of his viewpoint is that it was narrowly Christocentric rather than God-centered, and thus involved an attenuation and impoverishment of the message of the New Testament. However significant *was Christum treibet* may be for the understanding of the New Testament, it lacks the breadth of perspective and outlook given by understanding it, for example, in terms of the coming of the kingdom of God. This essentially eschatological message, conceived in terms of realized and unrealized eschatology, prevents one from contemplating the New Testament narrowly and exclusively in terms of Christ and personal salvation. Again, if Luther had

[22] *Luther and the Scriptures* (Columbus, 1944) pp. 13 ff.

seen the New Testament in the broader context provided by the Biblical idea of the covenant, he likewise would have been better prepared, without sacrifice of the doctrines of grace, and indeed reinforcing them, to recognize more adequately the place assigned to the law of righteousness. Luther to be sure is hardly to be accused of antinomianism, as Berkouwer has rightly insisted.[23] Nevertheless, the comprehensive significance of law hardly came into its own on his approach. And thus, formulating his criterion in narrow terms, and insisting upon the same manifestation of it in each writing of the New Testament, he missed much of the richness of the revelation of the New Testament organism of Scripture.

[23] G. C. Berkouwer, *Faith and Sanctification*, (Grand Rapids, 1952) pp. 165 ff.

www.ingramcontent.com/pod-product-compliance
Lightning Source LLC
Chambersburg PA
CBHW072127160426
43197CB00012B/2022